T0286954

Cambridge Elements

Elements in Quantitative Finance
edited by
Riccardo Rebonato
EDHEC Business School

A PRACTITIONER'S GUIDE TO DISCRETE-TIME YIELD CURVE MODELLING

WITH EMPIRICAL ILLUSTRATIONS AND MATLAB EXAMPLES

Ken Nyholm
European Central Bank, Frankfurt

CAMBRIDGE
UNIVERSITY PRESS

CAMBRIDGE
UNIVERSITY PRESS

University Printing House, Cambridge CB2 8BS, United Kingdom

One Liberty Plaza, 20th Floor, New York, NY 10006, USA

477 Williamstown Road, Port Melbourne, VIC 3207, Australia

314–321, 3rd Floor, Plot 3, Splendor Forum, Jasola District Centre,
New Delhi – 110025, India

79 Anson Road, #06–04/06, Singapore 079906

Cambridge University Press is part of the University of Cambridge.

It furthers the University's mission by disseminating knowledge in the pursuit of
education, learning, and research at the highest international levels of excellence.

www.cambridge.org
Information on this title: www.cambridge.org/9781108972123
DOI: 10.1017/9781108975537

First published 2020

A catalogue record for this publication is available from the British Library.

ISBN 978-1-108-97212-3 Paperback
ISSN 2631-8571 (online)
ISSN 2631-8563 (print)

Additional resources for this publication at www.cambridge.org/nyholm

A Practitioner's Guide to Discrete-Time Yield Curve Modelling

With Empirical Illustrations and MATLAB Examples

Elements in Quantitative Finance

DOI: 10.1017/9781108975537
First published online: December 2020

Ken Nyholm
European Central Bank, Frankfurt

Author for correspondence: Ken Nyholm, ken.nyholm@ecb.europa.eu

Abstract: This Element is intended for students and practitioners as a gentle and intuitive introduction to the field of discrete-time yield curve modelling. I strive to be as comprehensive as possible, while still adhering to the overall premise of putting a strong focus on practical applications. In addition to a thorough description of the Nelson-Siegel family of model, the Element contains a section on the intuitive relationship between P and Q measures, one on how the structure of a Nelson-Siegel model can be retained in the arbitrage-free framework, and a dedicated section that provides a detailed explanation for the Joslin, Singleton, and Zhu (2011) model.

Keywords: yield curve modelling, discrete-time, arbitrage-free models, Nelson-Siegel type models

JEL classifications: G1, E4, C5, C13

ISBNs: 9781108972123 (PB), 9781108975537 (OC)
ISSNs: 2631-8571 (online), 2631-8563 (print)

Contents

1 Empirical Analysis of Term Structure Data

1.1 Introduction

Before looking at the empirical behaviour of yields, we need to introduce some notation. Let y_t^τ denote a set of yields that together form a yield curve, that is, a vector that stacks individual annual yields, with the same dating, t, but that are observed at different maturities, τ. In the practical examples included in this Element, we will typically use $\tau = \{3, 12, 24, \ldots, 120\}$ months, but τ can naturally take any value, at which yields are observed. When referring to a panel of yield observations (of dimension number of dates by number of maturities; i.e. a collection of yield curves observed at different dates), we will either write y, $y(\tau)$, or Y.

In a factor model, X will denote the extracted factors, and H, G, or B, will typically denote the matrix that translates factors into yields; this matrix is often denoted the 'loading' matrix because it expresses how each of the extracted factors impact, or load on, the yields at different maturities. Vector autoregressive models will be written as $z_t = m + \Phi \cdot (z_{t-1} - m) + e_t$, when written in mean-adjusted form, and sometimes as $z_t = c + \Phi \cdot z_{t-1} + e_t$, when written in constant form (i.e. $m = [I - \Phi]^{-1} \cdot c$).

At this point it may also be worth recalling that the yield curve is a by-product of the financial market trading process. Agents trade bonds that are quoted in prices, $p_t(\tau)$. A risk-free bond, the ones we primarily deal with here, guarantees to pay Eur 1 (in reality some scaling of 1, most often Eur 100) at the maturity of the bond. The price today is therefore, as always in finance, the discounted value of the promised payment that falls in the future: $P_t(\tau) = 1 \cdot (1 + y_t(\tau))^{-\tau} \Leftrightarrow y_t(\tau) = (P_t(\tau))^{1/-\tau} - 1$, in discrete time, and $P_t(\tau) = 1 \cdot e^{-y_t^\tau \cdot \tau} \Leftrightarrow y_t(\tau) = -\frac{1}{\tau} \cdot log(P_t(\tau))$, in continuous time.

We will model exclusively zero-coupon bonds. These bonds are important because they form the basis for fixed income pricing: since all coupon paying bonds can be expressed as portfolios of zero-coupon bonds (of relevant maturities), once we know the prices of zero-coupon bonds, we can also find the market-clearing price for all existing coupon paying bonds, assuming that there is no idiosyncratic risk attached to these bonds, such as, for example, illiquidity risk. Most often, however, we do not work with prices, but instead focus on rates/yields, that is, on the annualised percentage return the bond gives, if we hold it to maturity. As implied by its name, a zero-coupon bond does not pay any coupons during its life, and its cashflow stream is therefore simple, as illustrated in Figure 1 for zero-coupon bonds of one, two, and ten-year maturities.

Typically, we get zero-coupon data from Bloomberg, Reuters, and other data providers. These data are available at daily, weekly, and monthly

Quantitative Finance

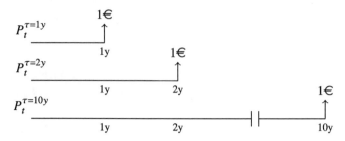

Figure 1 Zero-coupon cashflows

observation frequencies, and at predefined target maturities, for example, at $\{0.25, 1, 2, \ldots, 10, 15, 20, 30\}$ years.

1.2 Exploring Yield Curve Data

The example data used in this section are stored in the MATLAB work-space file named 'Data'. Data are obtained from public sources. The US data are downloaded from the Federal Reserve Board homepage.[1] These are the well-known and often-used Gurkaynak, Sack and Wright (2006) data. German yield curve data are obtained from the homepage of the German Bundesbank.[2]

For each segment, we have yields in per cent per annum across maturities, as well as model-based estimates for the expectations component and the term premium, both estimated at a ten-year maturity point. We will return to these latter two variables later on and for now only focus on the yield curve data. Let's load and plot these data: each data set contains monthly observations for the following variables: date and yields, and spans the period from January 1975 to December 2018, that is, a total of 528 time-series observations for each of the 6 included maturities per yield curve segment, which are $\{3, 12, 24, 60, 84, 120\}$ months.[3]

In addition to the time-series evolution of yields shown in Figure 2, it is also informative to see what the yield curve looks like in the cross-sectional dimension. For example, what does the average yield curve look like? And, what

---

[1] https://www.federalreserve.gov/pubs/feds/2006/200628/200628abs.html

[2] https://www.bundesbank.de/en/statistics/time-series-database

[3] The shortest maturity observed for the raw German data downloaded from the homepage of the German Bundesbank is six months. For the illustrative examples shown in this section, it is simpler if observations at equal maturities are available for the German and the US yield curve data. Hence, an interpolation technique is used to obtain a three-month maturity observation for the German data. The exact process used is documented in the MATLAB code in Section 1. In an actual analysis we would not do this because it is not needed. Yield curve models can easily handle data observed at different maturities: we employ this trick here simply for expositional reasons.

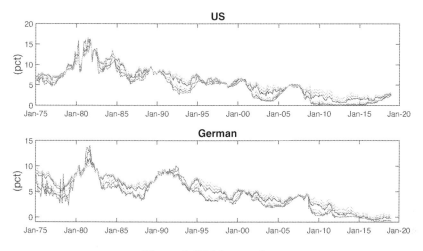

Figure 2   Yield curve data

The figure shows the time series of yields, observed monthly and covering the period from 1975 to end-2018, for maturities of six-month, one-year, two-year, five-year, seven-year, and ten-year for Germany, and for the US market the following maturities are shown three-month, one-year, two-year, five-year, seven-year, and ten-year. Yields for the USA, Germany, and the euro area are included in the plot. It is noted that the shortest maturity in the German market is six months (that is what is available from the German Bundesbank home page) while the shortest maturity available for the US data is three months.

are some of the most extreme shapes and locations that yield have displayed historically? These questions are explored in the following.

Note that one of the curves shown in Figures 3 and 4 may actually have materialised historically, since the calculations are done for each of the maturity points separately.

Going back to the time-series plots of the yields observed for the USA and German market segments, it is also interesting to observe that there is a very high degree of correlation among yields within a given market segment, and that a similarly high degree of correlation exists between market segments. It almost seems as if every little up- and down-ward movement in one maturity is mirrored by the other maturities in that market segment, with more pronounced movements the higher the maturity. Similarly, the secular swings that yields display over the twenty years of data are equally well visible across market segments.

A more structured view on the within and between segment correlation is illustrated in the following. For presentational purposes, correlations are shown only for a subset of the included maturities.

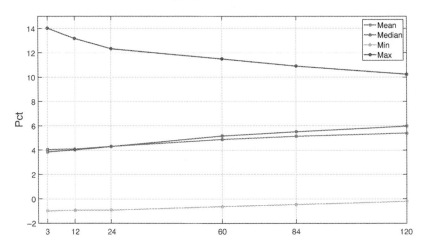

Figure 3 Generic shapes of the German yield curves

The figure shows the mean, median, min, and max of the German yields observed at a monthly frequency and covering the period from January 1975 to December 2018. The statistics are calculated across maturities. The x-axis shows the maturity of the yields in months (e.g. 120 months correspond to 10 years).

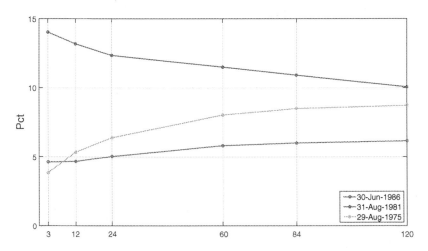

Figure 4 German yields with varying slopes

The figure shows German yield curves on the days when the slope $(y^{\tau=10y}-y^{\tau=3m})$ reached its minimum, maximum and average value, for the period from January 1975 to December 2018.

Figure 5 provides a visual representation of the correlation between German and US yields. If we had included other or additional yield curve segments, in addition to the three-month, five-year, and ten-year maturities, we would get qualitatively identical results. As expected based on the visual inspection of

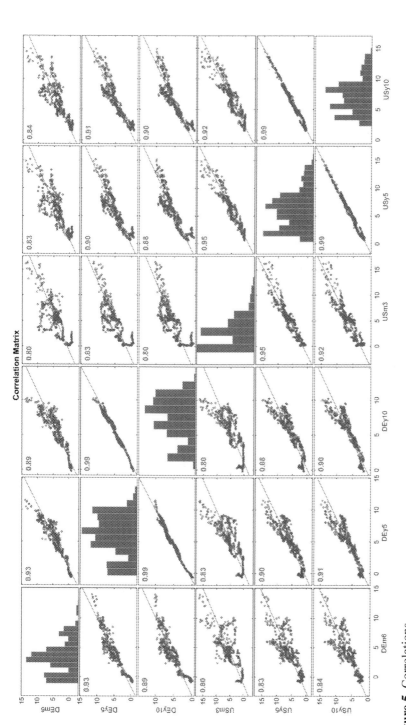

Figure 5 Correlations

The figure shows the pair-wise correlation between US and German yield levels observed at a monthly frequency and covering the period from January 1975 to December 2018. Correlations are calculated between the three-month, five-year, and ten-year maturity points. In each sub-element of the figure, the red number indicates the correlation coefficient, and the red line shows the fitted regression line. On the diagonal, histograms of the series are plotted.

the time series plots, the cross correlations confirm our suspicion: yields within and across yield segments are very highly correlated. Note that a red number in the Figure 3 correlation matrix indicates that the correlation is statistically significant from zero at a 1 per cent significance level.

We could repeat the above correlation analysis for the first differences of the yield series – this would, for example, make sense, if yields were believed to be I(1) processes (i.e. integrated of order one). And, if we did this, we would obtain a correlation picture that is qualitatively identical to the one discussed here.

Now, looking at the time series plots of the yield curve segments, one could conclude, based on a preliminary and casual visual inspection, that the behaviour displayed by yields is somewhat different from what most people have in the back of their mind when they think about the trajectory of a stationary I(0) process. While this is a relevant thought, the discussion of stationarity will be taken up later on, when we discuss the eigenvalues of estimated vector autoregressive processes (VAR models – not to be confused with VaR, i.e. value-at-risk). For now, we treat observed yields as coming from a stationary data-generating process.

How can the overwhelming degree of correlation between yields be exploited? The answer is: by using principal component analysis (PCA)/ factor models. At this stage, it is worth noting that virtually all term structure models, as well as many other important financial models (e.g. ATP and CAPM for equity return modelling), rely heavily on PCA modelling principles. In fact, this econometric technique is quite possibly the single most important modelling idea in the field of quantitative time-series finance. To my mind, it is as important as PDEs (partial differential equations) are to the branch of finance that deals with derivative pricing. It is therefore fairly important to master this technique.

Before embarking on the factor modelling principle, it is worth spending a few minutes explaining why it is generally not advisable to use raw lagged yields directly to explain current yields. Doing this would amount to applying the following VAR-model set-up, where Y is a vector of yields, c is a constant, Φ is a matrix of autoregressive coefficients, and e is a vector of residuals:

$$Y_t = c + \Phi \cdot Y_{t-1} + e_t \tag{1.1}$$

Arguments against this modelling strategy are, amongst others:

- The number of yields modelled may vary from market to market and over time. It is therefore not clear which maturities that should be included in the model.

- One may need to adapt the dimension of the model, depending on which market is modelled. This is inconvenient as well, as model results may not be comparable.
- Since correlation between yields is so high, we may run into the problem of multicollinearity.
- Projected yield curves and yield curve forecasts may turn out to violate standard regularities (e.g. individual yield curve points may be out of sync with the rest of the curve).
- The econometrician has very little control over the simulations; for example, it is difficult to steer the projections in a certain direction, if that is desired. Likewise, it is difficult to avoid certain (unrealistic) yield curve shapes and developments.

This last point is illustrated in Figure 6, using the German data.

It is dangerous these days to make statements about whether a given simulated yield curve has a realistic shape or not – and the future may prove me wrong – but despite what we have seen over the past years, I believe that the depicted simulated curves in Figure 7 are too oddly shaped to be considered for financial analysis (unless for some wild economic scenario): this applies to their shape and location, and to the overall simulated trajectory (Figure 6) for

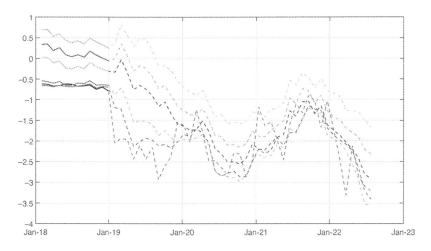

Figure 6 Naive yield curve forecasts

The figure shows how one can do naive forecasts of the yield curve, and what problems this may bring. A VAR model is fitted to individual maturity points using the full historical sample (from 1975 to end-2018) of German yields. Each maturity is then projected forty-two monthly periods ahead using the VAR. These projections are started at the last observation covered by the data sample.

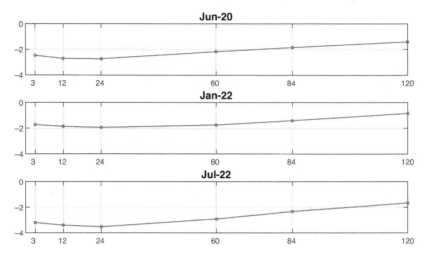

Figure 7 Randomly chosen projected yield curves

The figure shows randomly selected sample curves picked among the forty-two projected curves. The x-axis shows the maturities in months at which yields are recorded.

the yields over the coming forty-two months. One may of course have a rule-of-thumb and a routine that kicks out too oddly looking yield constellations and trajectories. Doing this will naturally change the distributional assumptions of the forecasted yields (since they are truncated at some pre-specified value) compared to the distribution exhibited by the historical data. One way to remedy this is to rely on approaches similar to Rebonato, Mahal, Joshi, Bucholz and Nyholm (2005), where historical residuals are block-bootstrapped (i.e. re-sampled) and the resulting simulated yields are smoothed to achieve shapes that are akin to those seen in historical data.

1.3 A First Look at Principal Component Models

Dimension reduction is one of the great feats of PCA / factors models: the core idea is that the majority of the variability of a given data set derives from a few underlying (sometimes not directly observable) factors. This concept is familiar; for example, the well-known CAPM prescribes that a single market factor is responsible for the expected return on all equities traded in the economy. Recall that the security market line is written as: $E[r_i] = r_f + \beta_i \cdot (r_m - r_f)$, where investors are rewarded only for taking market risk in excess of the risk free rate. r_m is the return on the market portfolio, that is, the underlying factor in this model, r_f is the observable risk free rate, and β_i is the sensitivity of the i'th security's return, r_i. In factor model language, r_f is the constant, r_m is the underlying factor, and β_i is the factor sensitivity that translates the factor

observation into something that is applicable to the i'th security. We can naturally operate with more than one factor. Typically, term structure models include
between one and five factors.

In general terms, and using matrix notation, we can write a factor model for
the yield data in the following way:

$$
\underbrace{Y_t}_{(\#\tau \times 1)} = \underbrace{G}_{(\#\tau \times \#F)} \cdot \underbrace{X_t}_{(\#F \times 1)} + \underbrace{\Sigma}_{(\#\tau \times \#\tau)} \cdot \underbrace{e_t}_{(\#\tau \times 1)} \quad e_t \sim N(0, I)
$$

$$(1.2)$$

where Y is the vector of yields observed at time t, G is the aforementioned
loading matrix, that translates the extracted factors X into into yields, Σ collects the standard deviations of the residuals, and e $N(0, 1)$. The dimensions of
the variables are recorded below each entry, with the $\#$-sign referring to the dimension of each variable: so, for example, $\#\tau x1$ reads 'number tau by 1'. Say
that yields are observed at the following $\{3, 12, 24, 36, 60, 120\}$ months: in this
case we would have: $\tau\{3, 12, 24, 36, 60, 120\}'$ so, $\#\tau = 6$, and since this is a
column vector, the number of columns included in τ is just 1. Consequently, the
dimension of τ is therefore 6x1. The dimension of the other included variables
are denoted in a similar way, with $\#F$ representing the number of included
factors. So, our first job when using factor models is to settle on an appropriate number of factors to extract (i.e. to choose $\#F$). We will always have
that $\#F < \#\tau$, utilising the high cross-sectional correlation between yields, as
shown in Figure 5, to reduce the dimensionlity of Y.[4]

Looking at the expression for Y_t in (1.2) indicates that if we know the factor
loadings Φ, then we can find the factors X_t using linear regression, or by inversion. Underline the previous sentence! – we will use this 'trick' extensively
when dealing with Nelson-Siegel type yield curve models later on. To preview
a bit, let's quickly see how to back out the factors X using the full set of data
– as mentioned, we will return to this issue in greater detail later on. First we
write the above expression in terms of the full data set:

$$
\underbrace{E[Y]}_{(\#\tau \times \#Obs)} = \underbrace{G}_{(\#\tau \times \#F)} \cdot \underbrace{X}_{(\#F \times \#Obs)}
$$

where *nObs* is the number of dates the data spans. Assume G is known.
Then, in the context of an OLS regression, G represents the explanatory

---

[4] If a purely statistical factor model is estimated on the yield curve data, we will obtain factors that
   are orthogonal. However, later on it will become clear that the choice of G defines the economic
   interpretation that can be attached to the extracted yield curve factors; and in this case we will,
   in general, not find orthogonal factors.

variables and X the parameters to be estimated. We can therefore find X in the following ways:

$$\hat{X} = G^{-1} \cdot Y \tag{1.3}$$

or

$$\hat{X} = (G' \cdot G)^{-1} \cdot G' \cdot Y \tag{1.4}$$

where the first equation in (1.3) represents a pure inversion, and the second is the standard OLS formula. Returning to the main topic of this section (i.e. factor models), let's see if the DE and US data hide some interesting underlying patterns (i.e. factors), and let's try to construct a completely data-driven joint model for these to yield curve segments on the basis of such underlying factors.

The intention here is only to show how factor models can be useful for modelling term structure data, without infusing any term structure modelling knowledge – in other words, the illustrated strategy may be what an econometrician would choose to do if she had not received any term structure schooling. Later on in the Element it will become clear, that such an econometrician can actually be quite successful at modelling term structure data!

A clarification about the term 'factor models' is warranted here. When I refer to 'factor models' and 'factors', I do in fact mean 'principal Components', (i.e. the outcome of applying the PCA function in MATLAB). So, throughout, it is assumed that yield curve factors can be formed as a linear combination of observed yields. Alternatively, if a true factor modelling approach was applied, the starting point would be some underlying latent factors that were causing the evolution observed in the yield curve, and we would try to extract these factors. As we shall see, we will typically revert to factors that are directly interpretable in terms of yield curve observables (e.g. the level, slope and curvature of the yields curve), or actual maturity points on the yield curve. We will not, however, include unobservable quantities, such as, for example, the effective stance of monetary policy, or the natural long-term rate, as factors in the models that we work with in this Element.

Individual eigenvalues express how much of the overall variability in the data set the respective eigenvector explains. To help decide how many factors we need to include in our model, we can therefore link the number of factors to the overall variance that we want our model to capture.

Table 1 shows the cumulative fraction explained by the first six extracted principal components/factors explain of the US and German data. It is seen that four factors capture 100 per cent of the historical variability of both US and German yields, confirming the high degree of cross-sectional correlation among yield levels documented. If we believe that some of the variability in the observed data is due to noise, we should chose to model fewer than four

Table 1 Cumulative variability explained by the extracted yield curve factors

	US	DE
1st	0.9884	0.9675
2nd	0.9982	0.9964
3rd	0.9998	0.9995
4th	1.0000	0.9999
5th	1.0000	1.0000
6th	1.0000	1.0000

The table shows the cumulative fraction of variability explained by the principal components extracted from US and euro area yield curve data (in levels). The data cover the period from January 1975 to December 2018 and are observed monthly. The following maturities are included in the data sets: {3, 12, 24, 60, 84, 120} months.

factors: we don't want a model that propagates idiosyncratic noise from the past into the future. Three factors also look to be on the high side, so a sensible choice may be to include two factors. In fact, the explained variability may suggest that only one factor is needed, since the most important factor explains 95 per cent of the variability in the US data, and 98 per cent of the variability in the German data. But, a model with just one factor is quite simplistic: while it naturally can portray realistic shapes of the yield curve observed at a given point in time, if the dynamic evolution of the yield curve factors are modelled and used to project yield curves, a one-factor model is only able to generate parallel shifts in yields from t to $t + j$, with $j > 0$. In the following we will therefore typically rely on model having thee to four factors.

For convenience, we will refer to distinct groups of yields as: 'yield curve segments'. There is of course no universal definition of what a segment is, and our use of this terminology is deliberately loose: we will use this 'terminology' as referring to a distinct a group of yields that intuitively (and economically) belong together. For example, US government zero-coupon yields can form a yield curve segment; German sovereign zero-coupon yields can form another segment; similarly, yields carrying a certain credit grade can form another yield curve segment. Although the segmentation of yields into these distinct 'segments' follows from the actual model application, it should be clear from the context what constitutes a yield curve segment.[5]

---

[5] In the interest of completeness, it should be mentioned that the use of the word "segment" in this context has nothing to do with the yield curve segmentation hypothesis, the theory where

Table 2 Root mean squared errors

	US						DE					
	3m	1y	2y	5y	7y	10y	3m	1y	2y	5y	7y	10y
RMSE	8	12	4	12	6	11	2	10	7	11	4	11

The table displays the fit of the joined yield curve model, comprising US and euro area German data, to the used data. The degree of fit is assessed via the root mean squared error (RMSE) denominated in basis points.

Say we want to jointly model US and German government zero-coupon yields. And, lets assume that for our practical application, that it makes sense to treat the US yields as the 'base' yields curve segment, and hence the German yields will be modelled as a spread/add-on to the base US yield curve segment. To investigate whether such a set-up, where one segment constitutes yields (here US yields) and the other segment constitutes yield spread (here German yields minus US yields, naturally observed for identical maturities) makes sense econometrically, we will investigate what the loading structures look like, and whether it is possible to approximate the German yield spreads sufficiently well using a factor structure. We will do this before looking in more detail at the complete model formulation and how we can include a model that captures well the time series dynamics of the yield curve factors.

Figure 8 shows the empirical loadings when two factors are extracted for the US yield curve segment, and when two factors are used to model the spread data. It is interesting to see how similar the loadings are: the loading for the first US factor is constant across all maturities; likewise, the first spread-segment factor has a constant impact across all maturities. The loadings across the sampled maturities for the second factor are also similar, and so are the loadings for the third factor.

The RMSEs delivered by this model are fine and what we would expect of a 3-factor model (see Table 2). To provide a visual comparison between observed and model fitted yields, Figure 9 shows the three-month and ten-year segments of the German and US yield curve segments.

1.4 Adding Time-Series Dynamics to the Factors

It is now natural to add dynamics to our empirical model, such that we can use it as a projection and scenario-generation tool. To do this, we assume that

---

bond traders are believed to have a preference for a given set of maturities: see e.g. Vayanos and Vila (2009), Greenwood and Vayanos (2014), Li and Wei (2013), and Eser, Lemke, Nyholm, Radde and Vladu (2019).

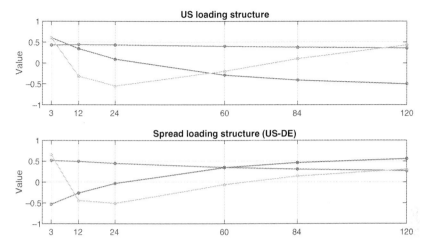

Figure 8 Yield curve data

The figure shows the empirical loadings for the US data (upper panel), and the German yield curve spread data (lower panel). The spreads are defined as the difference between the US and German yields observed for identical maturities: $S_t^{US-DE} = Y_t^{US}(\tau) - Y_t^{US}(\tau)$ for $\tau = \{3, 12, 24, 60, 84, 120\}$ months. The data used in this example are observed monthly and cover the period from 1975 to 2018 The loading structures are estimated using principal component analysis assuming that two factors are needed to provide a good characterisation of the US data, and that two factors are needed to model the spread data.

a VAR(p) model is an appropriate devise to capture the dynamic behaviour of the yield curve factors. First, we want to identify the log-order p. Following the BIC criterion[6], a VAR(1) model is applied as an adequate description of the law of motion for the four yield curve factors. Our purely empirically derived joint German and US yield curve model is then ready to be put to work. The model can be summarised in the following way:

$$\begin{bmatrix} y_{US} \\ y_{DE} \end{bmatrix}_t = \begin{bmatrix} G_{US} & 0 \\ G_{US} & G_{sprd} \end{bmatrix} \cdot \begin{bmatrix} X_{US} \\ X_{sprd} \end{bmatrix}_t + \Sigma e_t \qquad (1.5)$$

$$\begin{bmatrix} X_{US} \\ X_{sprd} \end{bmatrix}_t = \begin{bmatrix} c_{US} \\ c_{sprd} \end{bmatrix}$$

$$+ \begin{bmatrix} \Phi_{US,US} & \Phi_{US,sprd} \\ \Phi_{sprd,US} & \Phi_{sprd,sprd} \end{bmatrix} \cdot \begin{bmatrix} X_{US} \\ X_{sprd} \end{bmatrix}_{t-1} + \Sigma v_t \qquad (1.6)$$

---

[6] This is the Bayesian information criterion, which can be used to determine the optimal lags to include in a time-series model; see Lütkepohl (1991)[ch.4]

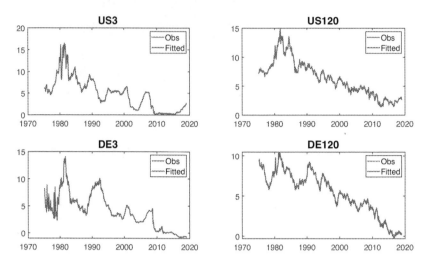

Figure 9 Observed and fitted yields

The figure shows the time-series evolution of selected maturity points for the US and German yield curve data. The figures show the observed and model-fitted yields for the 3-month and 120-month maturity points.

The eigenvalues of Φ are $[0.9569, 0.9569, 0.9720, 0.9921]$. Given that the maximum eigenvalue of the auroregressive matrix is less than one, the estimated VAR is stationary. So, lets see what kind of yield and return projections we can generate using this model. But, before we embark on this exercise, lets first backtest the model using a pseudo out-of-sample forecasting experiment. Our data sample covers 468 monthly observations from January 1975 to April 2018, and the last five years of the sample is used for backtesting purposes. Naturally, this choice is somewhat arbitrary, since other equally appropriate combinations of the amount of data available for the first estimation of the model, and number of data points available for backtesting, naturally exists. The backtesting exercise is therefore structured in the following way:

- The model is estimated using data from January 1975 to May 2013.
- Factor projections are generated using the dynamic model for the yield curve factors, shown previously. Projections are generated for months one to six ahead, (i.e. for April, May,…,September 2013).
- The factor projections are converted to yields using the Yield Equation, shown previously.
- Projected yields are compared to observed yields at the appropriate horizon.
- As a comparison, random walk projections are also generated and compared to the relevant observed yields.

Table 3 Back-testing the joint model

	US					DE				
	3m	1y	2y	5y	10y	3m	1y	2y	5y	10y
					Model					
Fitted	6	8	2	6	5	2	8	2	12	13
Forecasted 1m ahead	15	11	13	19	22	8	9	9	19	18
Forecasted 2m ahead	21	13	18	24	29	11	10	10	23	21
Forecasted 3m ahead	27	15	23	29	34	13	11	13	27	25
Forecasted 4m ahead	31	19	28	33	37	17	14	16	31	29
Forecasted 5m ahead	34	22	32	37	41	20	16	19	35	34
Forecasted 6m ahead	36	25	35	40	43	24	20	23	39	39
					Random Walk					
Fitted	10	13	13	18	23	8	9	8	18	20
Forecasted 1m ahead	13	18	17	23	31	9	10	9	21	24
Forecasted 2m ahead	16	22	21	27	36	11	10	10	24	28
Forecasted 3m ahead	20	27	27	31	40	13	12	12	27	32
Forecasted 4m ahead	23	32	31	34	44	15	12	13	29	34
Forecasted 5m ahead	27	37	36	37	46	17	13	15	31	37
Forecasted 6m ahead	31	42	41	40	49	19	14	16	34	41

The table shows the s-step ahead prediction RMSEs in basis points for the joint model and the Random Walk model.

- One month is added to the dataset used to estimate the model and the aforementioned steps are repeated until the end of the dataset is reached

More can naturally be done, but this is left to the reader, should they have the urge to go more into detail at this stage. It is also left to the reader to evaluate the outcomes shown in Table 3 and to reach a conclusion on whether the model is useful for any practical purposes – apart from illustrative ones.

With this out of the way, let's now see what kind of forward-looking return distributions the model can generate. Assuming that we are working with continuously compounded yields, which we are, the holding period return on a τ-maturity bond over the period from t to $t+j$ is $r^{\tau}_{t,t+j} = p^{\tau-j}_{t+j} - p^{\tau}_t$, where p is the log bond price. The intuition here is that we buy a bond at time t with maturity τ, (p^{τ}_t), and sell it j periods later, at time $t+j$, where the bond is j periods closer to redemption, and its maturity is therefore $\tau - j$. Since $p^{\tau}_t = -\tau \cdot y^{\tau}_t$, we can rewrite the return in terms of yields as: $r^{\tau}_{t,t+j} = \tau \cdot y^{\tau}_t - (\tau - j) \cdot y^{\tau-j}_{t+j}$.

Table 4 Simulated return statistics

	US			SE		
	1y	5y	10y	1y	5y	10y
Mean	2.51	1.42	-0.88	-0.76	-2.93	-5.37
Std.	0.00	5.12	9.69	0.00	3.33	7.09

The table shows distribution statistics for the simulated return distributions for the five-year and ten-year segments of the curve.

As an example, we will use our model to simulate return distributions for the 12, 60, and 120 months segments of the curve, using the last observation in our data sample as a starting point. With this application in mind, it is clear that we cannot use the model directly. A bit of adjustment is needed since the empirical factor loadings only are available at the maturities at which data are observed, i.e. for maturities $\{3, 12, 24, 60, 84, 120\}$ months, and since we also need yield observations at maturities $\{0, 48, 108\}$ months to calculate the desired returns. We therefore need somehow to enlarge our loading matrix such that it also comprises loadings for these additional maturity points. We will see later on that this is an easy operation, if we have a parametric description of the loading matrix (such as e.g. in the Nelson-Siegel model). However, for now, we have to come up with a solution applicable to the empirical problem at hand by using inter-/extra-polation techniques.

The derived loadings are shown in Figure 10. It is observed that the expanded loadings are inline with the ones calculated for the maturities at which yields are observed. The expanded loadings are shown as blue lines while the original observations are indicated using red stars. It looks good, so it can be concluded that the chosen expansions methodology did a good job. We can now proceed with the generation of yield simulations and return calculations, and proceed with the generation of yield simulations and return calculations.

Figure 11 shows the simulated return distributions for the 5- and 10-year maturity points and Table 4 shows the two first moments of the simulated distributions. I have not shown the plots of the 1-year maturity points – why not? To illustrate the distributional properties of the simulated returns, the red lines in the plots show superimposed normal distributions. These distributions fit the returns quite well, as expected, since the estimated model for the yields relies on the normal distribution. We will see later on how we can escape the world of normality and how distributions can be generated that match assumptions about the expected future trajectory of the economy.

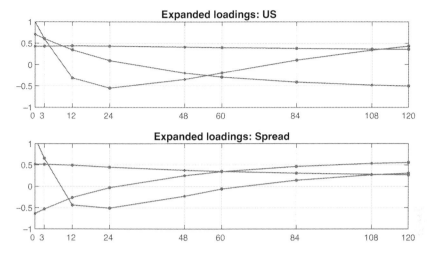

Figure 10 Model and observed yields

The figure shows the loading structures for the US and spread yield curve segments, including the additional loadings that are needed to calculate monthly returns. Since returns are calculated for the 60- and 120-month maturities, we need to approximate yields also at the 48- and 108-month maturities. The loadings for these points are seen in the figure.

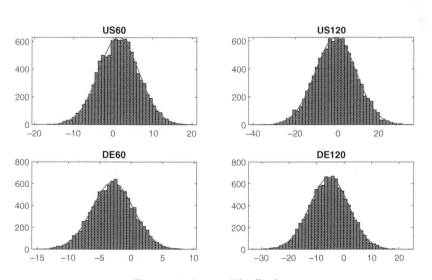

Figure 11 Return Distributions

The figure shows empirical return distributions evaluated against the normal distribution for the 5-year and 10-year segments of the examined yield curve data.

MATLAB code

filename: Empirical_Investigation_of_Observed_Yields.m

```
1   %%  Section 1: Empirical exploration of yield curve data
2   %
3   clear all;                          % clear all variables
4   close all;                          % close all figures
5   clc;                                % clear command window
6   disp('Please wait...')
7   load('Data_YCM.mat');
8
9   % adjusting the minimum maturity for the German data:
10  %   the 6 month maturity is the shortest observed maturity in the
11  %   downloaded german data. Using a principal component analysis
12  %   (more about this in the text) a three-month yield observation is
13  %   is fitted. This makes US and German yields available for an
14  %   identical set of maturities.
15  %
16  x_      = [1:1:11]';
17  tau_in  = [6 12:12:120]';
18  tau_out = [3 12:12:120]';
19  Dates   = DE_data(:,1);
20  Y_tmp   = DE_data(:,2:end);
21  [G, F ] = pca(DE_data(:,2:end),'Centered','off');
22  G_   = nan(11,11);
23  for (j=1:11)
24      G_(:,j) = interp1(tau_in,G(:,j),tau_out,'spline','extrap');
25  end
26  DE_data = [];
27  DE_data = [Dates (G_*F')'];
28
29  start_ = datenum('31-Jan-1975');      % defines the start date of the data samples.
30                                        %   can be changed to test whether the results
31                                        %   below are robust to other starting points.
32
33  indx_s   = find(US_data(:,1)==start_,1,'first');
34  indx_tau = [1 2 3 6 8 11];                % selected maturities
35  tauDE    = [3 12 24 60 84 120]';          % defines the maturities
36  tauUS    = [3 12 24 60 84 120]';
37  Y_US     = US_data(indx_s:end,indx_tau+1);  % ... first column holds the date ...
38  Y_DE     = DE_data(indx_s:end,indx_tau+1);  % contains the yield curve
39  dates    = US_data(indx_s:end,1);           %   observations nObs-by-nTau
40  [nObs,nTau] = size(Y_US);                    % number of time series observations and
41                                               %   number of maturities.
42
43  figure('units','normalized','outerposition',[0 0 1 1])
44      subplot(2,1,1), plot( dates, Y_US )
45      date_ticks = datenum(1975:5:2020,1,1);
46      set(gca, 'xtick', date_ticks), ylabel('(pct)')
47      datetick('x','mmm-yy','keepticks'), title('US')
48      set(gca, 'FontSize', 20)
49
50      subplot(2,1,2), plot(dates, Y_DE),
51      date_ticks = datenum(1975:5:2020,1,1);
52      set(gca, 'xtick', date_ticks), ylabel('(pct)')
53      datetick('x','mmm-yy','keepticks'), title('German')
54      set(gca, 'FontSize', 20)
55
56  print -depsc Empirical_YieldCurves_US_DE_EA
57
58  %% Cross sectional plots
59  figure('units','normalized','outerposition',[0 0 1 1])
60      plot(tauDE,[mean(Y_DE)' median(Y_DE)' min(Y_DE)' max(Y_DE)' ], ...
61          'o-','LineWidth',2), ...
62      xticks(tauDE'), grid, 'on';
63      xticklabels(tauDE' ), ...
```

```
64        ylabel('Pct'), legend('Mean', 'Median', 'Min', ...
65        'Max', 'Location','northeast')
66        ylim([-2 15])
67        set(gca, 'FontSize', 20)
68    print -depsc AverageYieldsDE
69
70    diff_S = Y_DE(:,end)-Y_DE(:,1);        % difference between the 10y and
71                                           % 6m yields (a measure for the slope)
72
73    [~, indxS_med] = min(abs(diff_S-median(diff_S)));  % finds the index of
74    [~, indxS_min] = min(abs(diff_S-min(diff_S)));     % the curve having the
75    [~, indxS_max] = min(abs(diff_S-max(diff_S)));     % median, min, and max
76                                                       % slope in the sample
77
78    figure('units','normalized','outerposition',[0 0 1 1])
79        plot(tauDE,[Y_DE(indxS_med,:)' Y_DE(indxS_min,:)'...
80                    Y_DE(indxS_max,:)'],'o-', 'LineWidth',2 ), ...
81        %title('Generic Slope-Based Shapes of the Yield Curve - Germany'), ...
82        legend( datestr(dates(indxS_med,1)), datestr(dates(indxS_min,1)), ...
83                datestr(dates(indxS_max,1)), 'Location', 'SouthEast' ), ...
84        xticks(tauDE), xticklabels(tauDE), ...
85        ylabel('Pct'), grid, 'on'; ...
86        ylim([0 15])
87        set(gca, 'FontSize', 20)
88    print -depsc GenericYieldCurveShapesDE
89
90
91    %% Correlation analysis
92    subData = array2table([Y_DE(:,1), Y_DE(:,4), Y_DE(:,6), Y_US(:,1), Y_US(:,4),
93                           Y_US(:,6)]);
94    subData.Properties.VariableNames = { 'DEm6', 'DEy5', 'DEy10', ...
95                                         'USm3', 'USy5', 'USy10' };
96    corrplot(subData,'type','Pearson','testR','on','alpha',0.01)
97
98    print -depsc YieldCorrPlot
99
100   %% Generating projections from a yields-only model
101   %
102   rng(42+42+42); % fixing the starting point for the random number generator
103                  %    to ensure replicability
104   nHist    = 12; % number of historical observations to inlude in the plot
105   nSim     = 42; % number of periods to be simulated
106   VAR_y    = varm(nTau, 1); % sets up a VAR1 model: 11 variables and 1 lag
107   est_DE   = estimate(VAR_y, Y_DE); % estimate VAR1 model on all obs.
108   sim_DE   = simulate(est_DE, nSim, 'Y0', Y_DE(end,:)); % simulate the model
109                                                         % star at last obs
110   simDates = [ dates(end-11:end,1); ...
111                dates(end,1)+(31:31:nSim*31)' ];
112                % concatenating the dates for the last 12 data observations
113                %    with the dates spanning the forecasts
114   data2plot = [ Y_DE(end-nHist+1:end,:); sim_DE]; % hist. + sim. data
115
116   figure('units','normalized','outerposition',[0 0 1 1])
117       plot(simDates, data2plot, '--', 'LineWidth',2), ...
118       hold on, grid, 'on'; ...
119       plot(simDates(1:nHist,1), Y_DE(end-nHist+1:end,:), '-', ...
120                                   'LineWidth',2)
121       %title('Forecasting German Yields the Incorrect way'), ...
122       set(gca, 'FontSize', 20)
123       datetick('x','mmm-yy')
124       print -depsc WrongProjections
125
126   figure('units','normalized','outerposition',[0 0 1 1])
127       subplot(3,1,1), plot(tauDE,sim_DE(17,:),'o-'), ...
128           ylim([-4 0]), grid,'on'; ...
129                                 title(datestr(simDates(17+nHist),'mmm-yy'))
130       xticks(tauDE), xticklabels({tauDE}),
131       set(gca, 'FontSize', 18)
132       subplot(3,1,2), plot(tauDE,sim_DE(36,:),'o-'), ...
```

```
133            ylim([-4 0]), grid,'on'; ...
134                        title(datestr(simDates(36+nHist),'mmm-yy'))
135     xticks(tauDE), xticklabels({tauDE}),
136     set(gca, 'FontSize', 18)
137     subplot(3,1,3), plot(tauDE,sim_DE(42,:),'o-'), ...
138            ylim([-4 0]), grid,'on'; ...
139                        title(datestr(simDates(42+nHist),'mmm-yy'))
140     xticks(tauDE), xticklabels({tauDE})
141     set(gca, 'FontSize', 18)
142     print -depsc FunnySimYields
143
144
145  %% A first look at factor models
146  %
147  [G_US, F_US, eig_US]   = pca(Y_US);      % run factor analysis on US data
148  [G_DE, F_DE, eig_DE]   = pca(Y_DE);      % run factor analysis on DE data
149
150  [ cumsum(eig_US./sum(eig_US)) cumsum(eig_DE./sum(eig_DE)) ]
151
152  nF      = 3;
153  Spread = Y_DE-Y_US;                        % the pure spread in percentage points
154  [G_Sprd, F_Sprd, eig_Sprd] = pca(Spread);  % run factor analysis on US data
155
156  figure('units','normalized','outerposition',[0 0 1 1])
157     subplot(2,1,1), plot(tauUS,G_US(:,1:nF),'o-', ...
158         'LineWidth',2),  ylim([-1 1]),  title('US loading structure'),
159     xticks(tauUS),xticklabels(tauUS'),
160     ylabel('Value'), grid, 'on'; set(gca, 'FontSize', 20)
161     subplot(2,1,2), plot(tauDE,G_Sprd(:,1:nF),'o-', ...
162         'LineWidth',2), ylim([-1 1]), title('Spread loading structure (US-DE)'),
163     xticks(tauDE), xticklabels(tauDE'),
164     ylabel('Value'), grid, 'on'; set(gca, 'FontSize', 20)
165     print -depsc EmpiricalLoadingStructures
166
167  %% Joint model for DE and US yields
168  %
169  Y2     = [ Y_US Y_DE ];                     % collecting the relevant yield segments
170  G_mdl  = [ G_US(:,1:nF) zeros(nTau,nF);    % loading structure for the joint model
171           G_US(:,1:nF) G_Sprd(:,1:nF)] ;
172  F_mdl  = G_mdl\Y2';
173  Y2_hat = (G_mdl*F_mdl)';                    % fitted yield curves
174  err    = Y2-Y2_hat;                         % fitting errors
175
176  RMSE_bps = 100*(mean(err.^2)).^(1/2)     % RMSE in basis points
177
178  Tab_rmse = array2table(round(RMSE_bps)); % just for the display of output
179  for (j=1:nTau)
180      Tab_rmse.Properties.VariableNames(1,j)      = {strcat(['US',num2str(tauDE(j,1))])
                }};
181      Tab_rmse.Properties.VariableNames(1,j+nTau) = {strcat(['DE',num2str(tauUS(j,1))])
                }};
182  end
183  disp(Tab_rmse)
184  disp('Min and Max RMSE')
185  disp(round([ min(RMSE_bps) max(RMSE_bps) ]))
186  %% Comparing observed and fitted yields
187  figure('units','normalized','outerposition',[0 0 1 1])
188  subplot(2,2,1), plot(dates,[Y2(:,1) Y2_hat(:,1)], 'LineWidth',2), ...
189                  set(gca, 'FontSize', 20)
190                  title(Tab_rmse.Properties.VariableNames(1,1)), ...
191                  datetick('x','yyyy'),
192                  legend('Obs','Fitted','Location','northeast')
193
194  subplot(2,2,2), plot(dates,[Y2(:,6) Y2_hat(:,6)], 'LineWidth',2), ...
195                  set(gca, 'FontSize', 20)
196                  title(Tab_rmse.Properties.VariableNames(1,6)), ...
197                  datetick('x','yyyy'),
198                  legend('Obs','Fitted','Location','northeast')
199
```

```
200   subplot(2,2,3), plot(dates,[Y2(:,7) Y2_hat(:,7)], 'LineWidth',2), ...
201                   set(gca, 'FontSize', 20)
202                   title(Tab_rmse.Properties.VariableNames(1,7)), ...
203                   datetick('x','yyyy'),
204                   legend('Obs','Fitted','Location','northeast')
205
206   subplot(2,2,4), plot(dates,[Y2(:,12) Y2_hat(:,12)], 'LineWidth',2), ...
207                   set(gca, 'FontSize', 20)
208                   title(Tab_rmse.Properties.VariableNames(1,12)), ...
209                   datetick('x','yyyy'),
210                   legend('Obs','Fitted','Location','northeast')
211                   print -depsc EvaluatingJointModel
212
213
214   %% Adding dynamics to the model
215   %
216   maxLags = 6;
217   aic_bic = zeros(maxLags,2);
218   for ( j=1:maxLags )
219       Mdl_      = varm(nF*2,j);
220       Mdl_est = estimate(Mdl_,F_mdl');
221       Info_    = summarize(Mdl_est);
222       aic_bic(j,:) = [ Info_.AIC Info_.BIC ];
223   end
224   disp('Optimal lag-order according to:')
225   disp('    AIC    BIC ')
226   disp( [find(min(aic_bic(:,1))==aic_bic(:,1)) ...
227          find(min(aic_bic(:,2))==aic_bic(:,2))])
228
229   Mdl_dynamics        = varm(nF*2,1);
230   Est_dynamics        = estimate(Mdl_dynamics, F_mdl');
231   sort(real(eig(Est_dynamics.AR{:,:})))
232
233   end_     = datenum('31-May-2013');   % end-date of the est data sample
234   indx_e  = find(dates==end_,1,'first')-1;
235   horizon_ = 6;                          % projection horizon
236   nCast    = nObs-indx_e-horizon_;       % number of times to re-estimate
237   err_mdl = NaN(horizon_+1,nTau*2,nCast); % container for the output
238   err_rw  = NaN(horizon_+1,nTau*2,nCast); % container for the random-walk
239   Mdl_cast = varm(nF*2,1);
240   for ( j=1:nCast )
241       % estimate on expanding data window
242       est_tmp  = estimate(Mdl_cast, F_mdl(:,1:indx_e+j)');
243       % forecast VAR model
244       F_cast   = forecast(est_tmp,horizon_,F_mdl(:,1:indx_e+j)');
245       % forecast random-walk
246       F_rw     = repmat(F_mdl(:,indx_e+j-1)',horizon_+1,1);
247       Y_obs    = Y2(indx_e+j:indx_e+j+horizon_,:);
248       F_cast   = [ F_mdl(:,indx_e+j)'; F_cast ];
249       Y_cast   = (G_mdl*F_cast')';  % convert forecasted factors into yields
250       Y_rw     = (G_mdl*F_rw')';    % convert random projections into yields
251       err_mdl(:,:,j) = (Y_obs-Y_cast)*100;
252       err_rw(:,:,j)  = (Y_obs-Y_rw)*100;
253   end
254   tab_Fcast_mdl_rmse = array2table( round( (mean(err_mdl.^2,3)).^(1/2)) );
255   tab_Fcast_mdl_rmse.Properties.VariableNames = Tab_rmse.Properties.VariableNames;
256   tab_Fcast_mdl_rmse.Properties.RowNames    = {'Fitted', 'Forecast 1m ahead', ...
257                                     'Forecast 2m ahead', ...
258                                     'Forecast 3m ahead', ...
259                                     'Forecast 4m ahead', ...
260                                     'Forecast 5m ahead', ...
261                                     'Forecast 6m ahead'};
262
263   tab_Fcast_rw_rmse  = array2table( round( (mean(err_rw.^2,3)).^(1/2)) );
264   tab_Fcast_rw_rmse.Properties.VariableNames = tab_Fcast_mdl_rmse.Properties.
265                                     VariableNames;
266   tab_Fcast_rw_rmse.Properties.RowNames     = tab_Fcast_mdl_rmse.Properties.RowNames;
267   disp('Projections from the estimated model')
268   disp('-----------------------------------')
```

```
269   disp(tab_Fcast_mdl_rmse)
270   disp('Projections assuming an Random-Walk model')
271   disp(tab_Fcast_rw_rmse)
272   disp('-----------------------------------')
273
274   %% Creating the expanded loading matrix
275   %   to facilitate monthly return calculations
276   %   for the 1, 60, 120 months maturity points
277   %
278   tau_new     = sort([tauUS;[0;48;108]]);
279   nTau_new    = length(tau_new);
280   % inter- and extra-polation of the Base loadings
281   G_ext       = interp1(tauUS,G_mdl(1:nTau,1:3),tau_new,'pchip');
282   % inter- and extra-polation of the Spread loadings
283   G_Sprd      = interp1(tauUS,G_mdl(nTau+1:end,4:6),tau_new,'pchip');
284   % expanded loading matrix
285   G_sim       = [ G_ext zeros(nTau_new,3); G_ext G_Sprd ];
286
287   figure('units','normalized','outerposition',[0 0 1 1])
288       subplot(2,1,1), plot(tau_new, G_sim(1:nTau_new,1:3),'-b*','LineWidth',2)
289       hold on, ylim([-1 1])
290       subplot(2,1,1), plot(tauUS, G_mdl(1:nTau,1:3),'r*','LineWidth',5),
291       title('Expanded loadings: US')
292       set(gca, 'FontSize', 20), xticks(tau_new), xticklabels({tau_new})
293       grid, 'on';
294       subplot(2,1,2), plot(tau_new, G_sim(nTau_new+1:end,4:6),'-b*','LineWidth',2)
295       hold on, ylim([-1 1])
296       subplot(2,1,2), plot(tauUS, G_mdl(nTau+1:end,4:6),'r*','LineWidth',5),
297       title('Expanded loadings: Spread')
298       set(gca, 'FontSize', 20), xticks(tau_new), xticklabels({tau_new})
299       grid, 'on';
300       print -depsc ExpandedLoadingMatrix
301
302   %% Calculates return distributions
303   % defines the end-date of the first data sample
304   end_        = datenum('31-Dec-2018');
305   indx_e      = find(dates==end_,1,'first');
306   horizon_    = 12;                          % simulation horizon
307   nSim        = 1e4;                         % number of simulation paths
308   nAssets     = length(tau_new)-length(tauDE);  % number of points on the curve
309                                             %     for which returns are generated
310   Sim_Ret     = NaN(nSim, nAssets);         % container for the simulated returns
311   Mdl_        = varm(nF*2,1);
312   % estimate the VAR model on the selected data
313   est_Mdl     = estimate(Mdl_, F_mdl(:,1:indx_e)');
314   Y0          = repmat(F_mdl(:,indx_e)',nSim,1);
315   F_sim1      = repmat(F_mdl(:,indx_e),1,1,nSim);
316   % Simulated paths for the factors
317   F_sim2      = simulate(est_Mdl, horizon_, 'Y0', Y0, 'NumPaths', nSim);
318   % combining obs and simulated data
319   F_sim3      = cat(1,F_sim1,F_sim2);
320   % transposing first two dimensions
321   F_sim       = permute(F_sim3,[2 1 3]);
322   % container for simulated yields
323   Y_sim       = NaN(2*nTau_new,horizon_+1,nSim);% dim: Tau x horizon x sim_path
324   % container for the simulated annual returns
325   R_sim       = NaN(nSim,nAssets*2);
326   e1          = [3;6;9;12;15;18];   % indicator for relevant maturity points
327   e2          = [1;5;8;10;14;17];   %     at time t, and t+1
328   tau_ret     = [tau_new;tau_new]./12;
329
330   for ( j=1:nSim )                          % calculating returns
331       Y_sim(:,:,j) = G_sim*squeeze(F_sim(:,:,j));
332       R_sim(j,:)   = (tau_ret(e1,1).*squeeze(Y_sim(e1,1,j)) - ...
333                       tau_ret(e2,1).*squeeze(Y_sim(e2,horizon_+1,j)))';
334   end
335   ret_Tab = array2table([ round(mean(R_sim).*100)./100; ...
336                           round(std(R_sim)*100)./100 ]); % organising results
337   ret_Tab.Properties.VariableNames = ...
```

```
338                         Tab_rmse.Properties.VariableNames(1,(2:2:12));
339     ret_Tab.Properties.RowNames = [{'Mean'};{'Std.'}];
340     disp('Summary of the simulated return distributions')
341     disp(ret_Tab)
342
343     figure('units','normalized','outerposition',[0 0 1 1])
344         subplot(2,2,1), histfit(R_sim(:,2),50,'Normal'), ...
345             set(gca, 'FontSize', 20), title(ret_Tab.Properties.VariableNames(2))
346         subplot(2,2,2), histfit(R_sim(:,3),50,'Normal'), ...
347             set(gca, 'FontSize', 20), title(ret_Tab.Properties.VariableNames(3))
348         subplot(2,2,3), histfit(R_sim(:,5),50,'Normal'), ...
349             set(gca, 'FontSize', 20), title(ret_Tab.Properties.VariableNames(5))
350         subplot(2,2,4), histfit(R_sim(:,6),50,'Normal'), ...
351             set(gca, 'FontSize', 20), title(ret_Tab.Properties.VariableNames(6))
352         print -depsc ReturnDistributions
353     disp('Done executing the code')
```

2 $\mathbb{P}$ and $\mathbb{Q}$ measures

2.1 Introduction

It is impossible to escape a treatment of the $\mathbb{P}$ and $\mathbb{Q}$ measures. Even if we choose only to rely on models that do not impose arbitrage restrictions, such as, for example, the Nelson-Siegel family (among others, Nelson and Siegel (1987), Diebold and Li (2006)), and Diebold and Rudebusch (2013)) we need, as a minimum, to appreciate what we are missing (and gaining), such that our modelling choice is made in full consciousness. The main point here is to bring into sharper focus the elements that are necessary for gaining an intuitive and practical understanding of the difference between the $\mathbb{P}$ and $\mathbb{Q}$ measures. In my opinion, this is sufficient for 'blue-collar' yield-curve implementation work (i.e. the work that ensures the correct implementation of existing models in the context of financial decision support frameworks).[7]

2.2 Switching between Measures

One of the central principles of financial theory is that asset prices (of equities, bonds, business projects, and so on) can be found as the sum of the discounted expected future cashflow stream, where the discount rate is set to match the riskiness of the cashflows being discounted. The risk adjustment is done by adding an appropriate risk premium to the discount rate, that is, the discounting is done using $1 + r_t + \theta$, where r_t is the risk-free rate and θ is the market-determined equilibrium risk-premium, scaled by the risk of the cashflows in question. Another key insight is that financial option pricing does not fit immediately into this framework.[8] The main reason for this is that these assets

---

[7] In-depth treatments of the topics touched upon in this section can be found in, for example, Campbell (2018), Cochrane (2005), Karatzas and Shreve (1996), and Mikosch (1998).

[8] You may wonder why I am bringing financial option pricing into play here, when the focus of attention is purely on fixed income pricing and yield curve modelling. But, please bear with me, I hope it will become clear.

have asymmetric (hockey-stick shaped) pay-off schedules, and our traditional $\mathbb{P}$-measure pricing tool-kits (such as the CAPM and APT) can only risk-adjust assets that have symmetric pay-off distributions.[9]

To solve this dilemma, Black, Scholes, and Merton, came up with a clever scheme where the ($\mathbb{P}$-measure) cashflows, as opposed to the discount rate, undergo a risk adjustment. This adjustment is achieved by weighting the state-contingent cashflows by a new set of probabilities, drawn from a new probability distribution, such that the *expected* value of the cashflows can be discounted using the risk-free rate (term structure). Since the risk-free rate is used for discounting, the distribution and the accompanying probability meas-ure, can be called *risk neutral*. This probability measure is also referred to as the *pricing measure*, because observed/theoretical prices are obtained using the ad-justed probability distribution. After all, the correct pricing of financial options was the primary motivation behind the ideas developed by Black, Scholes, and Merton, so *pricing measure* seems like a very appropriate name. In the finan-cial option pricing literature, as well as in the term structure literature, it has become common practice to associate the risk-neutral pricing measure with the letter $\mathbb{Q}$, and the historical/empirical measure with the letter $\mathbb{P}$.

The idea of adjusting the size of the cashflows to reflect the euro amount a risk-averse investor would accept, instead of taking on a risky bet, is also known from introductory investment science text books, as the 'certain-equivalent cashflow method'. Often tucked away in an appendix, this method is presen-ted as a way to determine a reference value for new products, or the premium companies should offer to entice new investors and make them participate in new equity or bond offerings. So, one way to see the $\mathbb{Q}$ measure is as a solution to the certain-equivalent cashflow adjustment process: a $\mathbb{Q}$ distribution assigns risk-adjusted probabilities to each possible cashflow–outcome combination for the assets that exist in the economy, such that all assets are priced correctly. This means that any asset that is priced in the economy, can be written in the following way:

$$P_t = e^{-r_t} \cdot \mathbb{E}_t^{\mathbb{Q}}\left[P_{t+1}\right] = e^{-r_t} \int_S c_{t+1}(s+1) \cdot f_t^{\mathbb{Q}}(s+1)ds(t+1), \qquad (2.1)$$

where P is the price, r is the risk-free rate, $c(s)$ is the cashflow in the possible (continuous) states=$s, \dots, S$ of the world, e.g. $c_t \sim N(\mu, \sigma^2)$, and $f^{\mathbb{Q}}$ gives the

---

[9] Think of how you would find the appropriately risk-adjusted discount rate, using the CAPM or APT, for pricing a call-option on the SP500 index. To determine the β of the call-option in the CAPM world, we would need the covariance between the call-option's return (pay-offs) and the return on the market portfolio: how do we calculate the covariance between a variable that has a pay-off of the form $max(0, S - X)$ (the option) and the market portfolio that can assumed to be normally distributed? Pursuing this question is not necessarily a meaningful endeavour.

accompanying (pricing) probability density function. If we are dealing with risk-free bonds, it is also known that $P_T = 1$ (i.e. that all bonds repay their principal at the maturity date.

Since risk-averse investors pay extra attention to outcomes of the world that they see as being undesirable (risky), the $\mathbb{Q}$ distribution is effectively a shifted/skewed version of the $\mathbb{P}$ distribution, where more probability mass is allocated to negative states of the world. We can write the relationship between the distributions in the following way:

$$f_t^{\mathbb{Q}}(s_{t+1}) = f_t^{\mathbb{P}}(s_{t+1}) \cdot \mathcal{R}_t(s_{t+1}), \tag{2.2}$$

where $\mathcal{R}$ is the risk-adjustment function that financial market participants agree on, and which therefore becomes embedded in observed prices.[10]

The more pessimistic (risk averse) the financial market participants are at a given point in time, the more attention (weight) is given to bad states of the world. But, what are these bad, or undesirable, outcomes, that demand a risk premium? The general answer is: states where the prices turn out to be low. For equities, we would therefore expect the mean of the $\mathbb{Q}$ distribution to be lower than that of the $\mathbb{P}$ distribution. Conversely, if we look at fixed income markets, and our focus is on the yield curve, we would expect the mean of the $\mathbb{Q}$ distribution to be higher than that of the $\mathbb{P}$ distribution, given the inverse relationship between bond prices and yields. This type of reasoning is of course only valid, when the risk premium is positive. On the other hand, if investors, for example, regard government bonds as a safe-heaven asset, then they are willing to pay a premium to acquire such securities, and the risk premium will, consequently, turn negative.

Participants in fixed-income markets will require compensations for risk factors that may lead to yield increases. And the higher the risk that yields increase, the higher the premium. So, if we first consider the shape of the term structure of term premia, it is natural to expect that it is upward sloping in the maturity dimension: The higher the duration of the bond, the more exposed it is to yield developments, compared to a bond with lower maturity, over the same holding period. Second, it is reasonable to consider the economic factors that impact the yield curve, and which therefore demand a risk premium. For default-free nominal bonds, the relevant factors are: the rate of economic growth, and the inflation rate. Uncertainty surrounding the future evolution of these macro gauges will therefore impact fixed-income term premia. Investors

---

[10] The function $\mathcal{R}$ is also called the Radon-Nikodym derivative, and it is assumed that $\mathcal{R}$ obey the conditions necessary such that $f^{\mathbb{Q}}$ behaves like, and can be interpreted as, a probability density function.

may also require compensation for holding illiquid bonds, that is, bonds that may take a longer time to sell than the investor would like to spend on this activity: here the compensation is of course not for the time spent but for the adverse price movement that may materialise during the time it takes to find a buyer for the bond.

Some bonds are also exposed to credit risk. The issuer of the bond may be subjected to a credit-downgrade, whereby the bonds will trade at lower prices, because they are now priced off a new and higher yield curve. A downgrade action by rating agencies will typically be expected by market participants so the downward drift in market prices will to some extent happen before the rating agencies' official announcement. Rating downgrades are not the only possible credit event. It is also possible that the issuer defaults. In this case, the bond holders will receive a certain recover percentage, depending on the prices, at which the available assets can be sold.

In summary, investors require compensations for having exposure to the following systematic risk factors:

- the economic growth rate
- the inflation rate
- credit migration risk (downgrade risk)
- default risk
- liquidity risk

However, in the remaining parts of the Element we will deal exclusively with credit- and liquidity-risk free bonds.

2.3 A Simplified Empirical Example

Later on, we will introduce the commonly used parametrisation of the market price of risk in the context of yield curve modelling, and go more into detail. For now, a simplified example is used to illustrate the idea.[11] Assume that fixed-income prices are governed by a single factor, the short rate, and that an AR(1) model gives a good characterisation of the dynamic behaviour of this factor:

$$r_t = c^{\mathbb{P}} + \alpha^{\mathbb{P}} \cdot r_{t-1} + \sigma \cdot e_t, \tag{2.3}$$

where r is the annualised three-month short rate, $c^{\mathbb{P}}$ is a constant, $\alpha^{\mathbb{P}}$ is the autoregressive coefficient, σ is the volatility of the process, and $e \sim N(0, 1)$.

---

[11] For the more traditional exposition using a binomial tree and the portfolio-replication strategy to derive the risk neutral probabilities, see e.g. Hull (2006), Rebonato (2018), and Luenberger (1998)

As is evident, the model is written under the empirical $\mathbb{P}$ measure, and in passing, it is noticed that this set-up is similar to a discrete-time version of Vasicek (1977):

$$\Delta r_t = a \cdot (b - r_{t-1}) + \sigma \cdot e_t, \tag{2.4}$$

$$\Updownarrow$$

$$r_t = c^{\mathbb{P}} + \alpha^{\mathbb{P}} \cdot r_{t-1} + \sigma \cdot e_t \tag{2.5}$$

with the parameter-mapping, $\alpha^{\mathbb{P}} = 1 - a$, and $c^{\mathbb{P}} = a \cdot b$. We will return to the Vasicek (1977) model in Section 2.4.

If we use (2.3) together with (2.1), we can obtain $\mathbb{P}$- and $\mathbb{Q}$-measure price expressions, denoted by $\tilde{P}_t^{\tau}$ and P_t^{τ} respectively, for a τ maturity bond at time t. First, the recursive structure of (2.1) is used to obtain:

$$
\begin{aligned}
\tilde{P}_t^{\tau} &= \mathbb{E}_t^{\mathbb{P}} \left[e^{-r_t \Delta t} \cdot \tilde{P}_{t+1}^{\tau-1} \right] \\
&= \mathbb{E}_t^{\mathbb{P}} \left[e^{-r_t \Delta t} \cdot e^{-r_{t+1} \Delta t} \cdot \tilde{P}_{t+2}^{\tau-2} \right] \\
&= \mathbb{E}_t^{\mathbb{P}} \left[e^{-r_t \Delta t} \cdot e^{-r_{t+1} \Delta t} \cdot e^{-r_{t+2} \Delta t} \cdot \tilde{P}_{t+3}^{\tau-3} \right] \\
&= \ldots
\end{aligned}
$$

and because $\tilde{P}_T^0 = 1$ (i.e. the bond repays its principal at maturity), this expression generalises to:

$$\tilde{P}_t^{\tau} = \mathbb{E}_t^{\mathbb{P}} \left[e^{-\sum_t^{\tau} r_t \Delta t} \right], \tag{2.6}$$

and by similarity, we can write:

$$P_t^{\tau} = \mathbb{E}_t^{\mathbb{Q}} \left[e^{-\sum_t^{\tau} r_t \Delta t} \right]. \tag{2.7}$$

Using monthly observations for the three-month maturity point on the US risk-free zero-coupon term structure, covering the period from 1961 to 2018, the following $\mathbb{P}$-measure parameter estimates are obtained:[12]

Based on (2.3), the comparable $\mathbb{P}$-measure prices, $\tilde{P}_t^{\tau}$ can be calculated, with $\Delta t = 1/12$ (because we use a monthly observation frequency), and using the parameter estimates in Table 5. The good thing is that with the above set-up (i.e. using the assumption of an AR(1) model for the short rate), there is a closed-form solution to the sum of the short rate that enters in equation (2.6):

$$\sum_t^{\tau} r_t = r_t \cdot \frac{1 - \alpha^{\tau}}{1 - \alpha} + \frac{c \cdot (\alpha^{\tau} - \alpha \cdot \tau + \tau - 1)}{(\alpha - 1)^2} \tag{2.8}$$

---

[12] Here we are using the data contained in the MATLAB file: Data_GSW_factors.mat.

Table 5 $\mathbb{P}$-measure estimates

	Estimate
$c^{\mathbb{P}}$	0.0763
$\alpha^{\mathbb{P}}$	0.9943
$\sigma^{\mathbb{P}}$	0.5886

Note that the superscript on the parameters are omitted in expression (2.8) because it is valid for any AR(1) model following the general notation used in equation (2.3).

With this, it is now possible to calculate $\mathbb{P}$ prices and compare them to observed $\mathbb{Q}$ prices, in order to gauge the size of the risk premium. When we use term structure models in practice, and apply them to observed market yields, it is easy to forget that yields are a by-product of the trading process: Investors observe market prices, and the trading commences until prices reach equilibrium, that is, until all investors agree that the price is right (even if this moment is only a micro-second). However, we model yields and not prices, and we are therefore used to thinking about the risk premium in yield-space (and we will continue doing so), but, in fact, the risk adjustment enters the stage through the pricing process, and is therefore originally a pricing concept, as also outlined. Before reverting to our normal yield-thinking mode, it may still be illustrative to see the risk premium as it materialises in price-space – even if this is only done using example prices.

On a randomly selected day, zero-coupon bond prices are sampled from the US market; see the row labelled $P^{\mathbb{Q}}$ in Table 6. Prices are sampled across the maturity spectrum, covering 3 to 120 months. The next row in the table gives the corresponding $\mathbb{P}$ prices, i.e. the prices that would prevail if equation (2.6) together with the parameter estimates shown in Table 5, were used to price the bonds. The difference between the two price rows is the risk premium, the compensation that investors require to hold bonds at different maturities, here given in price-space.

Table 6 $\mathbb{P}$ and $\mathbb{Q}$ example of prices and the price of risk

τ in months	3	12	36	60	84	120
$P^{\mathbb{Q}}$ (Eur)	99.12	96.22	88.56	81.53	74.71	64.82
$P^{\mathbb{P}}$ (Eur)	99.48	97.76	92.24	85.98	79.47	69.90
Price of risk (Eur)	0.36	1.54	3.69	4.45	4.75	5.08

Once the price of risk has been calculated in euro terms, we can fiddle with the parameters of the dynamic evolution of the yield curve factor in (2.3), such that we match the observed market prices as closely as possible. That is, we aim to find appropriate values for c^Q and α^Q, from this equation:

$$r_t = c^Q + \alpha^Q \cdot r_{t-1} + \sigma \cdot e_t, \tag{2.9}$$

This 'appropriate adjustment' constitutes the risk-adjustment in yield space, and we will see later on how exactly to map parameters between the two measures. For now, this link is (intentionally) left to be vague.

In our example, when the parameter-tinkering is done, we can draw the resulting distributions for the short rate, see Figure 12. Since the $\mathbb{Q}$ distribution falls to the right of the $\mathbb{P}$ distribution, it appears that a positive risk premium is present in the sampled data.

It is worth emphasising again, that the above is just an example. In general, we would not calibrate models using more observations than what was used here; in fact, models would typically be fitted to match a whole panel of yields covering no less than ten years of monthly time-series observations, where each monthly observation would cover several maturity points.

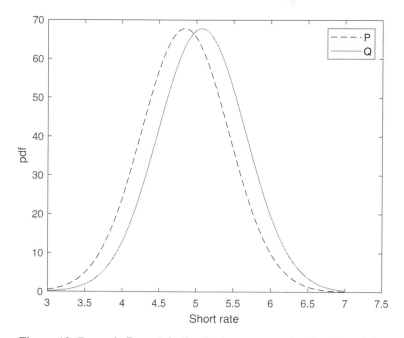

Figure 12 Example $\mathbb{P}$- and $\mathbb{Q}$ distributions on a randomly selected day
The figure shows an example of the relationship between the $\mathbb{P}$- and $\mathbb{Q}$ measure distributions. Only the mean differs between the two measures in this example.

2.4 A Generic Discrete-Time One-Factor Model

A discrete-time one-factor model is presented here as a prelude to the multi-factor models that we will concentrate on for the most part of the remainder of this Element. The model can be seen as the discrete-time counterpart of Vasicek (1977).

As previously, we assume that the underlying factor driving the yield curve is the short rate, and that the short rate is governed by a stationary AR(1) process:

$$r_t = c^{\mathbb{P}} + \alpha^{\mathbb{P}} \cdot r_{t-1} + \sigma \cdot e_t^{\mathbb{P}}. \tag{2.10}$$

The bond price is an exponential affine function of the short rate:

$$P_t^\tau = exp\left(A_\tau + B_\tau \cdot r_t\right), \tag{2.11}$$

and we can therefore write the yield at maturity τ as:

$$y_t^\tau = -\frac{1}{\tau} \cdot log\left(P_t^\tau\right) = -\frac{A_\tau}{\tau} - \frac{B_\tau}{\tau} \cdot r_t. \tag{2.12}$$

In order for bond prices to exclude arbitrage opportunities, a single stochastic discount factor (SDF, also called the pricing kernel) is assumed to exist, and to price all bonds (and other asset in the economy):

$$P_t^\tau = E_t^{\mathbb{P}}\left[M_{t+1} \cdot P_{t+1}^{\tau-1}\right], \tag{2.13}$$

it is typically assumed that the SDF is parameterised in the following way:

$$M_{t+1} = exp\left(-r_t - \frac{1}{2}\lambda_t^2 - \lambda_t e_{t+1}^{\mathbb{P}}\right), \tag{2.14}$$

and that:

$$\lambda_t = \lambda_0 + \lambda_1 r_t, \tag{2.15}$$

Armed with these prerequisites, the fun can begin. By inserting (2.14) and (2.11) into (2.13), we get:

$$
\begin{aligned}
P_t^\tau &= E_t^{\mathbb{P}}\left[exp\left(-r_t - \frac{1}{2}\lambda_t^2 - \lambda_t e_{t+1}^{\mathbb{P}}\right) \cdot exp\left(A_{\tau-1} + B_{\tau-1} \cdot r_{t+1}\right)\right] \\
&= E_t^{\mathbb{P}}\left[exp\left(-r_t - \frac{1}{2}\lambda_t^2 - \lambda_t e_{t+1}^{\mathbb{P}} + A_{\tau-1} + B_{\tau-1} \cdot r_{t+1}\right)\right]
\end{aligned} \tag{2.16}
$$

into which we substitute (2.10):

$$
\begin{aligned}
P_t^\tau = E_t^{\mathbb{P}}\Big[exp\Big(-r_t - \frac{1}{2}\lambda_t^2 - \lambda_t e_{t+1}^{\mathbb{P}} + A_{\tau-1} + B_{\tau-1} \cdot \\
\left(c^{\mathbb{P}} + \alpha^{\mathbb{P}} \cdot r_t + \sigma e_{t+1}^{\mathbb{P}}\right)\Big)\Big].
\end{aligned} \tag{2.17}
$$

Now, the terms can be separated into two groups: one group related to the future (i.e. $t + 1$), where the expectations operator is needed, and another group, which are known at time t, and where the expectations operator is therefore not needed:

$$P_t^\tau = E_t^\mathbb{P}\left[\exp\left(-r_t - \frac{1}{2}\lambda_t^2 - \lambda_t e_{t+1}^\mathbb{P} + A_{\tau-1} + B_{\tau-1} \cdot \left(c^\mathbb{P} + \alpha^\mathbb{P} \cdot r_t + \sigma e_{t+1}^\mathbb{P}\right)\right)\right]$$

$$= E_t^\mathbb{P}\left[\exp\left(-r_t - \frac{1}{2}\lambda_t^2 - \lambda_t e_{t+1}^\mathbb{P} + A_{\tau-1} + B_{\tau-1} \cdot c^\mathbb{P}\right.\right.$$

$$\left.\left. + B_{\tau-1} \cdot \alpha^\mathbb{P} \cdot r_t + B_{\tau-1} \cdot \sigma e_{t+1}^\mathbb{P}\right)\right]$$

$$= \exp\left(-r_t - \frac{1}{2}\lambda_t^2 + A_{\tau-1} + B_{\tau-1} \cdot c^\mathbb{P} + B_{\tau-1} \cdot \alpha^\mathbb{P} \cdot r_t\right)$$

$$\cdot E_t^\mathbb{P}\left[\exp\left(-\lambda_t \cdot e_{t+1}^\mathbb{P} + B_{\tau-1} \cdot \sigma \cdot e_{t+1}^\mathbb{P}\right)\right]$$

$$= \exp\left(-r_t - \frac{1}{2}\lambda_t^2 + A_{\tau-1} + B_{\tau-1} \cdot c^\mathbb{P} + B_{\tau-1} \cdot \alpha^\mathbb{P} \cdot r_t\right)$$

$$\cdot E_t^\mathbb{P}\left[\exp\left(\left(-\lambda_t + B_{\tau-1} \cdot \sigma\right) \cdot e_{t+1}^\mathbb{P}\right)\right].$$

$$(2.18)$$

Since $\mathbb{E}\left[\exp(aX)\right] = \exp\left(\frac{1}{2}a^2\right)$ when $X \sim N(0,1)$, the expectations part of (2.18) can be written as:

$$E_t^\mathbb{P}\left[\exp\left(\left(-\lambda_t + B_{\tau-1} \cdot \sigma\right) \cdot e_{t+1}^\mathbb{P}\right)\right] = \exp\left[\frac{1}{2}\left(-\lambda_t + B_{\tau-1} \cdot \sigma\right)^2\right]$$

$$= \exp\left[\frac{1}{2}B_{\tau-1}^2\sigma^2 - B_{\tau-1}\lambda_t\sigma + \frac{1}{2}\lambda_t^2\right].$$

$$(2.19)$$

The derived expression for the expectations part (2.19) can now be reinserted into (2.18)

$$P_t^\tau = \exp\left(-r_t - \frac{1}{2}\lambda_t^2 + A_{\tau-1} + B_{\tau-1} \cdot c^\mathbb{P} + B_{\tau-1} \cdot \alpha^\mathbb{P} \cdot r_t\right.$$

$$\left. + \frac{1}{2}B_{\tau-1}^2\sigma^2 - B_{\tau-1}\lambda_t\sigma + \frac{1}{2}\lambda_t^2\right)$$

$$= \exp\left(-r_t + A_{\tau-1} + B_{\tau-1} \cdot c^\mathbb{P} + B_{\tau-1} \cdot \alpha^\mathbb{P} \cdot r_t + \frac{1}{2}B_{\tau-1}^2\sigma^2 - B_{\tau-1}\lambda_t\sigma\right).$$

$$(2.20)$$

Recall the expression for the market price of risk, shown in equation (2.15). Insert it in (2.20), and collect terms related to r_t:

$$P_t^\tau = \exp\left(-r_t + A_{\tau-1} + B_{\tau-1} \cdot c^\mathbb{P} + B_{\tau-1} \cdot \alpha^\mathbb{P} \cdot r_t + \frac{1}{2}B_{\tau-1}^2\sigma^2 - B_{\tau-1}\lambda_t\sigma\right)$$

$$= exp\left(-r_t + A_{\tau-1} + B_{\tau-1} \cdot c^{\mathbb{P}} + B_{\tau-1} \cdot \alpha^{\mathbb{P}} \cdot r_t + \frac{1}{2}B_{\tau-1}^2\sigma^2\right.$$
$$\left. - B_{\tau-1}\sigma(\lambda_0 + \lambda_1 \cdot r_t)\right)$$

$$= exp\left(A_{\tau-1} + B_{\tau-1} \cdot c^{\mathbb{P}} + B_{\tau-1} \cdot \alpha^{\mathbb{P}} \cdot r_t + \frac{1}{2}B_{\tau-1}^2\sigma^2\right.$$
$$\left. - B_{\tau-1}\sigma(\lambda_0 + \lambda_1 \cdot r_t) - r_t\right)$$

$$= exp\left(A_{\tau-1} + B_{\tau-1} \cdot c^{\mathbb{P}} + \frac{1}{2}B_{\tau-1}^2\sigma^2 - B_{t-1}\sigma\lambda_0\right.$$
$$\left. + B_{\tau-1} \cdot \alpha^{\mathbb{P}} \cdot r_t - B_{\tau-1}\sigma\lambda_1 \cdot r_t - r_t\right)$$

$$= exp\left(A_{\tau-1} + B_{\tau-1} \cdot c^{\mathbb{P}} - B_{t-1}\sigma\lambda_0 + \frac{1}{2}B_{\tau-1}^2\sigma^2\right.$$
$$\left. + \left(B_{\tau-1} \cdot \alpha^{\mathbb{P}} - B_{\tau-1}\sigma\lambda_1 - 1\right) \cdot r_t\right)$$

$$= exp\left(\underbrace{A_{\tau-1} + B_{\tau-1}\left(c^{\mathbb{P}} - \sigma\lambda_0\right) + \frac{1}{2}B_{\tau-1}^2\sigma^2}_{A_\tau} + \underbrace{\left[B_{\tau-1}\left(\alpha^{\mathbb{P}} - \sigma\lambda_1\right) - 1\right]}_{B_\tau} \cdot r_t\right).$$

$$(2.21)$$

Matching coefficients between equations (2.11) and (2.21), it is seen that:

$$A_\tau = A_{\tau-1} + B_{\tau-1}\left(c^{\mathbb{P}} - \sigma\lambda_0\right) + \frac{1}{2}B_{\tau-1}^2\sigma^2 = A_{\tau-1} + B_{\tau-1}c^{\mathbb{Q}} + \frac{1}{2}B_{\tau-1}^2\sigma^2$$
$$(2.22)$$

$$B_\tau = B_{\tau-1}\left(\alpha^{\mathbb{P}} - \sigma\lambda_1\right) - 1 = B_{\tau-1}\alpha^{\mathbb{Q}} - 1 \qquad (2.23)$$

First, notice the nice interpretation of the constant and the autoregressive coefficient. When excluding arbitrage opportunities, by imposing a common risk-adjusted pricing equation for all assets that trade in the economy, see equation (2.13), the coefficients that determine the dynamics of the yield curve factor, r_t, under the market-pricing measure $\mathbb{Q}$, are being risk adjusted. We see that: $c^{\mathbb{Q}} = c^{\mathbb{P}} - \sigma\lambda_0$, and $\alpha^{\mathbb{Q}} = \alpha^{\mathbb{P}} - \sigma\lambda_1$, appear as the $\mathbb{Q}$-measure parameters, where σ has an interpretation as the amount of risk, and $\lambda_{0,1}$ can be interpreted as the price of risk. Second, the expressions for A_τ and B_τ have iterative structures, such that A_τ depends on $A_{\tau-1}$, and B_τ depends on $B_{\tau-1}$. This structure is no coincidence. It emerges as a natural consequence of the imposed sequential nature of the above pricing equation. With this structure, it is now possible to derive closed-form expressions for these parameters.

Starting with the general expression for B_τ in (2.23), gives:

$$B_1 = B_0\alpha^{\mathbb{Q}} - 1$$
$$B_2 = B_1\alpha^{\mathbb{Q}} - 1 = \left(B_0\alpha^{\mathbb{Q}} - 1\right)\alpha^{\mathbb{Q}} - 1 = B_0\left(\alpha^{\mathbb{Q}}\right)^2 - \alpha^{\mathbb{Q}} - 1$$

$$B_3 = B_2 \alpha^Q - 1 = \left(B_0 \left(\alpha^Q \right)^2 - \alpha^Q - 1 \right) \alpha^Q - 1$$

$$= B_0 \left(\alpha^Q \right)^3 - \left(\alpha^Q \right)^2 - \alpha^Q - 1$$

$$B_4 = B_0 \left(\alpha^Q \right)^4 - \left(\alpha^Q \right)^3 - \left(\alpha^Q \right)^2 - \alpha^Q - 1. \tag{2.24}$$

When the bond matures its price is $P_t^0 = exp\,(A_0 + B_0 \cdot r_t) = 1$, which implies that $A_0 = 0$ and $B_0 = 0$. The above expression therefore generalises in the following way:

$$B_\tau = - \sum_{j=0}^{\tau-1} \left(\alpha^Q \right)^j$$

$$= -\frac{1 - \left(\alpha^Q \right)^\tau}{1 - \alpha^Q} \tag{2.25}$$

where the last line results from the closed-form expression of the summed power series. Doing the same exercise for the A_τ term, now that B_τ is known, gives:

$$A_\tau = -\frac{c^Q}{1 - \alpha^Q} \cdot \left[\tau - \frac{1 - \left(\alpha^Q \right)^\tau}{1 - \alpha^Q} \right]$$

$$+ \frac{\sigma^2}{2 \left(1 - \alpha^Q \right)^2} \cdot \left[\tau + \frac{1 - \left(\alpha^Q \right)^{2\tau}}{1 - \left(\alpha^Q \right)^2} - 2 \cdot \frac{1 - \left(\alpha^Q \right)^\tau}{1 - \alpha^Q} \right] \tag{2.26}$$

Given the relationship between bond prices and yields in (2.12), the resulting yield equation for the discrete-time one-factor model can be written as:

$$y_t^\tau = -\frac{1}{\tau} A_\tau - \frac{1}{\tau} B_\tau r_t + \sigma_y u_t$$

$$= a_\tau + b_\tau r_t + \sigma_y u_t \tag{2.27}$$

with

$$a_\tau = \frac{c^Q}{\tau \left(1 - \alpha^Q \right)} \cdot \left[\tau - \frac{1 - \left(\alpha^Q \right)^\tau}{1 - \alpha^Q} \right]$$

$$- \frac{\sigma^2}{2\tau \left(1 - \alpha^Q \right)^2} \cdot \left[\tau + \frac{1 - \left(\alpha^Q \right)^{2\tau}}{1 - \left(\alpha^Q \right)^2} - 2 \cdot \frac{1 - \left(\alpha^Q \right)^\tau}{1 - \alpha^Q} \right] \tag{2.28}$$

$$b_\tau = \frac{1 - \left(\alpha^Q \right)^\tau}{\tau \left(1 - \alpha^Q \right)}. \tag{2.29}$$

2.4.1 Estimating the Short-Rate Model

Using example data collected from the US market, we can estimate our derived model. To this end, MATLAB's state-space toolbox (SSM) is used. Since the model relies on the short rate being the underlying factor that drives the dynamics of the model, it is assumed that the three-month rate can play this role. And the model is therefore parameterised such that the yield curve factor is observed.

The model looks like this:

$$\underbrace{r_t}_{1\times1} = \underbrace{c^{\mathbb{P}}}_{1\times1} + \underbrace{\alpha^{\mathbb{P}}}_{1\times1} \cdot \underbrace{r_{t-1}}_{1\times1} + \underbrace{\sigma_r}_{1\times1} \underbrace{e_t}_{1\times1} \tag{2.30}$$

$$\underbrace{Y_t}_{\#\tau\times1} = \underbrace{a_\tau}_{\#\tau\times1} + \underbrace{b_\tau}_{\#\tau\times1} \cdot \underbrace{r_t}_{1\times1} + \underbrace{\Sigma_y}_{\#\tau\times\#\tau} \underbrace{u_t}_{\#\tau\times1}, \tag{2.31}$$

with (2.30) being the state equation, and (2.31) being the observation equation, and with the dimension of the variables and parameters provided in brackets under the respective entries. Here $\#\tau$ refers to the number of maturities at which the yield curve is observed, at a give point in time. To set up the model in MATLAB's SSM toolbox requires a bit of reworking of the model, such that it fits into the required format. Indeed, it is required that the equations of the model match the following generic set-up:

state equation: $X_t = R \cdot X_{t-1} + S \cdot e_t$

observation equation: $Y_t = T \cdot X_t + U \cdot u_t.$

To align the one-factor model with this, the following is done for the state equation:

$$\underbrace{\begin{bmatrix} r_t \\ 1_t \end{bmatrix}}_{X_t} = \underbrace{\begin{bmatrix} \alpha^{\mathbb{P}} & c^{\mathbb{P}} \\ 0 & 1 \end{bmatrix}}_{R} \cdot \underbrace{\begin{bmatrix} r_{t-1} \\ 1_{t-1} \end{bmatrix}}_{X_{t-1}} + \underbrace{\begin{bmatrix} \sigma_r \\ 0 \end{bmatrix}}_{S} e_t,$$

where $1_t = 1$ is a constant that is equal to 1 for all values of t. The observation equation takes the following form:

$$\underbrace{\begin{bmatrix} y_t \\ r_t \\ 1_t \end{bmatrix}}_{Y_t} = \underbrace{\begin{bmatrix} b_\tau & a_\tau \\ 1 & 0 \\ 0 & 1 \end{bmatrix}}_{T} \cdot \underbrace{\begin{bmatrix} r_t \\ 1_t \end{bmatrix}}_{X_t} + \underbrace{\begin{bmatrix} \Sigma_y \\ 0 \\ 0 \end{bmatrix}}_{U} u_t.$$

It is well known that a one-factor model is not flexible enough to capture both the time- and cross-sectional behaviour of yields. In fact, it appears that when one-factor models are used in the industry, they are applied to fit the yield curve at a given point in time, and while the model parameters should be stable over time, in reality they are not, so model parameters in these models are frequently re-estimated. There is therefore not much hope for the practical usefulness of the aforementioend state-space model. However, as an example, it is useful to carry on.

As a complement to the state-space approach, we can also explore the possibility that the amount of risk in the economy is time-varying. With the intention to be as practical as possible, a two-step estimation approach is pursued to identify the relevant parameters of this model. First, the $\mathbb{P}$ dynamics are estimated, and the resulting parameter estimates are kept constant during the second stage of the estimation procedure. Second, the $\mathbb{Q}$ parameters are estimated (subject to the estimates obtained in step 1). For the sake of clarity, it is recalled that the first step takes care of the time-series dimension of the data, while the second step is concerned with the cross-sectional fit of the model, that is, with the maturity dimension.

step 1:
$$r_t = c^{\mathbb{P}} + \alpha^{\mathbb{P}} \cdot r_{t-1} + \sigma_t e_t \tag{2.32}$$
$$\sigma_t^2 = \omega + \kappa \sigma_{t-1}^2 + \gamma e_t^2 \tag{2.33}$$

Having obtained the parameter estimates: $\hat{c}^{\mathbb{P}}$, $\hat{\alpha}^{\mathbb{P}}$, and the time series of time-varying variances, $\hat{\sigma}_t^2 \; \forall \, t$, the next step can be completed:

step 2:
$$a_{\tau,t} = f\left(\hat{c}^{\mathbb{P}}, \hat{\alpha}^{\mathbb{P}}, \hat{\sigma}_t, \lambda_0, \lambda_1, \tau\right) \tag{2.34}$$
$$b_{\tau,t} = f\left(\hat{\alpha}^{\mathbb{P}}, \hat{\sigma}_t, \lambda_1, \tau\right) \tag{2.35}$$

which amounts to estimating the market price of risk parameters, λ_0 and λ_1. This can be done by minimising the sum of the squared errors between model and observed yields.

$$min_{\{\lambda_0,\lambda_1\}} = \sum_t \sum_\tau \left[Y - \hat{Y}\right]^2 = \sum_t \sum_\tau [Y - (a_\tau + b_\tau \cdot r_t)]^2. \tag{2.36}$$

The results from the above two estimation approaches and model specifications are sketched in the following.[13] The model fits are compared to that of a completely empirically determined one-factor model, where the factor is the observed short rate.[14]

---

[13] The results are generated using the MATLAB scripts named: "P_and_Q_Measure_Vasicek_2_-step_approach.m" and "P_and_Q_Measure_Vasicek_State_Space.m", that accompany the Element. See the Appendix MATLAB code, for a print of the code.
[14] This empirical model is estimated in MATLAB like this:

```
1  %% Empirical one-factor short-rate model
2  %
3  F      = [ones(nObs,1) RDNS.yields(:,1)];
4  H      = F\RDNS.yields;
5  Y_fit = F*H;
6  RMSE = (mean((RDNS.yields - Y_fit).^2)).^(0.5);
```

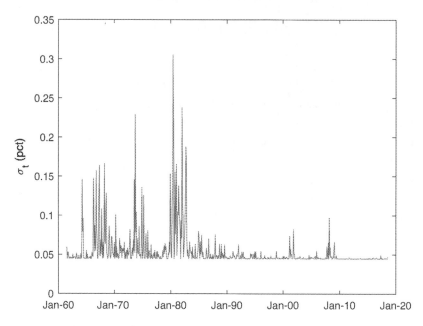

Figure 13 Time-varying volatility of the short-rate factor

The figure shows the estimated time-varying volatility of the short-rate factor, obtained from am AR(1)-GARCH(1,1) model applied to monthly data.

As anticipated, figure 14 shows that all three one-factor models have difficulties in matching the time-series evolution of yields. In fact, the average root mean squared error of the models, across all maturities, is of a similar magnitude and far too large to qualify these models as applicable to capture both the time-series and cross-sectional behaviour of yields. This observation underscores the usefulness of such one-factor models as a means to fit the prevailing term structure, on a day-to-day or intraday basis, for example, for pricing purposes and for detecting rich and cheap bonds at a given time-point. For that purpose, such models are great.

2.5 Summary

The main objective of this section is to illustrate, in an intuitive a practical way, what we mean, when we refer to the $\mathbb{P}$ and $\mathbb{Q}$ measures in the context of yield curve models. This topic can be a stumbling block, and a source of confusion, when entering into this literature the first time. Sure, we can read, accept, and

---

where Y contains the data for the 3-month to 10-year yields. Each column of Y contains the time-series observations for one maturity. Hence, the first column holds the short rate (the 3-month yield).

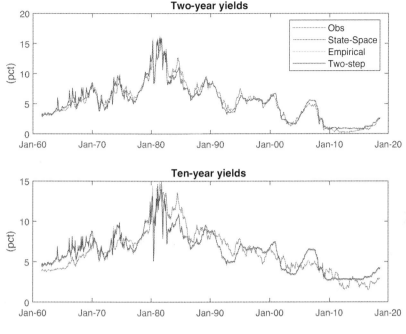

Figure 14 Model fit

The figure shows the two-year and ten-year observed and fitted yields. The models described in the text are used and comprise discrete-time Vasicek models estimated using a state-space approach, a simple empirical approach, and a two-step procedure allowing for time-varying volatility.

replicate what is written in text books and academic papers, but it may be difficult to discern from this a true sense of understanding. As mentioned in the introduction, my goal here is a modest one. But, I hope, after all, that the previous discussion may help to illustrate, and thereby further the understanding, of the $\mathbb{P}$ and $\mathbb{Q}$ measures, and the derived yield curve modelling frameworks.

(1) The arbitrage constraint amounts to assuming and imposing the existence of a unique pricing equation on the market being modelled. By pricing all assets that trade on this market, the unique pricing equation ensures that model prices for all assets are consistent with their exposure to the risk factors included in the model.

(2) Zero-coupon bonds are priced under the $\mathbb{Q}$ measure as the discounted value of its terminal payment, that is, the payment the bond makes when it matures, using the risk-free rate as the discount rate. The recursive structure of the discounting approach, together with the unique pricing equation, implies that the loading structure (i.e. the matrix that converts

yield curve factors into model yields), also can be found via a set of recursive equations.

(3) For many models, it is possible to solve these recursive equations in closed form, which makes model estimation faster.

(4) It is possible to find arbitrage-free counterparts to many of the yield curve models typically used by practitioners: for example, the Nelson-Siegel model and the Svensson-Soderlind models.

(5) When used appropriately, there is not much difference between arbitrage-free models, and models that do not impose arbitrage constraints. Still, the arbitrage-free models represent internally consistent frameworks and give additional information about the market being modelled, for example, on the market prices of factor risks.

MATLAB code

A discrete-time Vasicek model: state-space estimation

> filename: P_and_Q_Measure_Vasicek_State_Space.m

```
1   %% State-space estimation of the Vasicek model
2   % Used in the section: the P and Q measures of the lecture notes
3
4   %% Load yield factors and construct yield curves
5   %
6   path_=[pwd,'\MATLAB_classes'];
7   addpath(path_);
8   load('Data_GSW.mat');
9   GSW_          = GSW;                  % creates an instance of the GSW class
10  GSW_.tau      = [3 12:12:120]';      % vector of maturities
11  GSW_.beta     = GSW_factors(:,2:5);  % yield curve factors
12  GSW_.lambda   = GSW_factors(:,6:7);  % lambdas
13  GSW_          = GSW_.getYields;      % getting yields
14  figure
15      plot(GSW_factors(:,1),GSW_.yields(:,[1 11]));
16      datetick('x','mmm-yy'), title('US yields'), legend('3m','10y')
17
18  RDNS              = TSM;              % creates an instance of the TSM class
19  RDNS.yields       = GSW_.yields;     % adds yields to the model
20  RDNS.tau          = GSW_.tau;        % adds maturities
21  RDNS.biasCorrect  = 0;
22  RDNS.DataFreq     = 12;
23  RDNS.nF           = 3;
24  RDNS              = RDNS.getSRB3;     % estimates a 3 factor SRB model
25  figure
26      plot(GSW_factors(:,1), RDNS.beta'),
27      title('Extracted yield curve factors')
28      datetick('x','mmm-yy'),
29      legend('Short rate','Slope','Curvature')
30  figure
31      plot(GSW_factors(:,1),[RDNS.beta(1,:)' RDNS.yields(:,1)]),
32      title('Model and Observed short rate'),
33      datetick('x','mmm-yy'), legend('Model','Observed')
34  figure
35      plot(GSW_factors(:,1),[RDNS.TP(:,11) ACM(:,2)]),
36          title('10Y Term Premium'),
37          datetick('x','mmm-yy'), legend('SRB','ACM')
38
```

```
39    [nObs,nTau] = size(RDNS.yields);
40
41    %% Estimating the parameters of the discrete-time one-factor model
42    % Data are scaled to monthly decimals (percentage annual yields are
43    % converted to monthly decimal rates, because the formulas for the
44    % yield curve loadings are calculated for monthly step-sizes and thus
45    % for monthly rates.
46    %
47    scl_        = 1200;
48    Y           = [ RDNS.yields./scl_ ...
49                    RDNS.yields(:,1)./scl_ ...
50                    ones(nObs,1) ];
51
52    cP  = 0.01;
53    aP  = 0.95;
54    s   = 1.15;
55    L0  = 0;
56    L1  = 0;
57    sY  = 1.25.*ones(nTau,1);
58
59    p0  = [ cP; aP; s; L0; L1; sY ];
60    lb_ = [ 0.00; 0.00; 0; -inf; -inf; zeros(nTau,1) ];
61    ub_ = [ 1.00; 1.00; 1;  inf; inf; 1000.*ones(nTau,1) ];
62
63    % constraints that ensure that all yield volatilities, ie. the
64    % entries of the variance-covariance matrix in the observation
65    % equation are equal for all maturities included in the analysis.
66    %
67    nP  = size(p0,1);
68    Aeq = zeros(nTau-1,nP);
69    Aeq(1,[6 7])   = [1 -1];Aeq(2,[7 8])  =[1 -1];Aeq(3,[8 9])  = [1 -1];
70    Aeq(4,[9 10])  = [1 -1];Aeq(5,[10 11])=[1 -1];Aeq(6,[11 12])= [1 -1];
71    Aeq(7,[12 13]) = [1 -1];Aeq(8,[13 14])=[1 -1];Aeq(9,[14 15])= [1 -1];
72    Aeq(10,[15 16])= [1 -1];
73    beq = zeros(size(Aeq,1),1);
74
75    Mdl_sr = ssm(@(p) pMap(p, RDNS.tau));
76    options = optimoptions(@fmincon,'Algorithm','interior-point',...
77                           'MaxIterations',1e6, ...
78                           'MaxFunctionEvaluations',1e6, ...
79                           'TolFun', 1e-6, 'TolX', 1e-6);
80
81    disp('... Estimating the model using the SSM module')
82    [ EstMdl_sr, pHat, pCov, logl, outFlags ] = ...
83            estimate( Mdl_sr,Y,p0,'Display','iter','Aeq',Aeq,'beq',beq,...
84                    'lb',lb_,'ub',ub_,'univariate',true,'options',options )
85
86    x_filter  = filter( EstMdl_sr, Y );  % extract filtered state variables
87    sr_filter = x_filter(:,1);           % filtered short rate
88
89    cP_  = pHat(1,1);
90    aP_  = pHat(2,1);
91    s_   = pHat(3,1);
92    L0_  = pHat(4,1);
93    L1_  = pHat(5,1);
94    sY_  = pHat(6:end,1);
95    mP   = (cP_/(1-aP_))*scl_;
96
97    a_tau_ = EstMdl_sr.C(1:nTau,2);
98    b_tau_ = EstMdl_sr.C(1:nTau,1);
99    Y_fit  = (a_tau_ + b_tau_*sr_filter')';
100
101   RMSE   = 100.*(mean((scl_.*Y(:,1:11)-scl_.*Y_fit).^2)).^(1/2)
102
103   figure
104       plot(GSW_factors(:,1),[sr_filter Y(:,12)]),
105       title('Yield curve factor')
106       datetick('x','mmm-yy'), legend('obs','fit')
107   figure
```

```
108        plot(GSW_factors(:,1),[Y_fit(:,1) Y(:,1)]),
109        title('3M rate')
110        datetick('x','mmm-yy'), legend('fit','obs')
111    figure
112        plot(GSW_factors(:,1),[Y_fit(:,2) Y(:,2)]),
113        title('1Y rate')
114        datetick('x','mmm-yy'), legend('fit','obs')
115    figure
116        plot(GSW_factors(:,1),[Y_fit(:,3) Y(:,3)]),
117        title('2Y rate')
118        datetick('x','mmm-yy'), legend('fit','obs')
119    figure
120        plot(GSW_factors(:,1),[Y_fit(:,4) Y(:,4)]),
121        title('3Y rate')
122        datetick('x','mmm-yy'), legend('fit','obs')
123    figure
124        plot(GSW_factors(:,1),[Y_fit(:,5) Y(:,5)]),
125        title('4Y rate')
126        datetick('x','mmm-yy'), legend('fit','obs')
127    figure
128        plot(GSW_factors(:,1),[Y_fit(:,6) Y(:,6)]),
129        title('5Y rate')
130        datetick('x','mmm-yy'), legend('fit','obs')
131    figure
132        plot(GSW_factors(:,1),[Y_fit(:,11) Y(:,11)]),
133        title('10Y rate')
134        datetick('x','mmm-yy'), legend('fit','obs')
135
136    %%
137    function [R,S,T,U,Mean0,Cov0,StateType] = pMap( p, tau )
138    %
139    % Setting up the matrices necessary to estimate the state-space model
140    %
141    nTau_1 = length(tau);
142    nTau   = max(tau);
143
144    cP  = p(1,1);
145    aP  = p(2,1);
146    s   = p(3,1);
147    L0  = p(4,1);
148    L1  = p(5,1);
149    sY  = p(6:end,1);
150
151    cQ  = cP - s*L0;
152    aQ  = aP - s*L1;
153
154    [ a_tau, b_tau ] = find_a_b(s,cQ,aQ,tau);
155
156    R = [ aP cP; 0 1 ];
157    S = [ s; 0 ];
158    T = [ b_tau a_tau; 1 0; 0 1 ];
159    U = [ diag(sY); zeros(2,nTau_1) ];
160
161    % ... other assignments
162        Mean0     = [];
163        Cov0      = [];
164        StateType = [ 0; 1 ];
165    end
166
167    function [a_n, b_n] = find_a_b(s,cQ,aQ,tau)
168    % determines the loadings and the constant vector using the
169    % recursive equations and closed form expressions.
170    %
171    flagg = 1;    % 1-> closed form results, 0->iterative solution
172
173    a_nF = @(a_,n_,c_,s_)  -c_/(1-a_)*( n_ - (1-a_.^n_)/(1-a_) )...
174                           +(s_^2)/(2*((1-a_)^2)).*(n_ + ...
175                           (1-a_.^(2*n_))./(1-a_^2) - 2*(1-a_.^n_)./(1-a_) );
176    b_nF = @(a_,n_)  -(1-a_.^n_)./((1-a_));
```

```
177
178  if (flagg==0)
179      nTau = max(tau(:));
180      ttau = (1:1:nTau)';
181      a_t  = zeros(nTau,1);
182      b_t  = zeros(nTau,1);
183      for (j=2:nTau+1)
184          b_t(j,1) = b_t(j-1,1)*aQ - 1;
185          a_t(j,1) = a_t(j-1,1) + b_t(j-1,1)*cQ - 0.5*s^2*(b_t(j-1,1))^2;
186      end
187      a_n = -a_t(tau+1,1)./tau;
188      b_n = -b_t(tau+1,1)./tau;
189  else
190      a_n = -a_nF(aQ,tau,cQ,s)./tau;
191      b_n = -b_nF(aQ,tau)./tau;
192  end
193  end
```

A discrete-time Vasicek model: two-step estimation procedure

> filename: P_and_Q_Measure_Vasicek_2_step_approach.m

```
1   %% Two-step estimation procedure for the discrete-time Vasicek model
2   % Used in the section: the P and Q measures of the lecture notes
3
4   %% Load yield factors and construct yield curves
5   %
6   path_=[pwd,'\MATLAB_classes'];
7   addpath(path_);
8   load('Data_GSW.mat');
9   GSW_        = GSW;                       % instance of the GSW class
10  GSW_.tau    = [3 12:12:120]';            % vector of maturities
11  GSW_.beta   = GSW_factors(:,2:5);        % yield curve factors
12  GSW_.lambda = GSW_factors(:,6:7);        % lambdas
13  GSW_        = GSW_.getYields;            % getting yields
14  figure
15      plot(GSW_factors(:,1),GSW_.yields(:,[1 11]));
16      datetick('x','mmm-yy'), title('US yields'), legend('3m','10y')
17
18  RDNS             = TSM;                   % instance of the TSM class
19  RDNS.yields      = GSW_.yields;          % adds yields to the model
20  RDNS.tau         = GSW_.tau;             % adds maturities
21  RDNS.biasCorrect = 0;
22  RDNS.DataFreq    = 12;
23  RDNS.nF          = 3;
24  RDNS             = RDNS.getSRB3;         % est. a 3 factor SRB model
25  figure
26      plot(GSW_factors(:,1), RDNS.beta'),
27      title('Extracted yield curve factors')
28      datetick('x','mmm-yy'),
29      legend('Short rate','Slope','Curvature')
30  figure
31      plot(GSW_factors(:,1), [RDNS.beta(1,:)' RDNS.yields(:,1)]),
32      title('Model and Observed short rate')
33      datetick('x','mmm-yy'), legend('Model','Observed')
34  figure
35      plot(GSW_factors(:,1), [RDNS.TP(:,11) ACM(:,2)]),...
36      title('10Y Term Premium')
37      datetick('x','mmm-yy'), legend('SRB','ACM')
38
39  [nObs,nTau] = size(RDNS.yields);
40  %% Time-varying volatility and the Vasicek model
41  % Below we implement a two-step approach to estimating the Vasicek model
42  % with time-varying volatility, as outlined in the lecture notes.
```

```
43   %
44   Y    = RDNS.yields./1200;   % US Yields in decimal form
45   tau = RDNS.tau;             % for maturities 3, 12:12:120 months
46   %
47   % ... Step 1
48   Sr             = Y(:,1);                        % 3-month rate = short rate
49   Mdl_AR_garch   = arima('ARLags',1,'Variance',garch(1,1), ...
50                      'Distribution','Gaussian');  % AR(1)-GARCH(1,1) model
51   Est_AR_garch   = estimate(Mdl_AR_garch,Sr);     % estimate the model
52   [eps,s2]       = infer(Est_AR_garch,Sr);        % extract cond. variances
53   cP             = Est_AR_garch.Constant;
54   aP             = Est_AR_garch.AR{:};
55   s              = sqrt(s2);
56
57   %
58   % ... Step 2
59   p0  = [0;0];
60   lb_ = [-100;-100];
61   ub_ = [ 100; 100];
62   %
63   % minimise the squared residuals defined in the function
64   %     Est_Vasicek - see below
65   [pHat,fval,flagg,output,lamb_,G_,H_] = fmincon(@Est_Vasicek,p0,...
66                                          [],[],[],[],lb_,ub_,...
67                                          [],[],Y,s,cP,aP,tau,Sr)
68
69   [err2,Y_hat,a_tau,b_tau] = Est_Vasicek(pHat,Y,s,cP,aP,tau,Sr);
70   Y_hat = 12.*Y_hat;
71   RMSE  = 10000.*(mean((12.*Y-Y_hat).^2)).^(1/2);
72
73   figure
74       plot(GSW_factors(:,1),sqrt(s2))
75       datetick('x','mmm-yy')
76       ylabel('\sigma_t')
77   %   print -depsc P_Q_distribution
78
79   function [err2,Y_hat,a_tau,b_tau] = Est_Vasicek(p,Y,s,cP,aP,tau,Sr)
80   % This function calculates the difference between model and observed
81   % yields that can be used to estimate the parameters $\lambda_0$ and
82   % $\lambda_1$
83   %
84   nObs = size(s,1);
85   nTau = max(tau);
86
87   a_nF = @(a_,n_,c_,s_)  -c_/(1-a_)*( n_ - (1-a_.^n_)/(1-a_) )...
88                          +(s_^2)/(2*((1-a_)^2)).*(n_ + ...
89                          (1-a_.^(2*n_))./(1-a_^2) - 2*(1-a_.^n_)./(1-a_) );
90   b_nF = @(a_,n_)  -(1-a_.^n_)./((1-a_));
91
92   L0 = p(1);
93   L1 = p(2);
94   cQ = cP - L0.*s;
95   aQ = aP - L1.*s;
96   a_tau = NaN(size(tau,1),nObs);
97   b_tau = NaN(size(tau,1),nObs);
98   Y_hat = NaN(nObs,size(tau,1));
99   for (j=1:nObs)
100      a_tau(:,j) = -a_nF( aQ(j,1), tau, cQ(j,1), s(j,1) )./tau;
101      b_tau(:,j) = -b_nF( aQ(j,1), tau )./tau;
102      Y_hat(j,:) = (a_tau(:,j) + b_tau(:,j)*Sr(j,1))';
103  end
104  err2  = sum(sum((Y-Y_hat).^2));
105  end
```

3 The Basic Yield Curve Modelling Set-Up

3.1 Introduction

Our staring point is the empirical observation that yields observed across the maturity spectrum are highly cross-correlated, and that their time-series dynamics tend to exhibit some degree of autocorrelation. A good and practical modelling approach may therefore be to stack yields at different maturities, but observed at the same point in time, in a vector, and to collect all the vectors into a single panel of yield observations. The question is now, how do we model such a panel of correlated data points in a parsimonious way, while ensuring that as much of the information relevant to us is preserved? In coming up with an answer to this question, we will pursue a route that is purely empirically founded; the treatment of the arbitrage-free pricing set-up will follow in later sections. Here we will mainly follow the modelling ideas of Litterman and Scheinkman (1991), Nelson and Siegel (1987), Diebold and Li (2006), and in general, Diebold and Rudebusch (2013). In terms of estimation techniques, both state-space approaches and two-step OLS will be covered.

3.2 The Factor Structure of Yields

Let Y be a data set of yield curve observations covering time and maturity dimensions. Figure 15 shows an example of what Y can look like. The shown data are US zero-coupon yields, observed at a monthly frequency for the period from June 1961 to July 2018, and covering maturities from 3 to 120 months. As in other parts of this text, these are the data we will work with.

To illustrate further, Y can be sliced in two dimensions (obviously!): a single slice of Y in the maturity dimension, Y_t, contains yield observations at different maturity points, at the date where the slice is carved out of the data set; in other words, Y_t constitutes a yield curve observed at time t. We can also slice the data in the date dimension, and then collect the time-series observations of a given maturity point on the yield curve. These two ways of slicing Y are illustrated in Figure 16.

Now, if we want to model the observations contained in Y, the natural starting point is to assume, test, and estimate a time-series model for Y_t. But, we have already seen empirically in Section 1, that this may not be the best of ideas because of the strong cross-sectional relationship that exist between yields observed at different maturities. We have also seen that a more viable strategy is to model a few yield curve factors, and to find out how these yield curve factors map into observed yields – as described in the papers referred in Section 3.1, and the related large body of related literature.

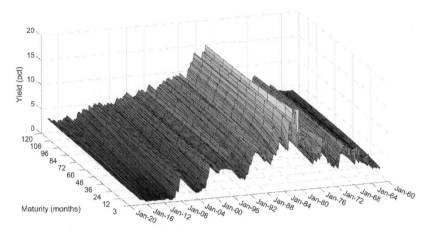

Figure 15 Yield curve data

The figure shows the US example data used throughout these notes. Monthly yield data are observed since 1961 to 2018, for maturities from 3–120 months. These data are from Gurkaynak et al. (2006) and made available and updated by the Federal Reserve Board.

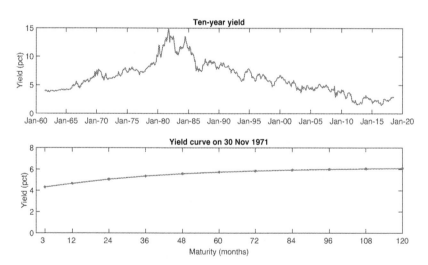

Figure 16 The maturity and time dimension of yield curve data

The figure shows the two dimensions of yield curve data. The upper panel displays the time-series dimension, and the lower shown the maturity dimension.

In its most general linear form, such an approach can be written as a two-equation dynamic system, which we typically refer to as a state-space model:[15]

---

[15] This does not necessary mean that we need to estimate the model using the Kalman filter. If, for example, we are working with observable yield curve factors, then an OLS estimation approach

state equation:

$$X_t = \underbrace{k}_{\#F\times1} + \underbrace{\Phi}_{\#F\times\#F} \cdot \underbrace{X_{t-1}}_{\#F\times1} + \underbrace{\Sigma_X}_{\#F\times\#F} \cdot \underbrace{e_t}_{\#F\times1}$$

observation equation:

$$Y_t = \underbrace{a}_{\#\tau\times1} + \underbrace{b}_{\#\tau\times\#F} \cdot \underbrace{X_t}_{\#F\times1} + \underbrace{\Sigma_Y}_{\#\tau\times\#\tau} \cdot \underbrace{u_t}_{\#\tau\times1}.$$

where ($\#F$) is the number of factors, and ($\#\tau$) is the number of maturity points modelled.

The state equation governs the dynamic evolution of the yields curve factors, X, where k is a vector of constants, Φ is a matrix of autoregressive coefficients, Σ_X is the cholesky decomposition of the covariance matrix (i.e. it is a lower triangular matrix of covolatilities), and e_t is a vector of standard normal innovations, $e_t \sim N(0, 1)$, so, $E[X_t|X_{t-1}] \sim N(\mu_X, \Sigma_X \Sigma'_X)$. The observation equation translates the yield curve factors into yields, Y_t, as they are observed in the market place. In the state equation, a is a constant vector, b is the matrix that maps factor space into yield space, Σ_Y is a diagonal matrix of maturity specific yield volatilities, and $u_t \sim N(0, 1)$.

It was shown in Section 1 that a principal component analysis can cast light on the empirical factor structure underlying yields. What is hypothesised here is addition that: (a) the factor structure can be parameterised in a parsimonious way (this idea was spearheaded by Nelson and Siegel (1987)), and that (b) the factors can be modelled by standard time-series models such as a VAR(1), as originally proposed by Diebold and Li (2006). To test out these ideas, we employ MATLAB's state-space modelling toolbox (SSM). Using MATLAB's built0in toolboxes generally comes at the cost of having to conform with a required model set-up and so on. This is of course the same for the SSM module, although the barrier-of-entry with this toolbox may at first sight seem higher than with other toolboxes. Still, in my estimation, it is worth the effort (although one also has to forego the fun of implementing the Kalman-filter from scratch), because the added benefits far outweigh this initial investment of time.

To use the SSM toolbox, it is required that the model to be estimated follows this generic set-up:

state equation: $X_t = R \cdot X_{t-1} + S \cdot e_t$

observation equation: $Y_t = T \cdot X_t + U \cdot u_t,$

---

suffices. On the other hand, if factors enter non-linearly and are unobservable, then we need to use an appropriate filtering technique such as, for example, the unscented Kalman filter (see, e.g. Julier and Uhlmann (2004), Julier and Uhlmann (1997), and Wan and Merwe (2001)).

which means that the constants need to be integrated into the R and T matrices. This is done by including additional state variables that are preconditioned to be constant, and set equal to 1 at each observation point. Apart from this, it should be relatively straight forward to set up the model. The below set-up assumes that three factors are included in the model – but it is naturally easy to accommodate any number of factors by appropriately adjusting the dimensions of the parameter matrices.

State equation

$$
\begin{bmatrix} X(1) \\ X(2) \\ X(3) \\ \hline 1_{\#\tau} \end{bmatrix}_t = \left[\begin{array}{ccc|cccc} \Phi_{1,1} & \Phi_{1,2} & \Phi_{1,3} & k_1 & 0 & 0 & 0_{1,\#\tau-3} \\ \Phi_{2,1} & \Phi_{2,2} & \Phi_{2,3} & 0 & k_2 & 0 & 0_{1,\#\tau-3} \\ \Phi_{3,1} & \Phi_{3,2} & \Phi_{3,3} & 0 & 0 & k_3 & 0_{1,\#\tau-3} \\ \hline & 0_{\#\tau,3} & & & & I_{\#\tau} & \end{array} \right] \cdot \begin{bmatrix} X(1) \\ X(2) \\ X(3) \\ \hline 1_{\#\tau} \end{bmatrix}_{t-1}
$$

$$
+ \left[\begin{array}{ccc} \Sigma_{X(1,1)} & 0 & 0 \\ \Sigma_{X(2,1)} & \Sigma_{X(2,2)} & 0 \\ \Sigma_{X(3,1)} & \Sigma_{X(3,2)} & \Sigma_{X(3,3)} \\ \hline 0_{\#\tau,1} & 0_{\#\tau,1} & 0_{\#\tau,1} \end{array} \right] e_t,
$$

where $1_{\#\tau}$ is a constant unit vector of dimension $\#\tau$, and $I_{\#\tau}$ is the identity matrix of dimension $(\#\tau \times \#\tau)$. The rest of the dimension assignments follow the same principle.

The observation equation takes the following form:

Observation equation

$$
\begin{bmatrix} y^{3m} \\ y^{12m} \\ \vdots \\ y^{120m} \\ \hline 1_{\#\tau} \end{bmatrix}_t = \left[\begin{array}{cccc|ccccc} b_{1,3m} & b_{2,3m} & b_{3,3m} & a_{3m} & 0 & \cdots & & 0 \\ b_{1,12m} & b_{2,12m} & b_{3,12m} & 0 & & \ddots & \cdots & 0 \\ \vdots & \vdots & \vdots & \vdots & \vdots & & \ddots & 0 \\ b_{1,120m} & b_{2,120m} & b_{3,120m} & 0 & 0 & 0 & & a_{120m} \\ \hline 0 & 0 & 0 & & & I_{(\#\tau \times \#\tau)} & & \end{array} \right] \cdot \begin{bmatrix} X(1) \\ X(2) \\ X(3) \\ \hline 1_{\#\tau} \end{bmatrix}_t
$$

$$
+ \left[\begin{array}{ccccc} \Sigma_{y,(1,1)} & 0 & 0 & \cdots & 0 \\ 0 & \Sigma_{y,(2,2)} & 0 & \cdots & 0 \\ 0 & 0 & \ddots & \cdots & 0 \\ \vdots & \vdots & \vdots & \ddots & \vdots \\ 0 & 0 & 0 & 0 & \Sigma_{y,(\#\tau,\#\tau)} \\ \hline & & 0_{\#\tau,\#\tau} & & \end{array} \right] u_t
$$

With the model now adhering to the notation used by MATLAB, it can be implemented and estimated using the SSM toolbox. This is done in the script included in the Annex part 4.2.2. Two model implementations are embedded in the code: one allows for the estimation of a fully empirical version of the model, where no prior structure is imposed on the constant vector, a, and the loading structure b in the observation equation; the other constrains a and b to follow the prescription by Nelson and Siegel (1987) using the parametrisation suggested by Diebold and Li (2006). This means that:

$$a = 0 \tag{3.1}$$

$$b_\tau = \left[1 \quad \frac{1-e^{(-\gamma \cdot \tau)}}{\gamma \cdot \tau} \quad \frac{1-e^{(-\gamma \cdot \tau)}}{\gamma \cdot \tau} - e^{(-\gamma \cdot \tau)} \right]. \tag{3.2}$$

Note that the notation is changed slightly compared to what is traditionally used. We use γ to denote the time-decay parameter, which is most often denoted by λ in the literature. This is done to avoid notational confusion, since λ is elsewhere in this Element used to denote the market price of risk.

When running the code shown in Annex part 4.2.2 (in its two guises by adjusting the input in line 52, choosing either 'Emp', for empirical, or 'NS', for the Nelson-Siegel model) we can compare the loadings and extracted factors. Since the empirical model is virtually unspecified in its generic form, it is not clear what to expect in terms of an outcome. In essence, this model is too flexibly specified, since there is nothing that locks down the scale and sign of the factors, and by the same token, there is noting ensuring that a reasonable and interpretable structure will emerge for the loadings contained in b. In principle, we have a linear regression model, $y = a + b \cdot x$, we only know y, and we try to determine a, b, and x, by using some clever estimation technique (i.e. the Kalman filter). Clearly, there are many combinations of $a + b \cdot x$ that will fulfil the equation. We must therefore expect that, depending on the starting values, the iterative algorithm can converge to a multitude of maxima all providing exactly the same fit to data. If we would like to have a model that facilitates economic analysis, it is useful to attach a certain meaning to the factors, and that this meaning remains constant over time (i.e. across the multiple times the model will be re-estimated, as time progresses). We will look more carefully at this in the next section; for now we will push ahead, and see what we get when we run the code.

Figure 17 shows the loadings that are generated by the two models, and Figure 18 shows the extracted factors. Using these two estimates, which amount to b and X in the above-outlined model-notation, together with the constant, a, we can assess how well the estimated models fit the observed yields. This is done by means of the RMSE (root-mean-squared-error) expressed in basis points. Model predictions are denoted by $\hat{y}^{Emp}$ and $\hat{y}^{NS}$, respectively, and calculated in the following way:

$$\hat{y} = \hat{a} + \hat{b} \cdot \hat{X}. \tag{3.3}$$

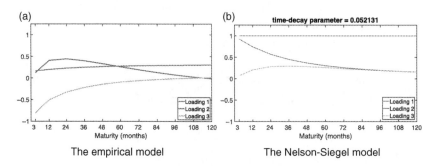

Figure 17 Estimated loadings

Panel (a) shows the loading structure of the empirical model specification, i.e. the parameter estimates contained in the b-matrix from the observation equation: $y = a + b \cdot X$. Panel (b) shows the same for the Nelson-Siegel model. The displayed loading structures provide a graphical representation of the loadings for the three estimated factors (i.e. the loadings for each factor across the modelled maturity dimension).

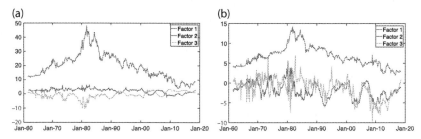

Figure 18 Estimated factors

Panel (a) shows the time-series evolution of the extracted yield curve factors, i.e. the estimates contained in the X-matrix from the observation equation: $y = a + b \cdot X$. Panel (b) shows the same for the Nelson-Siegel model.

Using the ˆ notation here underscores that estimates are used to produce the model predictions. This is an obvious fact, and this notation will therefore not be used throughout, unless the context is ambiguous. Another thing to note is that only the parameter estimates from the observation equation are used at the moment – but rest assured, we will return to the state equation, and use it extensively, in the section that looks at forecasting and scenario generation.

While it may not be evident to the naked eye, there is quite some commonality between the loading structures shown in Figure 17. Taking the Nelson-Siegel loadings as the starting point, the first factor has an equal impact on all yields, regardless of their maturity: that is, loading 1 equals unity across the maturity spectrum (see panel (b)). While the empirical model does not generate a constant value of one across the maturity spectrum for its first loading, the value is approximately constant. In the language of PCA analysis, where scale and signs of loadings and factors can switch around, this common feature (i.e. constancy across the maturity spectrum) is enough to declare, that the first factor has a similar interpretation for both model variants. And, by the virtue of its impact on the yield curve, shifting it upwards and downwards in a parallel fashion, this first factor can be seen as the duration risk factor. It is too early to say whether the duration factor is shifting the curve from the short, middle, or long end of the maturity dimension. To determine this, we need to look at the second factor. As is well known, in the Nelson-Siegel model, the second factor constitutes the slope of the yield curve, or rather, the negative slope, that is, the short-end yield minus the long-end yield. This is evident from the shape and location of Loading 2 in panel (b). At the short end of the maturity spectrum, this factor records its maximum impact, and its impact falls to zero (beyond the maturities shown in Figure 17) as the maturity increases, following a convex trajectory. Thinking, for example, about how the three-month yield is recovered from these two first-factor loadings of the Nelson-Siegel model, shows that the first factor is defined as the long-end level of the yield curve (and it is from here that parallel shifts are induced on the yield curve), and the second factor is the negative slope:

$$
\begin{aligned}
\text{short rate} &= \text{loading 1} \cdot \text{Factor 1} + \text{loading 2} \cdot \text{Factor 2} \\
&= 1 \cdot \text{Factor 1} + 1 \cdot \text{Factor 2} \\
&= 1 \cdot \text{level} + 1 \cdot (-\text{level} + \text{short rate}) \\
&= \text{short rate}.
\end{aligned}
$$

Following this logic, it is established that the Nelson-Siegel model imposes factor interpretations for the first two factors that are equal to a yield curve level factor, and to a negative (compared to the traditional definition) slope factor, respectively. In the example, we have also established that the first factor detected by the empirical model, is similar in shape to the level factor of the Nelson-Siegel model. The question is now, whether either of the two remaining loading structures in panel (a) of Figure 17 resembles the second Nelson-Siegel factor loading. It appears that Loading 3 exhibits a convex and increasing pattern, and if rotated around the x-axis, it compares well to the second Nelson-Siegel factor!

But, why does the empirical model swap the ordering of the factors around? Well, since we haven't given the model any information about how we want it to organise it does not know any better, and it orders the factors basically on the basis of the starting values given to the optimisation routine, and the path that the routine follows to reach the maximum. This is different when we do a PCA analysis, since most econometric packages order the extracted factors/principal components according to their eigenvalues, that is, according to the amount of variance that they each explain. And, since PCA analysis in principle underpins the Nelson-Siegel model, the ordering of the NS-factors follows this principle: by the way, obviously, it also makes a lot of economic and intuitive sense to order the factors in this way, since it corresponds to placing the most risky factor first in the hierarchy and the least risky factor last.

Finally, the two remaining factors – factor two from the empirical model and factor three from the Nelson-Siegel model – also match up in terms of patterns, with the weighting across maturities fitting that of a curvature impact, that is, having little impact in the short and long ends of the curve and larger impact in the middle part of the maturity spectrum.

Sorting out the relationship between the empirical and the Nelson-Siegel model specifications by visual inspection of the loading structure shown in Figure 17, as we have done above, has hopefully helped to further our intuitive understanding of yield curve factor-models. At least, this was the main purpose of this exercise. In my experience, it is in general helpful to think about yield curve factor models as the the multiplication of loadings and factors (plus a constant), so, $y = a + b \cdot X$, in visual terms as the multiplication of the load-ings, as, for example, shown in panel (a) of Figure 17, with the time series of factors, shown in panel (b) of Figure 18. Having such a visual representation in the back of the mind helps to lock down the entities that enter the model and facilitates an immediate intuitive sense of the economic interpretation of the factors.

There is an easier and (perhaps) more natural way to match up the factor interpretation across the two estimated models. Given that we have obtained the time series of the yield curve factors for each model, as shown in Figure 18, we can simply calculate the cross-correlations between the series. This is done in Table 7. And, luckily, the conclusions we drew are confirmed: there is a correlation of 0.99 between factor 1 of the empirical and Nelson-Siegel models, a correlation of 0.96 between the second factor from the empirical model and the third Nelson-Siegel factor, and finally a correlation of -0.85 between the third empirically determined factor and the second Nelson-Siegel factor. The negative sign of the latter correlation coefficient matches the fact that the loading structure for the third empirical factor had to be rotated around the x-axis (i.e. it had to be multiplied by -1) in order to obtain a pattern similar to that of the Nelson-Siegel model.

As the final issue in this section, we will have a look at how well the two models fit the data. To fix ideas, it is observed that the Nelson-Siegel model can be seen as a constrained version of the empirical model, since the Nelson-Siegel

Table 7 Factor correlations

	Emp F1	Emp F2	Emp F3	NS F1	NS F2	NS F3
Emp F1	1.00					
Emp F2	0.32	1.00				
Emp F2	−0.68	−0.28	1.00			
NS F1	**0.99**	0.23	−0.59	1.00		
NS F2	0.19	0.14	**−0.85**	0.08	1.00	
NS F3	0.48	**0.96**	−0.54	0.38	0.38	1.00

The table shows the correlations between the extracted factors from the empirically founded (Emp) model and from the Nelson-Siegel (NS) model.

model imposes a certain functional structure on the loadings contained in the b-matrix. In fact, at first sight, it seems that Nelson and Siegel chose to impose some rather severe constraints: where the empirical model relies on $\#\tau \times 3 = 33$ parameters, all to be estimated, the Nelson-Siegel model uses only one single parameter, namely the time-decay parameter γ, together with functions of γ and τ. On the other hand, we also know that the Nelson-Siegel model is hugely popular, and one of the tools often used by central banks asset managers. If the model produced a poor fit to data, it probably would not be so widely used. So, it is no surprise that the two-parameter functional-forms utilised by the Nelson-Siegel model do not impose any devastating constraints. This is, of course, because the chosen functional forms match well the patterns that result from PCA analysis on yields, and that yields in most markets, and across time, are well captured by these patterns.

Using the US data, Table 8 shows the root mean squared error (RMSE) for each model across maturities from three months to ten years. Both models fit data very well, and they both have very low average RMSEs. While the empirical model fits slightly better, we see that the cost of the constraints imposed by the Nelson-Siegel model are very small, at most 1 to 3 basis points. And, these results are obtained on data covering the period from 1960 to 2018, so this results seems to have general validity, and it surely not an artefact of a carefully selected data sample.

3.3 Rotating the Yield Curve Factors

As practitioners, we may, at times, be interested in imposing a certain economic meaning on one or more of the yield curve factors, while still staying within the comforting remit of the Nelson and Siegel (1987) and Diebold and Li (2006)

Table 8 RMSE (basis points)

τ in months	3	12	24	36	48	60	72	84	96	108	120
Empirical model (bps)	6	13	4	4	6	5	4	2	1	4	6
Nelson-Siegel (bps)	8	14	5	3	5	5	4	3	1	3	6
Difference	-2	-1	-1	1	-1	0	0	-1	0	1	0

Model fits are compared for the two estimated versions of the model: the empirical one and the Nelson-Siegel model. The table shows the root mean squared error (RMSE) for each model. For each maturity point covered by the data, the RMSE is calculated as $\left[mean\left[\left(y_{\tau(i)} - \hat{y}^j_{\tau(i)} \right)^2 \right] \right]^{\left(\frac{1}{2} \right)}$, where $y_{\tau(i)}$ and $\hat{y}^j_{\tau(i)}$ are time series for the i'th maturity point, $j \in \{Emp, NS\}$.

modelling frameworks.[16] For a given task, we may find that it is convenient to work directly with the short rate: for example, if yield curve scenarios need to be generated for risk assessment purposes, where a set of predefined scenarios are defined in terms of the future path of the monetary policy rate. In this case, it seems reasonable to model the short rate directly, rather than to backward engineer how the Nelson-Siegel level and slope factors would need to evolve, to match the predefined scenario paths for the short rate. It could may also be the case that a certain relationship between the short rate, the slope, and some macroeconomic variables, are believed to exist. For example, we may believe that a Taylor-rule (Taylor (1993)) inspired relationship holds between macroeconomic variables, and that slope is related to the perceived risk in the fixed income markets, and that scenarios need to be generated against this set-up. Again, it seems more fruitful to use on a Nelson-Siegel type model that relies on a short rate factor, rather than the level factor. Other examples are the evaluation of trading strategies and return decompositions. To the extent that trading positions are specified in terms of actual yield curve points, for example, long/short the 2y-10y spread positions, curvature positions (e.g. as combinations of the 2Y-5Y-10Y, and so on), it may be relevant to model yield curve points directly, rather than the level, slope, and curvature factors.

Under the requirement that the desired alternative factor interpretation can be expressed as a linear combination of the existing factors, it is possible to find a rotation matrix $\mathcal{A}$, where $I = \mathcal{A}^{-1} \cdot \mathcal{A}$, such that the desired factor structure emerges.[17]

---

[16] Factor rotation is a well-known concept in statistical analysis, see e.g. Johnson and Wichern (1992)[ch. 9.4].

[17] The matrix $\mathcal{A}$ will be orthogonal, so the rotation $I = \mathcal{A}' \cdot \mathcal{A}$ becomes $I = \mathcal{A}^{-1} \cdot \mathcal{A}$.

Consider the observation equation from the standard dynamic model. We can naturally expand this expression by I, without changing it in any way:

$$y_t = a + b \cdot X_t + \Sigma_y \cdot u_t$$
$$= a + b \cdot I \cdot X_t + \Sigma_y \cdot u_t$$
$$= a + b \cdot \mathcal{A}^{-1} \cdot \mathcal{A} \cdot X_t + \Sigma_y \cdot u_t. \qquad (3.4)$$

By doing this, we have obtained new interpretations of the factors and the factor loadings, that are in accordance with the chosen $\mathcal{A}$ matrix.

$$\tilde{b} = b \cdot \mathcal{A}^{-1} \qquad (3.5)$$
$$\tilde{X}_t = \mathcal{A} \cdot X_t. \qquad (3.6)$$

Later on, we will see how to choose $\mathcal{A}$, for now the objective is to see how the state equation changes:

$$\tilde{X}_t = \mathcal{A} \cdot X_t = \mathcal{A} \left(k + \Phi \cdot X_{t-1} + \Sigma_X \cdot e_t \right) \qquad (3.7)$$
$$= \mathcal{A} \cdot k + \mathcal{A} \cdot \Phi \cdot X_{t-1} + \mathcal{A} \cdot \Sigma_X \cdot e_t \qquad (3.8)$$
$$= \mathcal{A} \cdot k + \mathcal{A} \cdot \Phi \cdot \mathcal{A}^{-1} \cdot \tilde{X}_{t-1} + \mathcal{A} \cdot \Sigma_X \cdot e_t, \qquad (3.9)$$
$$= \tilde{k} + \tilde{\Phi} \cdot \tilde{X}_{t-1} + \tilde{\Sigma}_X \qquad (3.10)$$

where the second-to-last line follows from (3.6). The parameters of the rotated model can be read from equation (3.9), and are:

$$\tilde{k} = \mathcal{A} \cdot k \qquad (3.11)$$
$$\tilde{\Phi} = \mathcal{A} \cdot \Phi \cdot \mathcal{A}^{-1} \qquad (3.12)$$
$$\tilde{\Sigma}_X = \mathcal{A} \cdot \Sigma_X. \qquad (3.13)$$

In practical applications of rotated models, it is naturally enough to rotate the loading matrix, b, in the observation equation, and then to proceed with the estimation as usual. Doing this will result in the extraction of rotated factors as well. Equations (3.11)-(3.13) are only needed if a standard model has been estimated and it subsequently needs to be rotated, or if a rotated model has been estimated and it needs to be un-rotated.

How is $\mathcal{A}$ determined? This naturally depends on the desired factor interpretation. I present two simple cases where the factors have interpretations as: [short rate, slope, curvature], and as the [2Y yield, 5Y yield, 10Y yield].

3.3.1 A Short-Rate Based Model

As we have seen many times, the original Nelson-Siegel factors are level, slope, and curvature. To obtain a factor structure that equals the short rate, the slope, and the curvature, the following $\mathcal{A}$-matrix will do the trick ("SRB stands for short rate based"):

$$\mathcal{A}^{SRB} = \begin{bmatrix} 1 & 1 & 0 \\ 0 & -1 & 0 \\ 0 & 0 & 1 \end{bmatrix}.$$

Lets insert it and see if it rotates that factors as desired:

$$\begin{bmatrix} \text{short rate} \\ \text{slope} \\ \text{curvature} \end{bmatrix} = \begin{bmatrix} 1 & 1 & 0 \\ 0 & -1 & 0 \\ 0 & 0 & 1 \end{bmatrix} \cdot \begin{bmatrix} \text{level} \\ \text{-slope} \\ \text{curvature} \end{bmatrix} = \begin{bmatrix} \text{level-slope} \\ \text{slope} \\ \text{curvature} \end{bmatrix}.$$

It is important to recall that nothing is gained, in terms of model fit or improved forecasting performance, after a rotation is performed. This is clear since $I = \mathcal{A} \cdot \mathcal{A}^{-1}$. Only the factor interpretation is changed.

3.3.2 Using Yields as Factors

Another rotation that may be relevant for practical work, is a rotation towards an interpretation of the factors as yield curve maturity points. In Figure 19, the Nelson-Siegel factors are rotated to have interpretations as the [2y, 5y, 10y] yields. To achieve this, we need to establish a link between the Nelson-Siegel factors and the desired factor interpretation. Often, it is mentioned in the literature that the following relationships hold: [level = 10y yield], [-slope = 3m yield – 10y yield], and [curvature = 2× 2y yield – 10y yield – 3m yield]. From this we could, in principle, obtain a rotation matrix that approximately would give us the factor interpretation that we are looking for. But, it may be better to devise a general methodology that also would work, should we want to implement other types of factor interpretations/rotations. This can be done in a (perhaps) surprisingly simple way, by using linear regression. Of course, a prerequisite for this methodology to work is that the factors we rotate towards are observable or can be estimated.

Second, we see whether the rotated model fits the observed yields as well as the Nelson-Siegel model does. This assessment can be made on the basis of the RMSE across maturities. Table 9 shows the obtained numbers. As expected, the RMSEs of the rotated model are exactly the same as those obtained from the original Nelson-Siegel model.[18]

---

[18] It is worth noting that the RMSEs reported in Table 9 deviate slightly from the ones reported in Table 8. This is due to the difference in estimation methods applied: the results obtained in Table 8 rely on a state-space implementation, where as the results in Table 9 are based on a stepwise OLS implementation (via the TSM (term structure model) object-oriented class), where the time-decay parameter is determined to a precision of three decimals.

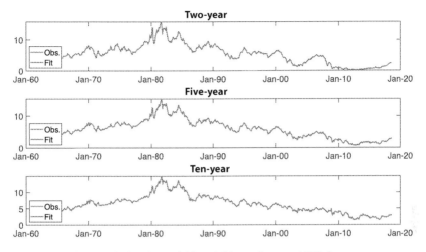

Figure 19 2y, 5y, and 10y yields, and rotated NS factors

The figure compares the yield curve factors of a rotated dynamic Nelson-Siegel model, where the factors are the 2y, 5y, and 10y yield curve points, with the actually observed 2y, 5y, and 10y yield curve points. The lines fall on top of each other, therefore only one line is visible in the panels.

To fulfil our current factor appetite, we fill the entries of the rotation matrix via the three OLS regressions (see Appendix with the MATLAB code to see how this can be implemented in practise):

$$y_{2Y} = \mathcal{A}^y_{(1,:)} \cdot \hat{X}^{NS}$$
$$y_{5Y} = \mathcal{A}^y_{(2,:)} \cdot \hat{X}^{NS}$$
$$y_{10Y} = \mathcal{A}^y_{(3,:)} \cdot \hat{X}^{NS}. \tag{3.14}$$

The regressions are run with the normalisation constraint that the impact of the level factor is equal to 1 for all rotated factors. Doing this gives:

$$\mathcal{A}^y = \begin{bmatrix} 1.00 & 0.56 & 0.28 \\ 1.00 & 0.31 & 0.26 \\ 1.00 & 0.15 & 0.16 \end{bmatrix}. \tag{3.15}$$

Even if we firmly believe that this approach will work, it may be a good idea to perform a double check. First, we can visually inspect how well the rotated factors match the observed counterparts. This is done in Figure 19, with convincing results: the lines are indistinguishable.

Table 9 RMSE (basis points)

τ in months	3	12	24	36	48	60	72	84	96	108	120
NS (OLS) (bps)	8.42	14.03	4.89	3.57	5.31	5.60	4.54	2.59	1.16	3.48	6.45
Rotated (bps)	8.42	14.03	4.89	3.57	5.31	5.60	4.54	2.59	1.16	3.48	6.45

RMSEs are calculated for the dynamic Nelson-Siegel model estimated using a two-step OLS methodology, as implemented in the object-oriented term structure model (TSM) class, and for the model presented in the text, where the Nelson-Siegel factors are rotated to be the time series of the 2y, 5y, and 10y yield curve points.

3.4 The Building Blocks That Shape the Yield Curve

Even if we resist the strong temptation to impose arbitrage constraints on our model, we will still be able to extract and analyse the fundamental building blocs that shape the location and dynamics of the yield curve. These are: (a) the term structure of term premia, and (b) the term structure of rate expectations. To assess the current economic environment in terms of risks and expectations to future economic growth, it is important to have reliable estimates of the term premium and the expected risk-free term structure. As also mentioned in Section 2 describing the $\mathbb{P}$ and $\mathbb{Q}$ measures, the term premium, $\theta_{t,\tau}$, at time t for some maturity τ, is a summary measure for the risks that financial agents are deemed to face, when trading fixed income securities. The items displayed in italics font are typically not included in the list, when we deal with risk-free sovereign bonds, as we do here. However, they are included just to remind us of these additional systematic risk factors when we start working with corporate bonds and possibly less liquid market segments:

- uncertainty about the economic growth rate
- uncertainty about the inflation rate
- *credit migration risk*
- *default risk*
- *liquidity risk*

The term premium-free ($\mathbb{P}$ measure) term structure is constructed mechanically as the average of the short-rate ($\mathbb{P}$) expectation over future periods. It is risk free, because the one period (short) rate is risk-free, period after period. Another way to realise this, is to consider that a model needs to be fitted to historically observed short-rate data, that represent past realisations of the risk-free rate.

Following Gürkaynak and Wright (2012), the risk-free term structure can be calculated as:

$$y_{t,\tau}^{rf} = \frac{1}{\tau} \cdot \mathbb{E}_t \sum_{j=0}^{\tau-1} r_{t,t+j},$$

(3.16)

and, the term premium, $\theta_{t,\tau}$, as the difference between the model fitted yield, $\hat{y}_{t,\tau}$ and the risk-free yield, $y_{t,\tau}^{rf}$:

$$\theta_{t,\tau} = \hat{y}_{t,\tau} - y_{t,\tau}^{rf}.$$

(3.17)

To illustrate how we can obtain rate expectations and term premia also from models that do not exclude arbitrage by construction, and to see to what extent they differ from model to model, we perform the following case studies, comparing the:

(A) three-factor SRB model with the standard Nelson-Siegel parametrisation.
(B) three- and four-factor SRB models.
(C) three-factor SRB model with and without bias correction (what bias correction entails will be outlined in the folllowing).
(D) three-factor SRB model with different assumptions on the mean of the short rate.
(E) three-factor SRB model with published term premium and rate expectations from the Adrian, Crump and Mönch (2013) and Kim and Wright (2005) models.

Before embarking on this task, we need to introduce the three- and four-factor versions of the short-rate based (SRB) model. The state and transition equations of the four-factor model will be presented, since the three-factor model is simply a constrained version of the four-factor model; the constraint being that the fourth factor is deleted in the three-factor version of the model. We will use a discrete-time version of the model, and we will derive it formally in a later section. For now, only the relevant equations are presented, as in the case of the Nelson-Siegel model, as shown in equations (3.1) and (3.2).

The four-factor model is shown in equations (3.18) and (3.19).

$$X_t = \mu + \Phi \cdot (X_{t-1} - \mu) + \Sigma_X \cdot e_t$$

(3.18)

$$y_{t,\tau} = b_\tau \cdot X_t + \Sigma_Y \cdot u_t$$

$$= \begin{bmatrix} 1 \\ 1 - \frac{1-\gamma^\tau}{(1-\gamma)\cdot\tau} \\ \frac{1-\gamma^\tau}{(1-\gamma)\cdot\tau} - \gamma^{\tau-1} \\ -\frac{1}{2}(\tau-1)(\gamma-1)\gamma^{(n-2)} \end{bmatrix}' \cdot X_t + \Sigma_Y \cdot u_t$$

(3.19)

Note that the VAR(1) model in (3.18) is written in mean-adjusted form, so μ is the mean of the included factors. Since we know that the the first factor in X_t is the short rate, we can work on equation (3.16), and turn it into a closed-from expression, in the following way:

$$
\begin{aligned}
y_{t,\tau}^{rf} &= \frac{1}{\tau} \cdot \mathbb{E}_t \sum_{j=0}^{\tau-1} r_{t,t+j} \\
&= \frac{1}{\tau} \cdot \left[r_t + \mathbb{E}_t \sum_{j=1}^{\tau-1} r_{t,t+j} \right] \\
&= \frac{1}{\tau} \left\{ X_t' \cdot \delta_1 + \left[\mathbb{E}_t \sum_{j=0}^{\tau-2} \mu + \Phi \cdot (X_{t+j} - \mu) \right]' \cdot \delta_1 \right\} \\
&= \frac{1}{\tau} \left\{ X_t' \cdot \delta_1 + \left[(\tau - 1) \cdot \mu + \frac{\Phi^\tau - \Phi}{\Phi - I} \cdot (X_t - \mu) \right]' \cdot \delta_1 \right\}
\end{aligned}
\qquad (3.20)
$$

where δ_1 is a vector of appropriate dimension that selects the first element of the vector generated inside the brackets, that is, $\delta_1 = [1, 0, 0, 0]'$ when we work with a four-factor model, and $\delta_1 = [1, 0, 0]'$, when working with a 3-factor model. The reason for separating out the $(X_t' \cdot \delta_1)$ part is to highlight that this equals r_t, and the factor, $(\Phi^\tau - \Phi)(\Phi - I)^{(-1)}$, originates as the limit of the sum of the power series implied by line 3 of (3.20).

It may be worth highlighting that it is much simpler to use the close-form expression in (3.20) compared to calculating the rate expectation using the summation over all τ, as implied by (3.16). The closed-form expression is both faster and less computationally intensive. While this is not a big deal when using monthly data, it may be an issue if we estimate the model on daily data. Imagine we want to calculate the ten-year rate expectation, and we have estimated our model on daily data, and we that have data for the period from January 1961 to July 2018, a total of around $14,800$ days. When using (3.20), we would then need to roll forward the state equation (3.18) for 3,650 observation points, for each of the 14,800 days covered by our sample; implying that we would need to calculate Φ^k for $k \in \{1, 2, \ldots, 3,650\}$ at each observation point, a total of 54mill calculations. Compared to this, it is easier to use (3.20), because only 14,800 calculations are needed, one for each day. A second thing that is worth mentioning is that either of the two outlined calculation methods can be efficiently completed using the eigenvalue decomposition[19] of Φ^k:

---

[19] Can be obtained in MATLAB using the `eig` command.

$$\Phi^k = V \cdot D^k \cdot V^{-1}, \tag{3.21}$$

where V is the matrix of eigenvectors, and D is a diagonal matrix of eigenvalues. Recall that it requires much less computational effort to calculate the power of a diagonal matrix, because one just needs to raise each diagonal element of the matrix to the desired power.

Case (C) in our list aims to investigate the relevance of bias-correcting the VAR(1) model, included in the state equation. When estimating a VAR model using OLS on relatively few time-series data points, as is often the case in yield curve applications, the parameters of the VAR can be biased downwards. This implies that the estimated factors can exhibit a lower degree of persistency, compared to their true process parameters. I think Bauer, Rudebusch and Wu (2012) were the first to highlight this issue. Our bias correction method, which is implemented in MATLAB via the term structure class (TSM) that accompany this Element, is based on the description in Engsted and Pedersen (2014), of the analytical approach suggested by Pope (1990).

The persistence of the factors is naturally important for the decomposition of the yield curve into rate expectations and term premium components. Imagine, for example, that the short rate factor exhibits a very low degree of persistency, in fact so low that the process converges to its sample mean within three to seven years, for any of the short-rate levels observed in the sample. Consequently, if we focus on the ten-year rate expectation, it will equal the sample mean for all dates covered by the sample, and the resulting time series of ten-year rate expectations is just a constant flat line equal to the sample mean, lets say, for example, 4.88 per cent. Then we will obtain a time series of ten-year term premium estimates that is equal to $\hat{y}_{t,\tau=10years} - 4.88\%$, and assuming that the model fits data well, then this is very close to being equal to the observed series of 10-year yields minus 4.88 per cent. Not a very believable result. At the other end of the absurdity scale is a super-highly persistent process. Imagine a process where the short-rate hardly moves (in expectations) from its starting point, and for example, takes 10,000 years for the process to converge to its sample mean. Calculating the term premium in this case amounts approximately to calculating the slope of the yield curve (again assuming a good fit of the model), at any date covered covered by the sample. An equally unbelievable outcome. So, the persistency of the estimated VAR model typically has a large impact on the model-derived expectations/term premium decomposition: we will check this empirically in the following.

All estimations done in the context of the five case studies are performed used the TSM class. To learn more about this object-oriented class, you can type `help TSM` at the command prompt. The basics of it is:

(1) To create an instance of the TSM class. An instance is, so to say, your private copy of the class, that you can work with. To create an instance, type: `<name>=TSM`, for example: `SRB_1 = TSM`.

(2) The created instance can now be populated with data: `SRB_1.yields=Y` (assuming that the data to be used for the estimation of the model are stored in the matrix `Y`), `SRB_1.tau=tau`, (assuming that the vector of maturities is stored in `tau`), and `SRB_1.DataFreq=12`, if data are sampled at a monthly time-interval. And so on. It should be noted that the variable names used in the TSM class are not optional, so the name that appears after the dot (i.e. in the example above `.yields`, `.tau`, and `.DataFreq`), has to be used as shown in the help file – the TSM class does not understand if yields, for example, are assigned to a container called `SRB_1.YieldsForTheModel`, or any other user-defined name. On the other hand, the name of the class instance (i.e. `SRB_1`) can be chosen freely.

(3) Given that all data have been passed successfully to the created instance, any of the models covered by the class can be estimated. Four models are covered at the moment, but this number will increase over time. The following are covered: the dynamic Nelson-Siegel model, the dynamic Svensson-Soderlind model, the 3-factor SRB model, and the 4-factor SRB model.

(4) Any of the models can be estimated using the command `.get<model name>`. For example, to estimate the three-factor SRB model we would write: $SRB_1 = SRB\_1.getSRB3$. This estimates the desired model and stores the results in the created class instance called `SRB_1`. The other models are estimated using the commands `.getDNS`, `.getDSS`, and `.getSRB4`, respectively.

(5) The output covers, among other things, model parameters, time series of extracted yield curve factors, RMSE, the term structure of term premia (at the provided maturities), and the term structure of rate expectations (at the provided maturities).

To complete the scenarios outlined, we will implement the five steps from the list. More details on the coding can be found in MATLAB Appendix in Section 4.2.2. Comparisons will be drawn in terms of rate expectations and term premia, typically at the ten-year maturity point; model fit in terms of RMSEs,

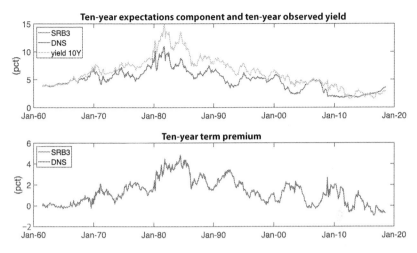

Figure 20 The SRB3 and DNS models

The figure shows the ten-year term premium estimates from the three- and four-factor SRB models. In the figure, the upper panel shows the ten-year term expectations component, and the lower panel shows the ten-year premium. Estimates from the standard *SRB3* model is shown in blue, and the mean adjusted version is shown in red. For comparison, the observed 10-year yield is plotted in yellow, in the upper panel.

and persistency of the VAR(1) model featuring in the state equation and judged on the basis of the eigenvalues of $\hat{\Phi}$.

Case (A): Comparing the 3-factor SRB model with the standard dynamic Nelson-Siegel model

Figure 20 draws a comparison between the 3-factor SRB model, and the dynamic Nelson-Siegel (DNS) model. While these models have different factor interpretations – the SRB-model explicitly includes the short rate, and the DNS model explicitly includes the long-term rate (i.e. the yield curve level) – they are very similar, and intimately linked via the rotation matrix $\mathcal{A}$. However, since the SRB model is derived in discrete-time (as we will see later on), and the DNS model is derived in a continuous time, the link between the two models, via a rotation-matrix, does not produce mathematically identical models.[20] It is actually not possible to rotate the DNS model into the SRB model, as it is used here, because of the mentioned difference between the models. But, it is possible to rotate the DNS model into a continuous-time SRB model, and the difference between this rotated model, and the SRB model (in discrete-time)

---

[20] The practical difference is that the SRB model's loading structure is defined in terms of power functions, while the DNS model relies on exponentials. The continuous-time limit of a power function is the exponential function: recall, for example, the link between discretely and continuously compounded interest rates: $lim_{n\to\infty} \left(1 + \frac{r \cdot T}{n}\right)^n = e^{rT}$.

Table 10 Case A: RMSE and eigenvalues

	RMSE (basis points)								
τ **in months**	**3**	**12**	**24**	**36**	**48**	**60**	**72**	**84**	**120**
SRB3	8.50	14.08	4.89	3.54	5.28	5.56	4.51	2.57	6.38
SRB3, bias corrected	8.42	14.03	4.89	3.57	5.31	5.60	4.54	2.59	6.45

	Eigenvalues of $\hat{\Phi}$		
	1	2	3
SRB3	0.990	0.957	0.808
DNS	0.990	0.957	0.807

RMSEs are calculated and shown in basis points for the two models under investigation, together with the eigenvalues of $\hat{\Phi}$, sorted in descending order.

is very, very small. So, this is the degree of intimacy between the two models used in this section.

The similarity between the models is confirmed in Figure 20, with the plots of the 10-year rate expectation and term premia being indistinguishable from one model to the next. A minor difference is observed on the third eigenvalue, where the SRB model is insignificantly more persistent than the DNS model; likewise, minor and non-significant differences are seen in terms of in-sample fits. For practical purposes in the area of extracting past information from the 3-factor SRB and DNS models, they are identical. In a later section of the Element, we will see whether this conclusion also carries over to the forecasting performance of the models.

Case (B): Comparing 3- and 4-factor SRB models

Including an additional factor into the SRB model greatly improves the in sample fit, as seen in Table 11, but dispite this, there is hardly any difference to detect between the models' output in terms of rate expectations and term premia, as seen in Figure 21. This result echoes the mantra that the potential merits of a model should never be judged only on its in-sample perform-ance. Clearly, as more yield curve factors are added, the in-sample fit will, by definition, improve. One can think of a good in-sample fit, as being a min-imum requirement for including a given model into the toolbox of models that one relies on: as long as a model provides a reasonably good in-sample fit, say below 10–20 basis points per maturity bucket, then it is worthwhile to consider whether other features makes it worthwhile to start using the model.

Table 11 Case B:RMSE and eigenvalues

	RMSE (basis points)								
τ in months	3	12	24	36	48	60	72	84	120
SRB3	8.50	14.08	4.89	3.54	5.28	5.56	4.51	2.57	6.38
SRB3, bias corrected	1.48	4.76	3.92	2.77	1.01	1.94	2.52	2.12	3.06

	Eigenvalues of $\hat{\Phi}$			
	1	2	3	4
SRB3	0.990	0.957	0.808	
SRB4	0.990	0.957	0.893	0.640

RMSEs are calculated and shown in basis points for the two models under investigation, together with the eigenvalues of $\hat{\Phi}$, sorted in descending order.

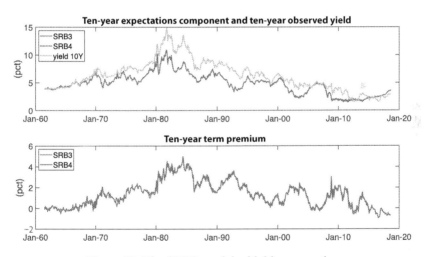

Figure 21 The SRB3-model with bias correction

The figure shows the ten-year term premium estimates from the three- and four-factor SRB models. In the figure, the upper panel shows the ten-year expectations component and the lower panel shows the ten-year premium. Estimates from the standard *SRB3* model is shown in blue, and the mean adjusted version is shown in red. For comparison, the observed ten-year yield is plotted in yellow, in the upper panel.

Case (C): Comparing 3-factor SRB models with and without bias correction

Bauer et al. (2012) remind us that Φ, in the VAR model: $X_t = \mu + \Phi \cdot (X_{t-1} - \mu) + \Sigma_X e_t$, most likely will be biased downwards in term structure applications, because lagged endogenous variables are included, and the VAR is estimated using OLS. Too-low persistency in the yield curve factors, and hence also in the short-rate process, may severely impact measures derived from the term structure dynamics, such as rate expectations and term premia estimates. On the other hand, it is worth noting that the potential bias is reduced, as the number of time-series observations is increased. For instance, Engsted and Pedersen (2014) show that the bias nearly disappears when the sample comprises 500 observations in the time-series dimension. However, the simulation study they conduct is based on a VAR that, at the outset, exhibits somewhat less persistency compared to what is typically encountered in term structure models. So, it is not clear that their result can be directly transferred to a term structure context.

Using the closed-form bias-correction methodology of Pope (1990), we compare the impact of bias correction on the 3-factor SRB model. Results are shown in Figure 22 and Table 12.

A higher degree of persistency implies that the short-rate process reverts in a more sluggish manner towards its sample mean. The impact of this on derived rate expectations and term premia estimates, is that the time-series evolution of the ten-year rate expectation (we use ten-years here because this is what is shown in the figure, but the conclusion holds for any maturity point) is that the rate expectation becomes more volatile, assuming that one or more rate cycles are contained in the data sample. The mirror image of this is, of course, that the term premia will evolve more smoothly. And, this is exactly what we observe in Figure 22.

Table 12 shows that the bias correction has absolutely no bearing on the in-sample fit. It is interesting to note that accounting for potential biases in $\hat{\Phi}$ only affects the relative weighting of the rate expectation and term premia components (that together make up the model fitted yield), and not of the overall fit of the model.

Case (D): The SRB model with a constraint on the mean of the short rate

For scenario analysis, or because the sample mean is judged to poorly reflect the true mean of one or more of the underlying yield curve factors, it may be relevant to impose constraints on the mean vector, μ, in the transition equation. Figure 23 shows the impact of doing this. For illustrative purposes, it is assumed that the true mean of the short rate is 2.00 per cent, and this is imposed on the optimisation algorithm estimating the VAR parameters; the in sample mean is 4.88 per cent, so changing it to 2.00 per cent is somewhat of a moderate to substantial change. In Figure 23 a comparison between the standard 3-factor SRB

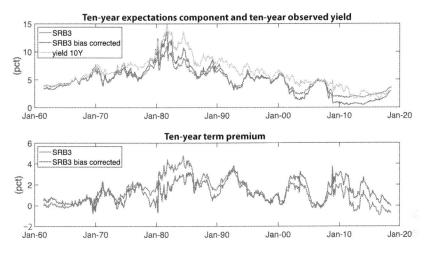

Figure 22 The SRB3-model with bias correction

The figure shows the ten-year term premium estimates from the 3-factor SRB model and a version of the model where Φ in the transition equation, $X_t = \mu + \Phi \cdot (X_{t-1} - \mu) + \Sigma_X e_t$, is bias corrected according to Pope (1990). In the figure, the upper panel shows the ten-year term expectations component, and the lower panel shows the ten-year premium. Estimates from the standard *SRB*3 model is shown in blue, and the mean adjusted version is shown in red. For comparison, the observed ten-year yield is plotted in yellow, in the upper panel.

Table 12 Case C: RMSE and eigenvalues

	RMSE (basis points)								
τ in months	3	12	24	36	48	60	72	84	120
SRB3	8.50	14.08	4.89	3.54	5.28	5.56	4.51	2.57	6.38
SRB3, bias corrected	8.50	14.08	4.89	3.54	5.28	5.56	4.51	2.57	6.38

	Eigenvalues of $\hat{\Phi}$		
	1	2	3
SRB3	0.991	0.957	0.808
SRB3, bias corrected	0.998	0.962	0.816

RMSEs are calculated and shown in basis points for the two models under investigation, together with the eigenvalues of $\hat{\Phi}$, sorted in descending order.

model (i.e. where sample means are used for μ), and the constrained version of the model. It is clear that this constraint has a significant influence on the 10-year rate expectation, and the 10-year term premium. In fact, the time-series

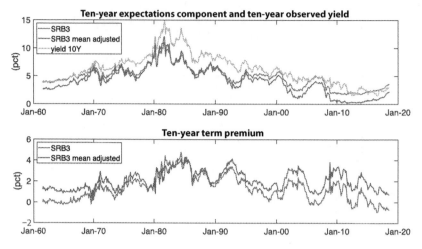

Figure 23 Mean adjusting the SRB3-model

The figure shows the 10-year term premium estimate from the 3-factor SRB model, and a version where the mean vector, μ, in $X_t = \mu + \Phi \cdot (X_{t-1} - \mu) + \Sigma_X e_t$, is altered. A constraint is imposed such that the mean of the short rate factor equals 2.00 per cent (changed from 4.88 per cent, which is its sample mean). The the slope and the curvature parameters are left at their sample means. In the figure, the upper panel shows the 10-year term expectatoins component and the lower panel shows the 10-year premium. Estimates from the standard *SRB*3 model is shown in blue, and the mean adjusted version is shown in red. For comparison, the observed 10-year yield is plotted in yellow in the upper panel.

evolution of the gauges shown in Figure 23 bears a lot of resemblance to the ones produced in Case C, where the bias correction is active, as shown in Figure 22.

Having a look at the eigenvalues in Table 13 confirms that not only is the mean of the short rate changed, also the persistence of the process has changed: the eigenvalue for the short-rate process (the first factor) in the plain *SRB*3 model is 0.9909; when constraining the mean, this eigenvalue increases to 0.9956; and finally, when bias correction is introduced, the eigenvalue equals 0.9976.

Why does the persistence of the VAR model change, when constraints are imposed on μ? One part of the system has to change such that the constrained set of means can be achieved, and the only part left in the equation is the Φ matrix, since the fit of the model, as seen in Table 13, is virtually unchanged. Let's consider the univariate case (which clearly generalises to the multivariate case), and assume that the yield curve factor is the short rate and it follows the AR(1) process:

Table 13 Case D: RMSE and eigenvalues

	RMSE (basis points)								
τ in months	3	12	24	36	48	60	72	84	120
SRB3	8.50	14.08	4.89	3.54	5.28	5.65	4.51	2.57	6.38
SRB3, mean adjusted	8.42	14.03	4.89	3.56	5.31	5.60	4.54	2.59	6.45

	Eigenvalues of $\hat{\Phi}$		
	1	2	3
SRB3	0.991	0.957	0.808
SRB3, mean adjusted	0.996	0.960	0.827

RMSEs are calculated and shown in basis points for the two models under investigation, together with the eigenvalues of $\hat{\Phi}$, sorted in descending order.

Case (E): Comparing the 3-factor SRB model with published term premium from the ACM and KW models

It is seen that Figure 24 confirms the notion highlighted in previous figures, that the main variation in term premia do not come from the applied model, but from the data sample used, and the thereby implied persistency of the underlying yield curve values and the convergence level for the factors (i.e. their sample mean). The KW premium estimate deviates most from the other two, and this is probably due to the different estimation window used. KW estimates only spans the period from 1990 and onwards, and the persistency and the sample mean of the factors is therefore likely different from the parameter estimates used in ACM and SRB3. We have seen that the *SRB*3 and *ACM* 10-year term premia are very similar, both in terms of dynamic behaviour and levels.

A relevant question to ask, with respect to published model estimates, is whether the parameter estimates are updated regularly, or whether they are kept constant over time. One would think that it would be better to update parameters such that the derived metrics make use of as much information as possible. However, updating parameters means that the newly produced estimates are not backward-comparable, since earlier estimates were based on another set of parameter estimates. This then opens the gate to potential confusion, since different vintages of term premia estimates would have to be published, one vintage for each parameter update, and it does not take much imagination to envisage the problems that can transpire from such a setting, especially when

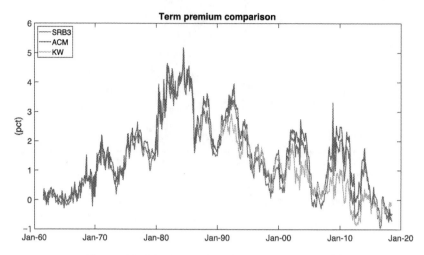

Figure 24 SRB3, ACM, and KW 10-year permia

The figure shows the ten-year term premium estimates from the three-factor SRB mode, the ACM model (Adrian et al. (2013)) and the KW model (Kim and Wright (2005)). The KW estimate is available from 1990 onwards. Both the ACM and KW estimates are downloaded from Bloomberg.

the metrics are used to support policy decisions on, for example, strategic asset allocation issues. Another issue is the standard choice to be made in terms of the length of the data history to include in the estimation of any model (i.e. the trade-off between additional parameter accuracy against the possibility of covering distinct economic regimes). In the end, this choice is not so trivial.

3.5 Modelling Yields at the Lower Bound

A non-negligible part of the term structure literature deals with the modelling of the yield curve and its dynamics, when the level of yields approaches zero, or hovers around some low level.[21] Such approaches have become increasingly popular, as the monetary policy rates have decreased steadily in Japan, the USA and UK, as well as the euro zone, at least since around 2008/2009. To illustrate, Figure 25 shows the evolution of the short end of the term structure in the mentioned economies.

The majority of this literature falls within the arbitrage-free framework, and it builds on Black (1995). Black suggests that the observed nominal rate, r_t,

---

[21] For a representative sample of the literature, see, Black, (1995), Christensen and Rudebusch (2013), Kim and Priebsch (2013), Bauer and Rudebusch (2014), Krippner (2015b), Wu and Xia (2015), and Lemke and Vladu (2017).

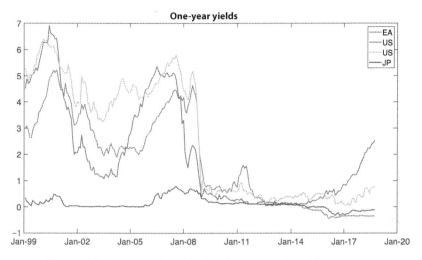

Figure 25 The maturity and time dimension of yield curve data

The figure shows the evolution of the 1-year yields in the euro area, the USA, UK, and Japan, from January 1999 to August 2018. The data used are obtained from Bloomberg, and the following series are used: EUSWE1 Curncy (euro area OIS rate), I11101Y Index (on-the-run US curve), GUKG1 Index (UK generic yield curve), GTJPY1Y Govt (JP generic yield curve). Data are observed monthly.

cannot be negative, because agents in the economy can hold cash at zero cost. We know now, that this is not necessarily completely true, since we have seen negative yields to a great extent, over the last years: just have another look at Figure 25 and observe that the 1-year yields is Japan and the euro area has been in negative territory since 2015. And, today (18 September 2018), according to Bloomberg, the German sovereign curve displays negative yields from the 3-month to the 6-year maturity points. So, there are storage costs, and the possibility of being robbed. For these, and possibly other reasons, it is possible to observe negative rates in the economy.[22] But, this does, of course, not invalidate the modelling idea proposed by Black (1995); rather than having a zero-lower bound, we can simply work with a lower bound, set at some reasonably low level.

Following Black (1995), the observed short rate, r_t, is modelled like a call-option, where the underlying asset is the unconstrained shadow short rate, s_t:

$$r_t = max(0, s_t) \tag{3.22}$$

---

[22] A negative rate can be interpreted as the storage cost of money, and/or the insurance premium to be paid to avoid running the possibility of being robbed while have large amounts of cash tucked away in the mattress at home – just imagine, for example, how many mattresses Goldman Sachs would need.

Here, we will also use Black (1995) as a starting point, but then we will deviate from the main-stream approach, and build a Nelson-Siegel inspired shadow short-rate model. This is done mainly for illustrative purposes, but also in the hope that it possibly could be useful from a yield curve practitioners view-point.

One of the arguments for using a shadow short-rate model is that traditional dynamic yield curve models have difficulties in matching the persistence displayed by yields when they evolve around a lower boundary, as, for example, shown in Figure 25 since 2009. As we have seen, yield curve factors are modelled using a stationary VAR model framework, and, consequently, yield curve factors, and thereby yields, will naturally converge back to their historical means, when projected forward. To circumvent this 'problem', the shadow-short rate idea allows for the evolution of an unobserved short-rate process, which is then truncated at some lower level, if the process at some point passes this threshold. In this way, if the underlying process (i.e. s_t), displays some level of persistence and stays in the truncation zone for an extended period of time, we will be able to replicate the observed dynamics of r_t, and then also the hovering dynamics of yields at longer maturities. There is one other potential benefit of shadow-rate models, and that is if the short rate is modelled together with macroeconomic variables. It is econometrically challenging to model the joint dynamic evolution of the short rate and macroeconomic variables, if the short rate appears to be truncated (i.e. if it stays around the lower bound for years). Allowing the shadow short rate to move freely makes it an ideal candidate to enter into a model where the evolution of the yield curve and macroeconomic variables are modelled jointly.

We need to find an appropriate functional form for the truncation function in (3.22). One shorthand approach is presented by Coche, Nyholm and Sahakyan (2017), and this is what we will rely on here:

$$\tilde{y}_\tau = \begin{bmatrix} 1 & 1 - \frac{1-\gamma^\tau}{(1-\gamma)\cdot\tau} & -\gamma^{\tau-1} + \frac{1-\gamma^\tau}{(1-\gamma)\cdot\tau} \end{bmatrix} \cdot \tilde{X}_t \tag{3.23}$$

$$\alpha(X) = \frac{\tanh(\psi_1 \cdot X_{(2,1)} + \psi_2) + 3}{2} \cdot \frac{\tanh(\psi_3 \cdot X_{(3,1)} + \psi_4) + 3}{2} \in [1,4] \tag{3.24}$$

$$y_\tau = r_L + \frac{\tilde{y}_\tau - r_L}{1 - e^{[-\alpha(\tilde{X})\cdot(\tilde{y}_\tau - r_L)]}} \tag{3.25}$$

Lets have a look to better understand what the components of this function are about. It is important to know that (3.24) and (3.25) work together with the short-rate-based (SRB) version of the Nelson-Siegel model, that is, where the factors have interpretations as [short rate, slope, curvature], as shown in (3.23). The variables $\tilde{y}$ and $\tilde{X}$, refer to the shadow yield curve and the shadow factors, respectively. The shadow factors are the shadow short rate, the shadow slope, and the shadow curvature.[23] Equation (3.25) indicates that the shadow yield curve, $\tilde{y}_t$, is transformed into the observed yield curve, y_t. This is similar to the traditional shadow-short-rate set-up, where the dynamics of the shadow rate impact the shape and location of the whole yield curve. The α-function in (3.24) generates a scalar-weight that is applied to the shadow yield curve, depending on the values at time t, of the shadow-slope and the shadow-curvature factors, contained in $\tilde{X}$. ψ_1-ψ_4 are scaling constants applied to the shadow slope and the shadow curvature. There are quite a number of moving parts – the impact of parameter constellations of ψ_1 to ψ_4, together with the value of the shadow factors contained in $\tilde{X}$ can be explored using the interactive MATLAB app called 'PG2TSM_SSR_original' contained in the MATLAB library accompanying this Element.

Two screenshots generated using the app are shown in Figure 26. This is done to give a brief view on how certain parameter settings affect the shape and location of the curves.[24]

One thing is to use the previously mentioned Shadow Short Rate App to fit the shadow short-rate model to a single yield curve. Although it would be entertaining (at least for a while), it would be too consuming to fit shadow short rates to the whole set of monthly US yields over the period from 1961 to 2018. Instead, we apply equations (3.23)–(3.24) to the whole data set at once, and minimise the overall sum of squared residuals to find the shadow short rate and the shadow slope; we impose the constraint that the shadow curvature is equal to the SRB curvature estimated on the observed yields. To obtain the estimates, the following steps are applied:

1. Estimate the SRB model via the TSM class, to obtain $\hat{X}_t$ $\forall t$ using (3.23).
2. Guess values for $\tilde{\hat{X}}_t$ $\forall t$, a handy way to make these guesses is to use $\hat{X}_t$.
3. Calculate $\hat{\alpha}_t | \{\tilde{\hat{X}}_t, \psi_1, \psi_2, \psi_3, \psi_4\}$, that is, one value for $\hat{\alpha}$ per observation point included in the data set, conditional on the generated shadow factors and the fixed parameters ψ_1 to ψ_4. This step is done via (3.24).
4. Calculate $\hat{y}_t$ $\forall t$ using (3.25).

---

[23] For practical reasons, when the model is estimated, we constrain the shadow curvature to be equal to the curvature obtained from the short-rate-based version of the Nelson-Siegel model.

[24] The app is flexible and allows for analysing other curves, and all parameters can be selected by the user.

(a)

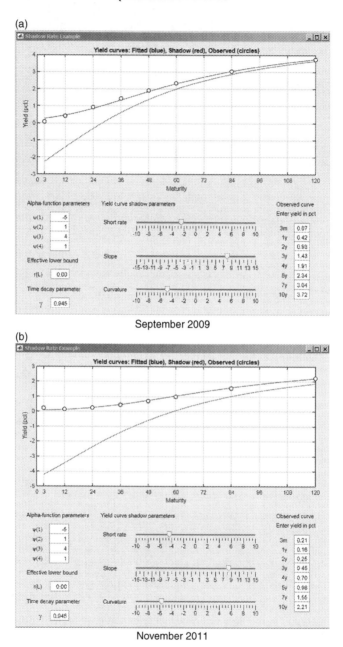

September 2009

(b)

November 2011

Figure 26 Examples using the MATLAB Shadow Short Rate App

Panel (a) shows an example using data from 30 September 2009. The black circles in the figure show the observed curve on this day. The red curve shows the shadow short rate, generated using the app. And, the blue line shows the corresponding fitted yield curve, the transformed shadow short rate using equations (3.23)–(3.24). Similarly, panel (b) shows a fitting example using data observed on 30 November 2011.

5. Calculate the sum of squared residuals between the observed yield curve data, y, and the fitted yield curves.

6. Ask MATLAB to minimise this quantity: $\sum_t \sum_{tau} (y - \hat{y})^2$, calculated in step 5, by repeating steps 2–5, until optimal parameter values for the shadow short rate and the shadow slope are obtained.

Following these steps produces a time series of shadow short rates as shown in Figure 27.

It is observed that the time-series behaviour of our measure[25] (red line) is similar to the estimate produced by Krippner (2015b) (purple line). The minimum value for both estimates occur on the same date (April 2013), and the dynamics towards and from this minimum point is roughly the same, with our measure falling a bit faster, and raising towards normalisation levels a bit slower, compared to Krippner's measure. In contrast to this, Fed Atlanta's

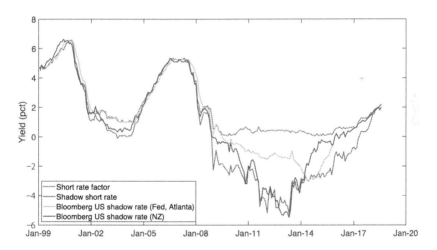

Figure 27 Shadow short-rate estimates

The figure shows the estimated shadow short rate using the estimation framework outlined in the text (red line), based on Coche et al. (2017). This estimate is compared with two officially published estimates downloaded from Bloomberg. One is produced by Fed Atlanta using the model presented in Wu and Xia (2015) (yellow line), and the other is produced by Leo Krippner (Reserve Bank of New Zealand) following Krippner (2015b) (purple line). Both of these series are available via Bloomberg as 'wuxiffrt index' and 'nzssus index', respectively. The last (blue) line shows the short-rate factor estimated by the SRB model.

---

[25] By 'our measure' I mean the estimate obtained from the methodology proposed by Coche et al. (2017). And, 'our' is used as an inclusive term here, that also comprises you, the reader: because, the code is available in the annex, and it can be used freely (at your own risk, of course).

shadow short-rate measure, based on Wu and Xia (2015) (yellow line), behaves in a distinctly different manner. It decreases very slowly, almost linearly, until October 2013, after which the decline picks up speed, and it reaches its minimum on May 2014.

A detailed chronology of the Fed's QE actions is provided in Krippner (2015a), and he further shows that the Krippner measure better reflects these actions than the Wu and Xia short-rate measure does. His conclusion is, therefore, that as a gauge of the effective monetary policy stance, when unconventional policies are enacted, the Krippner measure is more precise. The reason for this is probably, as also highlighted by Krippner (2015a), that Krippner's model includes two factors, and the model of Wu and Xia (2015) includes three factors. We typically model the yield curve using three factors, for example, the level, the slope, and the curvature. However, when yields are close to the effective lower bound, one of these dimensions will be redundant, because the short rate is fixed, and the level and the slope will consequently measure the same thing, namely the difference between a constant and the long end of the yield curve.[26] A two-factor model is therefore more appropriate to use in such cases. But, what happens then when the economy exits the lower bound period, and it again becomes relevant to use three factors? This is where the approach of Coche et al. (2017) comes into play. The derived shadow short-rate measure is based on three factors, the short rate, the slope, and the curvature – but one of the factors (the curvature) is frozen, and left unchanged, when the economy enters the effective lower bound period. And, when exit is observed (well, rather, judged to have occurred), the factor is again unfrozen. With the chosen factor structure, it is enough to reduce the dimensionality in the direction of the curvature, because the short short rate and the slope will not produce redundancies. This would have been the case, if the traditional factor interpretation as level, slope, and curvature had been chosen. To some extent, the Coche et al. (2017) methodology resembles that of a regime-switching model, where the regime is imposed exogenously on the curvature factor.

3.6 Summary

Honestly, the materials covered in this section went a bit beyond what I had planned at the outset. But, I hope that I have still managed to convey the main messages, at an acceptable and practical level, without messing things up too much. The main takeaways can be summarised in the following way:

---

[26] Let l, s, c, be the level, the negative of the slope, and curvature, respectively. If $r = 0$, or some other fixed lower bound, then we have that $r = 0 = l + s \Leftrightarrow -s = l$.

(1) Term structure models are best thought of in terms of a state-space model, where the state equation evolves the yield curve factors over time using a VAR(1) model, and the observation equation translates the yield curve factors into fitted yields using a loading matrix and possibly a constant as well.

(2) Even if a state-space model is used to characterise the dynamics and cross-sectional dimensions of yield curve data, it is not always necessary to estimate the model using the Kalman filter. A two-step OLS procedure is often faster and yields the same results.

(3) Assigning a certain economic and/or financial meaning to the yield curve factors is done via the choice of the loading matrix (in the observation equation).

(4) Yield curve factor models can be rotated, such that their factor interpretation changes, without affecting the model fit.

(5) Yield curves comprise information about future rate expectations and term premia. The distribution between these two important gauges is model and parameter dependant. Most important for the dissection of yields along these two dimensions is the model-implied mean for the short rate, and the persistence of the VAR(1) in the state equation.

(6) The persistence of the VAR can be changed via bias-correcting techniques applied to the (autoregressive) VAR parameters, and by imposing constraints on the mean vector in the VAR model.

(7) To better capture the behaviour of yields that evolve around some lower effective bound, it is possible to apply the concept of shadow short-rate models. These models rely on a truncation function that maps unrestricted factors into restricted factors that match observed yields. In essence, when such a non-linear truncation function is included into the modelling set-up, the state-space model becomes non-linear in the underlying factors and the Kalman filter is no longer usable. Instead, non-linear Kalman filters must be applied, or alternative methodologies, as presented in Section 3.5.

MATLAB code

Yield curve model estimation via the SSM toolbox

> filename: Basic_yield_curve_setup.m

```
1  %% Script for: the basic yield curve modelling setup
2  % Access to the MATLAB class GSW is required.
3  %
4  %% Loading and plotting data
5  %
6  path_=[pwd,'\MATLAB_classes'];
```

```
7   addpath(path_);
8   load('Data_GSW.mat');
9   GSW_         = GSW;                    % creates an instance of the GSW class
10  GSW_.tau     = [3 12:12:120]';         % vector of maturities
11  GSW_.beta    = GSW_factors(:,2:5);     % yield curve factors
12  GSW_.lambda  = GSW_factors(:,6:7);     % lambdas
13  GSW_         = GSW_.getYields;         % getting yields
14
15  dates = GSW_factors(:,1);
16  Y     = GSW_.yields;
17  tau   = GSW_.tau;
18  nTau  = size(tau,1);
19
20  figure('units','normalized','outerposition',[0 0 1 1])
21      surf(tau./12,dates,Y)
22      date_ticks = datenum(1960:4:2020,1,1);
23      set(gca, 'ytick', date_ticks);
24      datetick('y','mmm-yy','keepticks')
25      xticks(0:1:11), xticklabels({tau}),
26      xlabel('Maturity (months)'), zlabel('Yield (pct)'),
27      view([-109 38]),
28      ytickangle(-25),
29      set(gca, 'FontSize', 18)
30      print -depsc Y3D
31
32  nn = 3*42;
33  figure('units','normalized','outerposition',[0 0 1 1])
34      subplot(2,1,1), plot(dates,Y(:,11),'LineWidth',2), datetick('x','mmm-yy'),
35                      title('10 year yield'),
36                      ylabel('Yield (pct)')
37                      set(gca, 'FontSize', 18)
38      subplot(2,1,2), plot(tau,Y(nn,:)','*-','Linewidth',2),
39                      xlabel('Maturity (months)'),
40                      title(['Yield curve on ' datestr(dates(nn))]),
41                      ylabel('Yield (pct)'),
42                      ylim([0,ceil(max(Y(nn,:))+1)])
43                      xticks(tau), xticklabels({tau}),
44                      set(gca, 'FontSize', 18)
45      print -depsc Yslices
46
47  %% ................................................................
48  % ... Empirical factor structure and the Nelson-Siegel parameterisation
49  % ... This section uses the pMap function that appears at the end
50  % ... of this script.
51  % ................................................................
52
53  % ... Model selection
54  %
55  flagg   = 'Emp';                        % choose:  'NS'  -> Nelson-Siegel
56                                          % or    :  'Emp' -> Empirical model
57  [nObs,nTau] = size(Y);
58  Y_dat       = [Y ones(nObs,nTau)];
59
60  % ... assigning starting values ...
61  %
62  Phi0 = [ 0.99 0.00 0.00;
63           0.00 0.99 0.00;
64           0.00 0.00 0.99];
65  k0   = [ 0; 0; 0 ];
66  Sx0  = [ 1.00;
67           0.00; 1.00;
68           0.00; 0.00; 1.00 ];
69  b0   = [ ones(nTau,1) linspace(1,0,nTau)' zeros(nTau,1) ];
70  a0   = zeros(nTau,1);
71  Sy0  = 1.00*ones(nTau,1);
72
73  p0   = [ Phi0(:); k0(:); Sx0(:); b0(:); a0(:); Sy0(:) ];
74  nP   = size(p0,1);
75
```

```
76   % ... defining upper and lower parameter bounds
77   %
78   lb_=(*-}*)*)inf(nP,1); lb_(1:9,1)=(*-}*)1; lb_(10:12,1)=0;
79   lb_([13;15;18])=0; lb_(19:51,1)=-1;
80   lb_(52:62,1)=-1; lb_(63:73,1)=0;
81
82   ub_ = inf(nP,1); ub_(1:9,1)= 1.1; ub_(10:12,1)=1;
83   ub_([13;15;18]) = 1; ub_(19:51,1)=1;
84   ub_(52:62,1)=1; ub_(63:73,1)=1;
85
86   % ... parameter constraints ...
87   %
88   nP   = size(p0,1);
89   % ... equal yield vols across all maturities
90   Aeq = zeros(nTau-1,nP);
91   Aeq(1,[63 64])=[1 -1];Aeq(2,[64 65])=[1 -1];Aeq(3,[65 66])=[1 -1];
92   Aeq(4,[66 67])=[1 -1];Aeq(5,[67 68])=[1 -1];Aeq(6,[68 69])=[1 -1];
93   Aeq(7,[69 70])=[1 -1];Aeq(8,[70 71])=[1 -1];Aeq(9,[71 72])=[1 -1];
94   Aeq(10,[72 73])=[1 -1];
95   % ... no constants in the observation equation (i.e. a=0)
96   if (strcmp(flagg,'NS'))
97       Aeq(11:21,52:62) = eye(11);
98   end
99   % ... value of the constraints
100  beq = zeros(size(Aeq,1),1);
101
102  Mdl_    = ssm(@(p) pMap(p,flagg,tau));
103  options = optimoptions(@fmincon,'Algorithm','interior-point',...
104                              'MaxIterations',1e6, ...
105                              'MaxFunctionEvaluations',1e6, ...
106                              'TolFun', 1e-6, 'TolX', 1e-6);
107
108  [ EstMdl_, p_hat ] = ...
109          estimate( Mdl_,Y_dat,p0,'Display','iter','Aeq',Aeq,'beq',beq,...
110                  'lb',lb_,'ub',ub_,'univariate',true,'options',options );
111
112  x_filter = filter( EstMdl_, Y_dat );  % extract filtered state variables
113
114  % ... plotting the results
115  %
116  X_hat    = x_filter(:,1:3);
117  Phi_hat  = EstMdl_.A(1:3,1:3);
118  k_hat    = diag(EstMdl_.A(1:3,4:6));
119  b_hat    = EstMdl_.C(1:11,1:3);
120  a_hat    = diag(EstMdl_.C(1:11,4:14)); .
121  if (strcmp(flagg,'NS'))
122      L_hat    = p_hat(19);
123  end
124  Y_hat    = (a_hat + b_hat*X_hat')';
125  RMSE_bps = 100.*(mean((Y-Y_hat).^2)).^(0.5);
126
127  figure('units','normalized','outerposition',[0 0 1 1])
128      plot(dates,X_hat,'Linewidth',2), legend('Factor 1', 'Factor 2', 'Factor 3'),
129      date_ticks = datenum(1960:10:2020,1,1);
130      set(gca, 'xtick', date_ticks);
131      datetick('x','mmm-yy','keepticks')
132      set(gca, 'FontSize', 30)
133      if (strcmp(flagg,'NS'))
134          print -depsc EstFactors_NS
135      else
136          print -depsc EstFactors_Emp
137      end
138
139  figure('units','normalized','outerposition',[0 0 1 1])
140      plot(tau,b_hat,'Linewidth',2),
141      legend('Loading 1', 'Loading 2', 'Loading 3','Location','SE'),
142      xlabel('Maturity (months)'), ylim([-1 1.25]),
143      xticks([3 12:12:120]'), xticklabels({tau})
144      if (strcmp(flagg,'NS'))
```

```
145              title(['time-decay parameter = ', num2str(L_hat)])
146         end
147         set(gca, 'FontSize', 30)
148         if (strcmp(flagg,'NS'))
149             print -depsc EstLoadings_NS
150         else
151             print -depsc EstLoadings_Emp
152         end
153
154    disp(RMSE_bps)
155
156    %% ...........................
157    % ...  Rotation matrices
158    % ...........................
159    % .................................................
160    % ... rotating toward 2Y, 5Y and 10Y yields
161    % .................................................
162    NS_         = TSM;                   % create an instance of the TSM class
163    NS_.yields  = Y;                     % populating the model with input data
164    NS_.tau     = tau;
165    NS_.nF      = 3;
166    %NS_.mP_pre = [0;0;0];
167    NS_.DataFreq = 12;
168
169    NS_ = NS_.getDNS;                    % estimate Dynamic Nelson-Siegel model
170                                         %    using OLS
171
172    FunErr2 = @(p,dat_) sum(sum((dat_(:,1)-dat_(:,2:end)*p).^2));  % calc SSR
173
174    p0   = [1;0;0];  % starting values - no constant, only slope coefficients
175    Aeq  = [1 0 0];  % constraining the coefficient of the level factor to be =1
176    beq  = 1;
177    lb   = [0.99;0;0];  % just to help fmincon a bit
178    ub   = [1.01;1;1];
179
180    lst  = [3;6;11];
181    A_rotate = zeros(size(p0,1),size(p0,1));
182    for ( z=1:3 )
183        dat      = [NS_.yields(:,lst(z,1)) NS_.beta'];
184        [pHat]   = fmincon(FunErr2,p0,[],[],Aeq,beq,lb,ub,[],[],dat);
185        A_rotate(z,:) = pHat';
186    end
187
188    % ... double checking if the objective is achieved
189    X_rotate = A_rotate*NS_.beta;
190    b_rotate = NS_.B*inv(A_rotate);
191
192    figure('units','normalized','outerposition',[0 0 1 1])
193        subplot(3,1,1), plot(dates,[NS_.yields(:,3) X_rotate(1,:)'], ...
194                                                'LineWidth',2),
195        date_ticks = datenum(1960:10:2020,1,1);
196        set(gca, 'xtick', date_ticks), title('2 year');
197        datetick('x','mmm-yy','keepticks'), legend('Obs.','Fit','Location','SW')
198        set(gca, 'FontSize', 20)
199        subplot(3,1,2), plot(dates,[NS_.yields(:,6) X_rotate(2,:)'], ...
200                                                'LineWidth',2),
201        date_ticks = datenum(1960:10:2020,1,1);
202        set(gca, 'xtick', date_ticks), title('5 year'),
203        datetick('x','mmm-yy','keepticks'), legend('Obs.','Fit','Location','SW')
204        set(gca, 'FontSize', 20)
205        subplot(3,1,3), plot(dates,[NS_.yields(:,11) X_rotate(3,:)'], ...
206                                                'LineWidth',2),
207        date_ticks = datenum(1960:10:2020,1,1);
208        set(gca, 'xtick', date_ticks), title('10 year'),
209        datetick('x','mmm-yy','keepticks'), legend('Obs.','Fit','Location','SW')
210        set(gca, 'FontSize', 20)
211        print -depsc RotatedFactors2_5_10
212
213    RMSE_rotate = 100*(mean((Y - (b_rotate*X_rotate)').^2)).^(1/2)
```

```
214  [NS_.RMSE;RMSE_rotate]
215
216  %% .........................................................
217  %  ... Building blocks of the yield curve
218  %  .........................................................
219  %
220  % Case A: 3-factor SRB model and the DNS model
221  %
222  SRB3_ = TSM;
223  DNS_  = TSM;       % creating class instances
224
225  SRB3_.yields=Y; SRB3_.tau=tau; SRB3_.DataFreq=12; SRB3_.nF=3;
226  DNS_.yields=Y;  DNS_.tau=tau;  DNS_.DataFreq=12; DNS_.nF=3;       % allocating data
227
228  SRB3_ = SRB3_.getSRB3;
229  DNS_  = DNS_.getDNS;                            % estimate the models
230
231  RMSE_A = [ SRB3_.RMSE; DNS_.RMSE ];             % generating output
232  EIG_A  = [ sort(real(eig(SRB3_.PhiP))); ...
233               sort(real(eig(DNS_.PhiP))) ];
234
235  figure('units','normalized','outerposition',[0 0 1 1])
236      subplot(2,1,1), plot(dates,  [ SRB3_.Er(:,11) DNS_.Er(:,11) ...
237                                        Y(:,11)], 'LineWidth',2),
238      date_ticks = datenum(1960:10:2020,1,1);
239      set(gca, 'xtick', date_ticks), ylabel('(pct)')
240      datetick('x','mmm-yy','keepticks'), legend('SRB3','DNS','yield 10Y',...
241                                          'Location','NW')
242      set(gca, 'FontSize', 20)
243      title('10-year expectations component and 10-year observed yield')
244
245      subplot(2,1,2), plot(dates, [SRB3_.TP(:,11) DNS_.TP(:,11) ], ...
246                                        'LineWidth',2),
247      date_ticks = datenum(1960:10:2020,1,1);
248      set(gca, 'xtick', date_ticks), ylabel('(pct)')
249      datetick('x','mmm-yy','keepticks'), legend('SRB3','DNS',...
250                                          'Location','NW')
251      set(gca, 'FontSize', 20)
252      title('10-year term premium')
253      print -depsc Case_A_Er_TP
254
255  %
256  % Case B: 3- and 4-factor SRB models
257  %
258  SRB3_ = TSM;
259  SRB4_ = TSM;       % creating class instances
260
261
262  SRB3_.yields=Y; SRB3_.tau=tau; SRB3_.DataFreq=12; SRB3_.nF=3;
263  SRB4_.yields=Y; SRB4_.tau=tau; SRB4_.DataFreq=12; SRB4_.nF=4; % allocating data
264
265  SRB3_ = SRB3_.getSRB3;
266  SRB4_ = SRB4_.getSRB4;                          % estimate the models
267
268
269  RMSE_B = [ SRB3_.RMSE; SRB4_.RMSE ];            % generating output
270  EIG_B  = [ sort(real(eig(SRB3_.PhiP))); ...
271               sort(real(eig(SRB4_.PhiP))) ];
272
273  figure('units','normalized','outerposition',[0 0 1 1])
274      subplot(2,1,1), plot(dates,  [ SRB3_.Er(:,11) SRB4_.Er(:,11) ...
275                                        Y(:,11)], 'LineWidth',2),
276      date_ticks = datenum(1960:10:2020,1,1);
277      set(gca, 'xtick', date_ticks), ylabel('(pct)')
278      datetick('x','mmm-yy','keepticks'), legend('SRB3','SRB4', ...
279                                          'yield 10Y','Location','NW')
280      title('10-year expectations component and 10-year observed yield')
281      set(gca, 'FontSize', 20)
282
```

```
283
284       subplot(2,1,2), plot(dates, [SRB3_.TP(:,11) SRB4_.TP(:,11) ], ...
285                                              'LineWidth',2),
286       date_ticks = datenum(1960:10:2020,1,1);
287       set(gca, 'xtick', date_ticks), ylabel('(pct)'),
288       datetick('x','mmm-yy','keepticks'), legend('SRB3','SRB4', ...
289                                              'Location','NW')
290       title('10-year term premium')
291       set(gca, 'FontSize', 20)
292       print -depsc Case_B_Er_TP
293
294    %
295    % Case C: 3-factor SRB model with and without bias correction
296    %
297    SRB3_   = TSM;
298    SRB3_BC = TSM;       % creating class instances
299
300    SRB3_.yields=Y; SRB3_.tau=tau; SRB3_.DataFreq=12; SRB3_.nF=3;
301    SRB3_BC.yields=Y; SRB3_BC.tau=tau; SRB3_BC.DataFreq=12; SRB3_BC.nF=3;
302    % allocating data
303    SRB3_BC.biasCorrect = 1;                        % bias correction
304
305    SRB3_   = SRB3_.getSRB3;
306    SRB3_BC = SRB3_BC.getSRB3;                       % estimate the models
307
308    RMSE_C = [ SRB3_.RMSE; SRB3_BC.RMSE ];          % generating output
309    EIG_C  = [ sort(real(eig(SRB3_.PhiP))); ...
310               sort(real(eig(SRB3_BC.PhiP_bc))); ];
311
312    figure('units','normalized','outerposition',[0 0 1 1])
313       subplot(2,1,1), plot(dates,  [ SRB3_.Er(:,11) SRB3_BC.Er(:,11) ...
314                                      Y(:,11)], 'LineWidth',2),
315       date_ticks = datenum(1960:10:2020,1,1);
316       set(gca, 'xtick', date_ticks), ylabel('(pct)')
317       datetick('x','mmm-yy','keepticks'), legend('SRB3', ...
318                                      'SRB3 bias corrected', ...
319                                      'yield 10Y','Location','NW')
320       title('10-year expectations component and 10-year observed yield')
321       set(gca, 'FontSize', 20)
322       subplot(2,1,2), plot(dates, [ SRB3_.TP(:,11) SRB3_BC.TP(:,11)], ...
323                                              'LineWidth',2),
324       date_ticks = datenum(1960:10:2020,1,1);
325       set(gca, 'xtick', date_ticks), ylabel('(pct)')
326       datetick('x','mmm-yy','keepticks'), legend('SRB3', ...
327                                      'SRB3 bias corrected', ...
328                                      'Location','NW')
329       title('10-year term premium')
330       set(gca, 'FontSize', 20)
331       print -depsc Case_C_Er_TP
332
333    %
334    % Case D: 3-factor SRB model with different assumptions on
335    %                the mean of the short rate
336    %
337    SRB3_   = TSM;       % creating class instances
338    SRB3_ma = TSM;
339
340    SRB3_.yields=Y; SRB3_.tau=tau; SRB3_.DataFreq=12; SRB3_.nF=3;  % allocating data
341    SRB3_ma.yields=Y; SRB3_ma.tau=tau; SRB3_ma.DataFreq=12; SRB3_ma.nF=3;
342    SRB3_ma.mP_pre=[2.00;1.79;-1.19];
343
344    SRB3_   = SRB3_.getSRB3;                        % estimate the models
345    SRB3_ma = SRB3_ma.getSRB3;
346
347    RMSE_D = [ SRB3_.RMSE; SRB3_ma.RMSE ];          % generating output
348    EIG_D  = [ sort(real(eig(SRB3_.PhiP))); ...
349               sort(real(eig(SRB3_ma.PhiP)))  ];
350
351    figure('units','normalized','outerposition',[0 0 1 1])
```

```
352        subplot(2,1,1), plot(dates,   [ SRB3_.Er(:,11) SRB3_ma.Er(:,11) ...
353                                                  Y(:,11)], 'LineWidth',2),
354        date_ticks = datenum(1960:10:2020,1,1);
355        set(gca, 'xtick', date_ticks), ylabel('(pct)')
356        datetick('x','mmm-yy','keepticks'), legend('SRB3',...
357                                          'SRB3 mean adjusted', ...
358                                          'yield 10Y','Location','NW')
359        title('10-year expectations component and 10-year observed yield')
360        set(gca, 'FontSize', 20),
361        subplot(2,1,2), plot(dates, [SRB3_.TP(:,11) SRB3_ma.TP(:,11)], ...
362                                                  'LineWidth',2),
363        date_ticks = datenum(1960:10:2020,1,1);
364        set(gca, 'xtick', date_ticks), ylabel('(pct)')
365        datetick('x','mmm-yy','keepticks'), legend('SRB3', ...
366                                          'SRB3 mean adjusted', ...
367                                          'Location','NW')
368        title('10-year term premium')
369        set(gca, 'FontSize', 20)
370        print -depsc Case_D_Er_TP
371
372   %
373   % Case D: 3-factor SRB model against ACM and KW
374   %
375   SRB3 = TSM;      % creating class instances
376   SRB3.yields=Y; SRB3.tau=tau; SRB3.DataFreq=12; SRB3.nF=3;   % allocating data
377   SRB3   = SRB3.getSRB3;                              % estimate the model
378
379   figure('units','normalized','outerposition',[0 0 1 1])
380       plot(dates, SRB3.TP(:,11), 'lineWidth',2)
381       hold on
382       plot(ACM(:,1), ACM(:,2), 'lineWidth',2)
383       hold on
384       plot(KW(:,1), KW(:,2), 'lineWidth',2)
385       date_ticks = datenum(1960:10:2020,1,1);
386       set(gca, 'xtick', date_ticks), ylabel('(pct)')
387       datetick('x','mmm-yy','keepticks'), legend('SRB3','ACM','KW', ...
388                                          'Location','NW')
389       title('Term premium comparison')
390       set(gca, 'FontSize', 20)
391       print -depsc Case_E_Er_TP
392
393   %% ...............................................
394   %  ... Modelling yields at the zero lower bound
395   %  ...............................................
396
397   % ... plot of 1Y rates in EU, US, UK, JP
398   figure('units','normalized','outerposition',[0 0 1 1])
399       plot(Yield1Y(:,1), Yield1Y(:,2:end),'LineWidth',2),
400       date_ticks = datenum(1999:3:2020,1,1);
401       set(gca, 'xtick', date_ticks), title('1 year yields');
402       datetick('x','mmm-yy','keepticks'),
403       legend('EA','US','US','JP')
404       set(gca, 'FontSize', 20)
405       print -depsc EU_US_UK_JP_1Y_yields
406
407   % ... Calling the TSM class to estimate a short rate based (SRB) model
408   SRB        = TSM;                  % create an instance of the TSM class
409   SRB.yields  = Y;                   % populating the model with input data
410   SRB.tau    = tau;
411   SRB.mP_pre  = [];
412   SRB.DataFreq = 12;
413   SRB.nF      = 3;
414
415   % ... step 0: fix the parameters that need to be fixed
416   %
417   rL = 0.00;               % preset effective lower bound
418
419   % ... step 1: estimate the 3-factors from the short rate based model
420   %
```

```
421   SRB = SRB.getSRB3;
422   X_   = SRB.beta;            % factors: short rate, slope, curvature
423   B_   = SRB.B;               % loading structure
424   Y_   = SRB.yields;         % observed yields (also contained in Y)
425
426   % ... step2: estimate the shadow short rate and the shadow slope
427   %
428   X_tmp = X_';
429   p0    = X_tmp(:);
430   Aeq   = zeros(nObs,3*nObs);
431   Aeq(1:nObs,2*nObs+1:end) = eye(nObs);
432   beq   = X_(3,:)';
433   X_shadow = NaN(size(X_));
434   options_ = optimoptions(@fmincon,'Algorithm','sqp',...
435                                    'MaxIterations',1e8, ...
436                                    'MaxFunctionEvaluations',1e8, ...
437                                    'TolFun', 1e-4, 'TolX', 1e-4, ...
438                                    'display','iter');
439
440   FX_min       = @(p) Yshadow( p, Y_, B_, rL );
441   [ pHat_sr ]  = fmincon(FX_min, p0,[],[],Aeq,beq,[],[],[], options_);
442   alpha_       = pHat_sr(1:4,1);
443   X_shadow_hat = reshape(pHat_sr,nObs,3);
444
445   figure('units','normalized','outerposition',[0 0 1 1])
446       plot(dates, [ X_(1,:)' X_shadow_hat(:,1) ],'LineWidth',2)
447       hold on
448       plot(BB_US_shadow_rate(:,1),[BB_US_shadow_rate(:,3), ...
449                                    BB_US_shadow_rate(:,2)], ...
450                                      'LineWidth',2 )
451   %    yyaxis right
452   %    plot(BB_US_shadow_rate(:,1), -(BB_US_shadow_rate(:,4)),':g',...
453   %                    'LineWidth',2)
454       date_ticks = datenum(1999:3:2020,1,1);
455       set(gca, 'xtick', date_ticks)
456       datetick('x','mmm-yy','keepticks'),
457       legend('Short rate factor','Shadow short rate', ...
458              'Bloomberg US shadow rate (Fed, Atlanta)', ...
459              'Bloomberg US shadow rate (NZ)', ...
460              'Location','SW')
461       ylabel('Yield (pct)')
462       set(gca, 'FontSize', 20)
463       print -depsc Shadow_sr
464
465   figure('units','normalized','outerposition',[0 0 1 1])
466       plot(dates, [ X_shadow_hat ],'LineWidth',2)
467       date_ticks = datenum(1999:3:2020,1,1);
468       set(gca, 'xtick', date_ticks), title('Short rates');
469       datetick('x','mmm-yy','keepticks'),
470       legend('Sr','Slope','curvature')
471       set(gca, 'FontSize', 20)
472
473   %% functions
474   %
475   function [R,S,T,U,Mean0,Cov0,StateType] = pMap( p, flagg, tau )
476   %
477   % Parameter mapping function for MATLAB's SSM mudule
478   %
479       nTau = size(tau,1);
480
481       Phi  = [p(1) p(4) p(7)  ;
482               p(2) p(5) p(8)  ;
483               p(3) p(6) p(9) ];
484
485       k    = diag([p(10);p(11);p(12)]);
486
487       Sx   = zeros(3,3);
488       Sx(1,1)=p(13); Sx(2,1)=p(14); Sx(2,2)=p(15);
489       Sx(3,1)=p(16); Sx(3,2)=p(17); Sx(3,3)=p(18);
```

```
490
491        if (strcmp(flagg,'Emp'))
492            b = [ p(19:29,1) p(30:40,1) p(41:51,1) ];
493        elseif (strcmp(flagg,'NS'))
494            L = p(19,1); p(20:51,1)=0;
495            b = [ ones(nTau,1) ...
496                    (1-exp(-L.*tau))./(L.*tau) ...
497                    (1-exp(-L.*tau))./(L.*tau) - exp(-L.*tau)];
498        else
499            disp('The variable flagg must take on either of the following values')
500            disp('NS (Nelson-Siegel)')
501            disp('or, Emp (empirical model) ')
502        end
503
504        a  = diag(p(52:62,1));
505        Sy = diag(p(63:73,1));
506
507    % ... Assigning the parameters following MATLAB's notation
508    %
509        R = [ Phi k zeros(3,nTau-3); zeros(nTau,3) eye(nTau) ];
510        S = [ Sx; zeros(nTau,3) ];
511
512        T = [ b a; zeros(nTau,3) eye(nTau) ];
513        U = [ Sy; zeros(nTau,nTau) ];
514
515    % ... other assignments
516        Mean0     = [];
517        Cov0      = [];
518        StateType = [ 0 0 0 ones(1,nTau) ];
519    end
520
521    function [ err2, X_shadow, y_shadow, err ] = Yshadow( p0, Y_, B_, rL )
522    %
523    % calculating the sum of squared residuals from the static
524    %    shadow short rate model set-up
525    %
526        nObs = size(Y_,1);
527
528    % ... Defining the shadow rate transformations
529    %
530        alfa_  = @(Xshdw,zz) ( tanh(zz(1,1).*Xshdw(2,:)+zz(2,1)) ...
531                        +3 )./2 .*( tanh( zz(3,1).*Xshdw(3,:)+zz(4,1) )+3 )./2;
532
533        yFit_  = @(yS_,alpha_,rL_) rL_+(yS_-rL_)./(1-exp(-alpha_.*(yS_-rL_)));
534
535    % ... fixing some of the free parameters
536    %
537        zz_ = [ -5.00; 1.00; 4.00; 1.00 ];
538
539    % ... calculating shadow yields
540    %
541        X_shadow = reshape(p0,nObs,3)';
542        y_shadow = B_*X_shadow;
543        alpha    = alfa_(X_shadow,zz_);
544        yFit     = yFit_(y_shadow,alpha,rL)';
545        err      = Y_-yFit;
546        err2     = sum(sum(err.^2));
547
548    end
```

4 Modelling Yields under the $\mathbb{Q}$ Measure

4.1 Introduction

In this section, we will look at yield curve models that exclude arbitrage by construction. The treatment is purposefully pragmatic, and it will focus on, and emphasise, the pure mechanics of the modelling frameworks. A deep-dive into the mathematical underpinnings of these models, and a full account of how the literature has evolved over time, is beyond the purpose of this Element.

As a gentle introduction, a four-factor short rate based (SRB) model will be derived, based on Nyholm (2018). Then we will move on to Joslin, Singleton and Zhu (2011), a corner-piece in the literature, and see how they cut to the bone of the inner workings of term structure models.

4.2 A Discrete-Time Four-Factor SRB Model

Our purpose here is to illustrate how the standard linear modelling set-up (see, e.g., Duffie and Kan (1996), Dai and Singleton (2000), and Ang and Piazzesi (2003)) can be used to derive a tailor-made discrete-time arbitrage-free model that has a loading structure similar to that of a dynamic Svensson and Söderlind (1997) model, but where the first factor can be interpreted as the short rate, rather than as the yield curve level. Since this will result in a four-factor model, we get the three-factor model for free, so to say, since we can reduce the factor space by simply omitting the fourth factor and fourth factor loading.

Within the continuous-time setting Christensen, Diebold and Rudebusch (2011) have shown how to maintain the parametric loading structure of the Nelson and Siegel (1987) model, while ensuring that arbitrage constraints are fulfilled.[27] Discrete-time versions of the same model have been derived previously (Niu and Zeng (2012) and Li, Niu and Zeng (2012)). Christensen et al. (2011) show that five factors are needed to generate an arbitrage-free term structure model, where the factor loadings match precisely those of Svensson and Söderlind (1997). Instead of providing an exact fit, here we derive a parsimonious four-factor model with a closed-form loading structure that maintains the characteristics of the Svensson and Söderlind (1997) model, where only one time decay is used (recall that the original Svensson and Söderlind (1997) model relies on two time-decay parameters to define its loading structure).

As before, let X_t denote the vector of the modelled yield curve factors, at time t. Furthermore, let the dynamics of X_t be governed by vector autoregressive (VAR) processes of order 1 under both the empirical measure, $\mathbb{P}$, and the pricing measure, $\mathbb{Q}$:

$$X_t = k^{\mathbb{P}} + \Phi^{\mathbb{P}} \cdot X_{t-1} + \Sigma^{\mathbb{P}} \epsilon_t^{\mathbb{P}}, \qquad \epsilon_t^{\mathbb{P}} \sim N(0,1) \qquad (4.1)$$

$$X_t = k^{\mathbb{Q}} + \Phi^{\mathbb{Q}} \cdot X_{t-1} + \Sigma^{\mathbb{Q}} \epsilon_t^{\mathbb{Q}}, \qquad \epsilon_t^{\mathbb{Q}} \sim N(0,1). \qquad (4.2)$$

---

[27] See also, Krippner (2013) and Diebold and Rudebusch (2013).

with $\Sigma\Sigma' = \Omega$ being the variance of the residuals, and it is assumed that $\Sigma^{\mathbb{P}} = \Sigma^{\mathbb{Q}}$. It is noted that we do not use the mean-adjusted version of the VAR model here; the reason for this will become clear at the end of the section.

The risk-free one-period short rate is assumed to be a function of X_t, such that:

$$r_t = \rho_0 + \rho_1' X_t. \tag{4.3}$$

In the model that we derive, we want our factors, X, to have interpretations as the short rate, the slope, and curvature 1 and 2. Given that the first factor is the short rate, we impose the following constraints on (4.3): $\rho_0 = 0$ and $\rho_1 = [1, 0, 0, 0]'$.

As in the derivation of the discrete-time version of the Vasicek (1977), in one of the previous sections of this Element, we now impose absence of arbitrage on the model by introducing the unique pricing mechanism, that governs all traded assets:

$$P_{t,\tau} = \mathbb{E}_t[M_{t+1} \cdot P_{t+1,\tau-1}] \tag{4.4}$$

The idea here is that when the bond matures at time T, its value is known with certainty, since it is default-free: the bond pays its principal value on that day, so $P_{T,0} = 1$. At any time $t + j$ before maturity, the price of the bond can therefore be found as the one-period discounted-value of the price at time $t + j + 1$, all the way back to time t. Discounting is done using the stochastic discount factor (also called the pricing kernel), which is denoted by M_t:

$$M_{t+1} = \exp\left(-r_t - \frac{1}{2}\lambda_t'\lambda_t - \lambda_t'\epsilon_{t+1}^{\mathbb{P}}\right) \tag{4.5}$$

We recognise the univariate case of this expression, from when we derived the Vasicek (1977) model, but now we are dealing with a multifactor model, since X contains four factors. So, we also bring the expression for the time-varying market price of risk into the multi-variate domain by specifying:

$$\lambda_t = \lambda_0 + \lambda_1 \cdot X_t, \tag{4.6}$$

with λ_t being of dimension (4×1) in our application, because we have four factors, λ_0 is of dimension (4×1), and λ_1 is a matrix of dimension (4×4).

It is recalled that:

$$y_{t,\tau} = -\frac{1}{\tau}\log(P_{t,\tau}), \tag{4.7}$$

and that we can write the yield curve expression as a linear (plus a constant, i.e. affine) function:

$$y_{t,\tau} = -\frac{A_\tau}{\tau} - \frac{B_\tau'}{\tau}X_t. \tag{4.8}$$

The bond price is therefore exponential affine in terms of A_τ and B_τ:

$$P_{t,\tau} = \exp\left(A_\tau + B'_\tau X_t\right). \tag{4.9}$$

To derive closed-form expressions for A_τ and B_τ, the fundamental pricing equation is invoked (4.5):

$$P_{t,\tau} = \mathbb{E}_t\left[M_{t+1} \cdot P_{t+1,\tau-1}\right] \tag{4.10}$$

$$= \mathbb{E}_t\left[\exp\left(-r_t - \frac{1}{2}\lambda'_t\lambda_t - \lambda'_t\epsilon^{\mathbb{P}}_{t+1}\right) \cdot \exp\left(A_{\tau-1} + B'_{\tau-1}X_{t+1}\right)\right]. \tag{4.11}$$

The expression for X_{t+1} (see equation 4.1) is substituted:

$$P_{t,\tau} = \mathbb{E}_t\left[\exp\left(-r_t - \frac{1}{2}\lambda'_t\lambda_t - \lambda'_t\epsilon^{\mathbb{P}}_{t+1}\right)\right. \tag{4.12}$$

$$\left. \cdot\exp\left(A_{\tau-1} + B'_{\tau-1}\left(k^{\mathbb{P}} + \Phi^{\mathbb{P}}X_t + \Sigma\epsilon^{\mathbb{P}}_{t+1}\right)\right)\right], \tag{4.13}$$

and the terms are then separated into two groups: one to which the expectations operator should be applied, i.e. $t+1$ terms, and another group, which are known at time t:

$$P_{t,\tau} = \exp\left(-r_t - \frac{1}{2}\lambda'_t\lambda_t + A_{\tau-1} + B'_{\tau-1}k^{\mathbb{P}} + B'_{\tau-1}\Phi^{\mathbb{P}}X_t\right)$$

$$\cdot \mathbb{E}_t\left[\exp\left(-\lambda'_t\epsilon^{\mathbb{P}}_{t+1} + B'_{\tau-1}\Sigma\epsilon^{\mathbb{P}}_{t+1}\right)\right]. \tag{4.14}$$

The question is then, how can we calculate the expectations part of (4.14):

$$\mathbb{E}_t\left[\exp\left(-\lambda'_t + B'_{\tau-1}\Sigma\right)\epsilon^{\mathbb{P}}_{t+1}\right]. \tag{4.15}$$

To this end, the moment-generating function of the multivariate normal distribution is used. Since $\epsilon^{\mathbb{P}} \sim N(0, I)$, it is known that:

$$\mathbb{E}[\exp(d'\epsilon^{\mathbb{P}})] = \exp\left(\frac{1}{2}d' \cdot I \cdot a\right), \tag{4.16}$$

so, the expectation in (4.14) can be calculated, using $d' = (-\lambda'_t + B'_{\tau-1}\Sigma)$, as:

$$\exp\left[\frac{1}{2}(-\lambda'_t + B'_{\tau-1}\Sigma) \cdot I \cdot (-\lambda'_t + B'_{\tau-1}\Sigma)'\right]$$

$$= \exp\left[\frac{1}{2}(-\lambda'_t + B'_{\tau-1}\Sigma) \cdot I \cdot (-\lambda_t + \Sigma'B_{\tau-1})\right]$$

$$= \exp\left[\frac{1}{2}\left(\lambda'_t\lambda_t - \lambda'_t\Sigma'B_{\tau-1} - B'_{\tau-1}\Sigma\lambda_t + B'_{\tau-1}\Sigma\Sigma'B_{\tau-1}\right)\right], \tag{4.17}$$

and, since $B'_{\tau-1}\Sigma\lambda_t$ is a scalar, and for a scalar h, we know that $h = h'$, so $B'_{\tau-1}\Sigma\lambda_t = \lambda'_t\Sigma'B_{\tau-1}$. We can then write:

$$\mathbb{E}_t\left[\exp\left(-\lambda'_t + B'_{\tau-1}\Sigma\right)\epsilon^{\mathbb{P}}_{t+1}\right] = \exp\left(\frac{1}{2}\lambda'_t\lambda_t - B'_{\tau-1}\Sigma\lambda_t + \frac{1}{2}B'_{\tau-1}\Sigma\Sigma'B'_{\tau-1}\right).$$

This term is then reinserted into (4.14), giving:

$$P_{t,\tau} = \exp\left(-r_t + A_{\tau-1} + B'_{\tau-1}k^{\mathbb{P}} + B'_{\tau-1}\Phi^{\mathbb{P}}X_t - B'_{\tau-1}\Sigma\lambda_t \right.$$
$$\left. + \frac{1}{2}B'_{\tau-1}\Sigma\Sigma'B'_{\tau-1}\right).$$
$$(4.18)$$

It is recalled that $r_t = \rho'_1 X_t$, and that $\lambda_t = \lambda_0 + \lambda_1 X_t$. Inserting these expressions into (4.18), gives:

$$P_{t,\tau} = \exp\left(-\rho'_1 X_t + A_{\tau-1} + B'_{\tau-1}k^{\mathbb{P}} + B'_{\tau-1}\Phi^{\mathbb{P}}X_t - B'_{\tau-1}\Sigma(\lambda_0 + \lambda_1 X_t) \right.$$
$$\left. + \frac{1}{2}B'_{n-1}\Sigma\Sigma'B'_{\tau-1}\right).$$
$$(4.19)$$

Reorganising this expression into terms that load on X_t and terms that do not, help matching coefficients with respect to equation (4.9):

$$P_{t,\tau} = \exp\left(A_{\tau-1} + B'_{\tau-1}\left(k^{\mathbb{P}} - \Sigma\lambda_0\right) + \frac{1}{2}B'_{\tau-1}\Sigma\Sigma'B'_{\tau-1} \right.$$
$$\left. + B'_{\tau-1}\Phi^{\mathbb{P}}X_t - \rho'_1 X_t - B'_{\tau-1}\Sigma\lambda_1 X_t\right), \quad (4.20)$$

which is:

$$P_{t,\tau} = \exp\left(A_{\tau-1} + B'_{\tau-1}\left(k^{\mathbb{P}} - \Sigma\lambda_0\right) + \frac{1}{2}B'_{\tau-1}\Sigma\Sigma'B'_{\tau-1} \right.$$
$$\left. + \left[B'_{\tau-1}\left(\Phi^{\mathbb{P}} - \Sigma\lambda_1\right) - \rho'_1\right]X_t\right).$$
$$(4.21)$$

Matching the coefficients of (4.21) with those of (4.9) establishes the recursive formulas for A_τ and B_τ:

$$A_\tau = A_{\tau-1} + B'_{\tau-1}k^{\mathbb{Q}} + \frac{1}{2}B'_{\tau-1}\Sigma\Sigma'B'_{\tau-1} \qquad (4.22)$$

$$B'_\tau = B'_{\tau-1}\Phi^{\mathbb{Q}} - \rho'_1 \qquad (4.23)$$

with $k^{\mathbb{Q}} = k^{\mathbb{P}} - \Sigma\lambda_0$, and $\Phi^{\mathbb{Q}} = \Phi^{\mathbb{P}} - \Sigma\lambda_1$. Recall that $\rho_0 = 0$ in our model set-up. Using recursive substitution, we realise that the expression for B'_n also can be written in the following way:[28]

$$B_\tau = -\left[\sum_{k=0}^{\tau-1}\left(\Phi^Q\right)^k\right]' \cdot \rho_1.$$

(4.24)

It is convenient to write the loading structure in this way, when we want to find a closed-form solution for B_τ, because the expression in (4.24) is the sum of a matrix power series, and we know that this can be solved if Φ^Q comes from a stationary VAR model.

The last task remaining is then to find a Φ^Q matrix that, when inserted in (4.24), gives us loadings that are as similar as possible to the ones appearing in Svensson and Söderlind (1997), while still imposing the constraints mentioned previously that ensure that the first factor is the short rate. So, let's start the guessing game. What happens, for example, if we use the following matrix?

$$\Phi^Q = \begin{bmatrix} 1 & 1-\gamma & 1-\gamma & 1-\gamma \\ 0 & \gamma & \gamma-1 & \gamma-1 \\ 0 & 0 & \gamma & \gamma-1 \\ 0 & 0 & 0 & \gamma \end{bmatrix}.$$

(4.25)

A closed-form expressions for B_τ can then be derived by first finding $\left(\Phi^Q\right)^k$:

$$\left(\Phi^Q\right)^k = \begin{bmatrix} 1 & 1-\gamma^k & -k\gamma^{k-1}(\gamma-1) & -\frac{k}{2}\gamma^{k-2}\left((k+1)\gamma^2-2k\gamma+k-1\right) \\ 0 & \gamma^k & k\gamma^{k-1}(\gamma-1) & \frac{k}{2}\gamma^{k-2}\left((k+1)\gamma^2-2k\gamma+k-1\right) \\ 0 & 0 & \gamma^k & k\gamma^{k-1}(\gamma-1) \\ 0 & 0 & 0 & \gamma^k \end{bmatrix},$$

(4.26)

---

[28] We see this by the use of an example. For $\tau = 3$, we have:

$$\begin{aligned} B_1' &= -\rho_1' \\ B_2' &= B_1'\Phi^Q - \rho_1' = -\rho_1'\Phi^Q - \rho_1' \\ B_3' &= B_2'\Phi^Q - \rho_1' = (-\rho_1'\Phi^Q - \rho_1')\Phi^Q - \rho_1' \\ &= -\rho_1'\left(\Phi^Q\right)^2 - \rho_1'\Phi^Q - \rho_1' \\ &= -\rho_1'\left(\left(\Phi^Q\right)^2 + \left(\Phi^Q\right)^1 + \left(\Phi^Q\right)^0\right) \\ &= -\rho_1'\left[\sum_{k=0}^{2}\left(\Phi^Q\right)^k\right] \end{aligned}$$

so,

$$B_3 = -\left[\sum_{k=0}^{2}\left(\Phi^Q\right)^k\right]'\rho_1,$$

which generalises to equation (4.24).

and then by substituting (4.26) into (4.24), we get:

$$
B_\tau = - \begin{bmatrix} \tau \\ \sum_{k=0}^{\tau-1} 1 - \gamma^k \\ \sum_{k=0}^{\tau-1} -k\gamma^{k-1}(\gamma - 1) \\ \sum_{k=0}^{\tau-1} -\frac{k}{2}\gamma^{k-2}\left((k+1)\gamma^2 - 2k\gamma + k - 1\right) \end{bmatrix}. \tag{4.27}
$$

Solving (4.27) gives:[29]:

$$
B_\tau = - \begin{bmatrix} \tau \\ \tau - \frac{1-\gamma^\tau}{(1-\gamma)} \\ -\tau\gamma^{\tau-1} + \frac{1-\gamma^\tau}{(1-\gamma)} \\ -\frac{1}{2}\tau(\tau - 1)(\gamma - 1)\gamma^{\tau-2} \end{bmatrix}. \tag{4.28}
$$

An expression for the yield curve at time t is then obtained if Y_t collects $y_{t,\tau}$ $\forall \tau$ by increasing maturity, and if $a = -A_\tau/\tau$ and $b = -B'_\tau/\tau$ are defined similarly. The expression for the yield curve observed at time t is then:

$$
Y_t = a + bX_t + \Sigma_Y u_t. \tag{4.29}
$$

with:

$$
b = \begin{bmatrix} 1 \\ 1 - \frac{1-\gamma^\tau}{(1-\gamma)\cdot\tau} \\ -\gamma^{\tau-1} + \frac{1-\gamma^\tau}{(1-\gamma)\cdot\tau} \\ -\frac{1}{2}(\tau - 1)(\gamma - 1)\gamma^{\tau-2} \end{bmatrix}. \tag{4.30}
$$

4.2.1 The Relationship between the SRB Model and the Joslin, Singleton and Zhu (2011) Framework

Here we will briefly look at Joslin et al. (2011) (JSZ). This is a core paper in the literature because it shows that many of the existing model parametrisations are built from the same inner foundation, and are in fact identical up to a rotation. JSZ also present an algorithm to estimate arbitrage-free term structure models that is fast and that converges effortlessly. In addition, they provide insights on what to expect in terms of forecasting performance of certain term structure

---

[29] The first entry of (4.27) follows immediately, the second entry uses $\sum_{k=0}^{\tau-1} x^k = \frac{1-x^\tau}{1-x}$, the third and fourth entries can be found by consecutive substitution. For example, for $\tau = 5$ the third entry of (4.27) is: $4\gamma^4 - \gamma^3 - \gamma^2 - \gamma^1 - \gamma^0$, which generalizes to $(\tau - 1)\gamma^{\tau-1} - \sum_{k=0}^{\tau-2} \gamma^k$. Similarly, the fourth entry of (4.28) for $\tau = 5$ is: $-(0 + 1(\gamma - 1)\gamma^0 + 3(\gamma - 1)\gamma^1 + 6(\gamma - 1)\gamma^2 + 10(\gamma - 1)\gamma^3)$, which generalizes to $-\frac{1}{2}\tau(\tau - 1)(\gamma - 1)\gamma^{\tau-2}$.

models, and why some models have equal forecasting performance (to the degree of uncertainty present in the data). It is a true treat for the reader: if only the paper was easier to understand, it would be perfect.

From my reading of Joslin et al. (2011), the key takeaways are:

1. Gaussian dynamic term structure models (GDTSM) can be parameterised such that the parameters that govern the $\mathbb{P}$ measure, and thus the $\mathbb{P}$-measure forecasts of the yield curve factors, X, do not appear in the measurement-error density. This means that the $\mathbb{P}$- and $\mathbb{Q}$-measure parameters can be estimated separately.
2. It also means that constraints imposed under $\mathbb{Q}$ do not affect the dynamics of the yield curve factors under $\mathbb{P}$, so no-arbitrage constraints cannot help in providing better model forecasts.
3. For an N-factor GDTSM, the following parameters need to be specified:
   3.1 r_∞^Q, the long-run mean of the short rate under $\mathbb{Q}$
   3.2 γ^Q, mean reversion speed (eigenvalues) of the factor dynamics under $\mathbb{Q}$. Other notation uses λ for this parameter, but we have reserved λ for the market price of risk.
   3.3 $\Sigma^{\mathbb{P}}$, the conditional covariance matrix of the yield factors from the VAR model governing their dynamics.
4. The JSZ model characterisation-framework is based on the idea of 'similar' matrices, known from linear algebra, where similarity is defined on the basis of the Jordan form. JSZ apply this idea to GDTSMs: if a given model's $\mathbb{Q}$-dynamics can be rewritten in Jordan form, with ordered eigenvalues, then the model is identical (up to a rotation) to the JSZ canonical form.

If a comparison is made to the notation used in Joslin et al. (2011), it may be relevant to note that they specify VAR models in difference form. Throughout the Element, we have looked at VAR models in level form. Although it is not a big deal, I will continue using the level form here, and thus rewrite (and adapt their notation) to what we have been using so far.[30]

Let's start by looking at the issue from an intuitive angle on the basis of a general VAR model for the yield curve factors under the $\mathbb{Q}$ measure. As in Joslin et al. (2011), we choose a specific set of yield curve factors that are formed as linear combinations of yields. JSZ refer to these factors as being 'portfolios of yields' i.e. implying that they can be obtained by applying a weighting matrix

---

[30] A VAR model written in difference form looks like this: $\Delta X_t = k + \tilde{\Phi} X_{t-1} + \Sigma e_t$, which can be written as, $X_t - X_{t-1} = k + \tilde{\Phi} X_{t-1} + \Sigma e_t$, and as $X_t = k + \tilde{\Phi} X_{t-1} + X_{t-1} + \Sigma e_t$. So, the difference between the difference and level forms is that $\Phi = \tilde{\Phi} + I$, where Φ refers to the autoregressive matrix in the level form.

to the yield curve data in the following way[31]:

$$X_t = W \cdot y_t. \tag{4.31}$$

According to this definition, any linear combination of yields qualify, thus also principal components. We continue by writing a general VAR model for these factors:

$$X_t = k^{\mathbb{Q}} + \Phi^{\mathbb{Q}} \cdot X_{t-1} + \Sigma^{\mathbb{Q}} u_t, \tag{4.32}$$

We know that $\Phi^{\mathbb{Q}}$ governs the dynamics of the VAR model under the $\mathbb{Q}$ measure, and thus the shape of the yield loadings b_τ and the constant, a_τ. But, what are the core components of this matrix? If we look at the eigenvalue decomposition of $\Phi^{\mathbb{Q}}$, the eigenvalues express the degree of persistency of the matrix, that is, how fast (or slowly) it converges to its steady state (assuming, as always, that the VAR is stationarity). The eigenvectors of Φ (not of X, just to be clear) can be interpreted as the 'direction' the matrix points in, or the space that it spans; one way to use eigenvectors is to multiply them with a matrix having eigenvalues raised to the power of 's' on its diagonal. This operation will give the s-step ahead projection matrix.[32] We can naturally imagine many different sets of yield curve factors (one for each occasion), and all sets spanning different directions, and all formed according to (4.31). Some of these sets could, for example, be (a) the three first principal components; (b) level, slope, and curvature; (c) short-rate slope and curvature; and (d) the three-month yield, the three-year yield, and the ten-year yield. The crux of JSZ is that all these possible factors definitions (i.e. also our examples in (a)-(d)), can be converted (or rotated) into a common single basis form. So, in fact, the various factors definitions, and their associated models, are all (just) variations over a single core model; all having identical properties, but appearing to be different.

To express the GDTSM in its purest form, Joslin et al. (2011) rely on the Jordan decomposition of $\Phi^{\mathbb{Q}}$. The Jordan decomposition is a generalisation of the eigenvalue decomposition, see, for example, Hamilton (1994)[pp.730–31], in that it explicitly handles repeated eigenvalues. An eigenvalue decomposition can still be successfully completed, even if there are repeated eigenvalues, as long as the eigenvectors form a full-rank matrix. But this is not guaranteed to always be the case, hence the generalisation represented by the Jordan

---

[31] Joslin et al. (2011) denote the yield factors by $\mathcal{P}$, but we continue by using X to denote the factors.

[32] Recall from our discussion of the term premia in a previous section, that we can calculate the s-step ahead projection of the VAR as the s'th power of the diagonal matrix containing the eigenvalues, pre- and post- multiplied by the eigenvectors.

decomposition (formulas [A.4.26] and [A.4.27] from Hamilton (1994)):

$$
J = \begin{bmatrix}
J_1 & 0 & \cdots & 0 \\
0 & J_2 & \cdots & 0 \\
\vdots & \vdots & \cdots & \vdots \\
0 & 0 & \cdots & J_n
\end{bmatrix}
\tag{4.33}
$$

and

$$
J_i = \begin{bmatrix}
\gamma_i & 1 & 0 & \cdots & 0 \\
0 & \gamma_i & 1 & \cdots & 0 \\
0 & 0 & \gamma_i & \cdots & 0 \\
\vdots & \vdots & \vdots & \cdots & \vdots \\
0 & 0 & 0 & \cdots & \gamma_i
\end{bmatrix}
\tag{4.34}
$$

where the i'th eigenvalue is denoted by γ_i. Similarly to the eigenvalue decomposition, the Jordan decomposition is given by:

$$
\Phi^Q = V \cdot \Phi^J \cdot V^{-1}.
\tag{4.35}
$$

To facilitate the rotation from the Jordan form to any other observationally equivalent model, we start with the VAR model:

$$
X_t^J = k^J + \Phi^J \cdot X_{t-1}^J + \Sigma^J e_t^J,
\tag{4.36}
$$

where J refers to the Jordan form. A general rotation of this VAR model is implemented below:

$$
\begin{aligned}
X_t &= N + M \cdot X_t^J \\
&= N + M \cdot \left(k^J + \Phi^J \cdot X_{t-1}^J + \Sigma^J e_t \right) \\
&= N + M \cdot k^J + M \cdot \Phi^J \cdot X_{t-1}^J + M \cdot \Sigma^J e_t \\
&= N + M \cdot k^J + M \cdot \Phi^J \cdot M^{-1} \cdot (X_{t-1} - N) + M \cdot \Sigma^J e_t \\
&= N - M \cdot \Phi^J \cdot M^{-1} \cdot N + M \cdot k^J + M \cdot \Phi^J \cdot M^{-1} \cdot X_{t-1} + M \cdot \Sigma^J e_t \\
&= \underbrace{\left(I - M\Phi^J M^{-1} \right) N + Mk^J}_{k^Q} + \underbrace{M\Phi^J M^{-1}}_{\Phi^Q} \cdot X_{t-1} + \underbrace{M\Sigma^J}_{\Sigma^Q} e_t \\
&= k^Q + \Phi^Q \cdot X_{t-1} + \Sigma^Q e_t.
\end{aligned}
\tag{4.37}
$$

Line 4 follows from line 1, since $X_t = N + M \cdot X_t^J \Leftrightarrow X_t^J = M^{-1} \cdot (X_t - N)$.

We know from (4.3) that the short rate depends on the yield curve factors. In the SRB model, this link is simply defined by the parameter constraints $\rho_0 = 0$ and $\rho_1 = [1, 0, \ldots, 0]'$. However, for other factors, ρ_0 and ρ_1 contain parameters that need to be estimated. So, we need also to show how the introduced rotation affects the short-rate equation:

$$
\begin{aligned}
r_t &= \rho_0^J + \rho_1^J X_t^J \\
&= \rho_0^J + \rho_1^J M^{-1} (X_t - N) \\
&= \underbrace{\rho_0^J - \rho_1^J M^{-1} \cdot N}_{\rho_0} + \underbrace{\rho_1^J M^{-1} \cdot X_t}_{\rho_1} \\
&= \rho_0 + \rho_1 X_t.
\end{aligned}
\tag{4.38}
$$

With this behind us, we can now show that the SRB-model developed in Section 4.2 is a constrained member of the general family of Gaussian dynamic term structure model derived by Joslin et al. (2011).[33]

Now, let J be the Jordan matrix, and V be a rotation matrix such that equation (4.25) can be reformulated as:

$$
\Phi^Q = V \cdot J \cdot V^{-1}.
\tag{4.39}
$$

Choosing V to be:

$$
V =
\begin{bmatrix}
1 & -(\gamma - 1)^2 & \gamma - 1 & -1 \\
0 & \gamma^2 - 2 * \gamma + 1 & 1 - \gamma & 1 \\
0 & 0 & \gamma - 1 & -2 \\
0 & 0 & 0 & 1
\end{bmatrix},
\tag{4.40}
$$

implies that:

$$
J =
\begin{bmatrix}
1 & 0 & 0 & 0 \\
0 & \gamma & 1 & 0 \\
0 & 0 & \gamma & 1 \\
0 & 0 & 0 & \gamma
\end{bmatrix},
\tag{4.41}
$$

Since (4.41) is in Jordan form with repeated eigenvalues, there exists a mapping between the $\mathbb{Q}$-dynamics I propose in (4.25) and the framework suggested by JSZ. The proposed SRB model is therefore a constrained member of the JSZ family of models.[34]

---

[33] This is not overly surprising since the SRB model is a generalisation of the arbitrage-free Nelson-Siegel model suggested by Christensen et al. (2011)(CDR), and since Joslin et al. (2011) show that the CDR model is a constrained member of the JSZ family.

[34] The restriction of repeated eigenvalues, compared to the canonical JSZ form, is not rejected by the data used in the paper at a 5 per cent level, using a likelihood ratio test.

4.2.2 The Relationship between the Four-Factor SRB Model and the Svensson-Söderlind Model

Since the four-factor SRB model aims to replicate the Svensson and Söderlind (1997) loading structure as closely as possible, but by the use of a single time-decay parameter, γ, it may be relevant to draw a comparison between the two models.

It is recalled that the Svensson-Soderlind loadings are given by:

$$H = \begin{bmatrix} 1 \\ \frac{1-e^{-\kappa_1 n}}{\kappa_1 n} \\ \frac{1-e^{-\kappa_1 n}}{\kappa_1 n} - e^{-\kappa_1 n} \\ \frac{1-e^{-\kappa_2 n}}{\kappa_2 n} - e^{-\kappa_2 n} \end{bmatrix}, \tag{4.42}$$

and that the loading structure of the SRB model is given by $B = B_n/n$, where B is given by equation (4.28):

$$B = - \begin{bmatrix} 1 \\ 1 - \frac{1-\gamma^n}{(1-\gamma)\cdot n} \\ -\gamma^{n-1} + \frac{1-\gamma^n}{(1-\gamma)\cdot n} \\ -\frac{1}{2}(n-1)(\gamma-1)\gamma^{n-2} \end{bmatrix}. \tag{4.43}$$

Figure 28 compares the loading structures of the Svensson and Söderlind (1997) and the SRB models. The shape parameter of the SRB model is set to $\gamma = 0.945$, and the two Svensson-Söderlind shape parameters take on the values $\kappa_1 = 0.0381$ and $\kappa_2 = 0.1491$ (similar to what is found on US data). The loadings for the first factor are not shown in the figure, as they equal 1 for both models, across the included maturities. The first panel in the figure shows the loadings for the slope factor; and to facilitate easy comparison, the loading of the Svensson-Söderlind model is rotated to match that are the SRB model: let H_{slope} be the original slope loading for the Svensson-Söderlind model, panel 1 then plots $1 - H_{slope}$. The second and third panels compare the loadings for the first and second curvature loadings. Returning to the first panel. It shows that the loadings for the slope factor are quite similar across the two models, although the SRB loading assumes slightly higher values throughout the maturity spectrum, and also seems to arch upwards a bit more than the Svensson-Söderlind loading does. Level differences between the loading structures can naturally be subsumed by the corresponding factor values, so the shape attained by the loadings are of greater importance for the relative comparison between the models. Similarly, the second and the third panels show

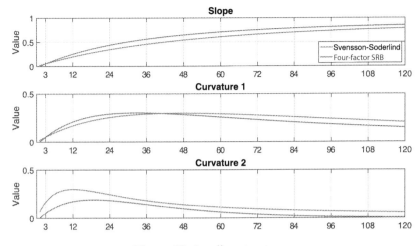

Figure 28 Loading structures

The figure compares the loading structures of the Svensson-Soderlind and the SRB models. The shape parameter of the SRB model is $\gamma = 0.945$, and the two Svensson-Soderlind shape parameters are estimated to be $\kappa_1 = 0.0381$ and $\kappa_2 = 0.1491$. The loadings for the first factor are not shown as they equal 1 for both models across the included maturities. The first panel shows the loadings for the slope factor, and to facilitate the comparison, the Svensson-Soderlind loading structure is rotated, to match that of the SRB model, and this is done in the following way: Let H_{slope} be the original slope loading for the Svensson-Soderlind model, panel 1 then plots $1 - H_{\text{slope}}$. The second and third panels compare the loadings for the first and second curvature loadings.

relatively good correspondence between the curvature loadings of the two models. Panel 2 indicates that the SRB model loading peaks around a maturity of 30 months, while the corresponding Svensson-Söderlind loading peaks around 40 months.

To test the impact of the detected differences in the loading structures, as noted, the models are fitted to the US data used in other sections of this Element. Table 14 documents that both models produce very low root mean squared errors and that the added flexibility of the Svensson-Söderlind model, via its reliance on two shape parameters, κ_1 and κ_2 (see equation (4.42)), as opposed to the one used by the SRB model (γ), gives it an economically insignificant edge of 1 basis points on average. The worst-fitted maturity of the SRB model is the one-year segment with a RMSE of 4.7 basis points, and the average RMSE across the eleven included maturities is 2.68 basis points. In comparison, the Svensson-Söderlind model produces the worst RMSE at the two-year segment of 3.0 basis points, with the average RMSE of 1.58 basis points across the included maturities.

Table 14 Root mean squared errors (basis points)

	3m	1y	2y	3y	4y	5y	6y	7y	10y	Average
SRB Model	2.8	4.7	4.1	2.5	1.6	2.3	2.3	2.1	3.4	2.6
Svensson-Söderlind	0.3	2.6	3.0	2.0	0.7	1.4	1.9	1.6	2.3	1.5

The table shows the root mean squared errors in basis points of the SRB and the Svensson and Söderlind (1997) models when estimated using monthly US yield curve data covering the period from January 1961 to November 2017. Data are observed at maturities spanning three months to ten years. The shape parameter of the SRB model is $\gamma = 0.945$, and the two Svensson-Söderlind shape parameters are estimated to be $\kappa_1 = 0.0381$ and $\kappa_2 = 0.1491$.

MATLAB code

Yield curve model estimation via the SSM toolbox

filename: Modelling_yields_under_Q.m

```matlab
1   %% Modelling yields under Q
2   % All we do here is to plot the loading structures of the Svensson-
3   % Soderlind and the 4-factor SRB models
4   %
5   path_=[pwd,'\MATLAB_classes'];
6   addpath(path_);
7
8   tau     = ( 1:1:120 )';
9   nTau    = size(tau,1);
10
11  Bfunc_SS = @(lambda_,tau_,nTau_) ...
12  [ ones(nTau_,1) (1-exp(-lambda_(1,1).*tau_))./ (lambda_(1,1).*tau_) ...
13  (1-exp(-lambda_(1,1).*tau_))./(lambda_(1,1).*tau_)-exp(-lambda_(1,1).*tau_) ...
14  (1-exp(-lambda_(2,1).*tau_))./(lambda_(2,1).*tau_)-exp(-lambda_(2,1).*tau_) ];
15
16
17  Bfunc_SRB4 = @(lambda_,tau_,nTau_) ...
18      [ ones(nTau_,1) 1-(1-lambda_.^tau_)./((1-lambda_).*tau_) ...
19      -(lambda_.^(tau_-1))+(1-lambda_.^tau_)./((1-lambda_).*tau_) ...
20      -0.5.*(tau_-1).*(lambda_-1).*lambda_.^(tau_-2) ];
21
22  L_SS    = [ 0.0381; 0.1491 ];
23
24  L_SRB4 = 0.945;
25
26  B_SS    = Bfunc_SS( L_SS, tau, nTau );
27  B_SRB4  = Bfunc_SRB4( L_SRB4, tau, nTau );
28
29  tau_plot = [3 12:12:120]';
30  figure('units','normalized','outerposition',[0 0 1 1])
31      subplot(3,1,1), plot( tau, 1-B_SS(:,2) , ...
32          'LineWidth',2),  ylim([0 1]),  title('Slope'),
33          ylabel('Value'), set(gca, 'FontSize', 20)
34      hold on
35      subplot(3,1,1), plot(tau,B_SRB4(:,2) , ...
36          'LineWidth',2), grid 'on'
37          xticks(tau_plot),xticklabels(tau_plot)
38          legend('Svensson-Soderlind','4-factor SRB','Location','SE')
```

```
39
40      subplot(3,1,2), plot( tau, B_SS(:,3) , ...
41          'LineWidth',2), ylim([0 0.5]), title('Curvature 1'),
42          ylabel('Value'), set(gca, 'FontSize', 20)
43      hold on
44      subplot(3,1,2), plot(tau,B_SRB4(:,3) , ...
45          'LineWidth',2), grid 'on'
46          xticks(tau_plot),xticklabels(tau_plot)
47
48      subplot(3,1,3), plot( tau, B_SS(:,4) , ...
49          'LineWidth',2), ylim([0 0.5]), title('Curvature 2'),
50          ylabel('Value'), set(gca, 'FontSize', 20)
51      hold on
52      subplot(3,1,3), plot(tau,B_SRB4(:,4) , ...
53          'LineWidth',2), grid 'on'
54          xticks(tau_plot),xticklabels(tau_plot)
55          print -depsc Loadings_SS_SRB4
```

5 Model Implementation

5.1 Introduction

In addition to the modelling explanations provided so far in this Element, it is also important to discuss how model implementation is achieved in practice. When looking at a model on the Internet or in a paper (here I am of course referring to a term structure model), it is not always clear how the authors manage to apply the model to data and how they obtain the relevant parameter estimates. The aim of the current section is therefore to discuss practical issues, supported by step-wise implementation guidelines.

5.2 A Brief Note on Model Implementation

Before getting started on outlining detailed implementation recipes and coding up the Joslin et al. (2011) model and the arbitrage-free version of the dynamic Nelson-Siegel model, following Nyholm (2018), this section describes the central building blocks that arbitrage-free models consist of. As we have seen in Section 4 these building blocks consists of the $\mathbb{P}$-measure dynamics, the $\mathbb{Q}$-measure dynamics, the parametrisation of the market price of risk, and the no-arbitrage pricing relationship. These elements, and how they interact, are illustrated in Figure 29.

The triangle in the figure is meant to illustrate that there are three ways to parameterise an arbitrage-free model. A model is parameterised by selecting two of the three corners in the triangle, and by letting the third, unselected, corner be implied by the parameter relationships recorded in the lower part of Figure 29. More specifically, you can choose to:

1. estimate the parameters governing the $\mathbb{P}$- and the $\mathbb{Q}$-dynamics, that is, the two lower parts of the triangle, leaving the parameters of the market price of

risk to be implied by the parameter relationships: $k^{\mathbb{Q}} = k^{\mathbb{P}} - \Sigma^{\mathbb{P}} \cdot \lambda_0$, and $\Phi^{\mathbb{Q}} = \Phi^{\mathbb{P}} - \Sigma^{\mathbb{P}} \cdot \lambda_1$.

2. estimate the parameters governing the $\mathbb{P}$ dynamics and the market price of risk, and letting the parameters of the $\mathbb{Q}$ dynamics be implied by the parameter relationships: $k^{\mathbb{Q}} = k^{\mathbb{P}} - \Sigma^{\mathbb{P}} \cdot \lambda_0$, and $\Phi^{\mathbb{Q}} = \Phi^{\mathbb{P}} - \Sigma^{\mathbb{P}} \cdot \lambda_1$.

3. estimate the parameters governing the $\mathbb{Q}$ dynamics and the market price of risk, and letting the parameters of the $\mathbb{P}$ dynamics be implied by the parameter relationships: $k^{\mathbb{Q}} = k^{\mathbb{P}} - \Sigma^{\mathbb{P}} \cdot \lambda_0$, and $\Phi^{\mathbb{Q}} = \Phi^{\mathbb{P}} - \Sigma^{\mathbb{P}} \cdot \lambda_1$.

A final issue to consider is what the main object of the estimation routine is going to be. In Figure 29, it is observed that the no-arbitrage relationship is specified in term of bond prices by $P_{t,\tau} = \mathbb{E}_t[M_{t+1} \cdot P_{t+1,\tau-1}]$. However, it is rarely the case that observed market prices are used to fit yield curve models.[35] The vast majority of models use yields as the primary object for writing up the objective function, meaning most models minimise the (squared) difference between observed and model yields, in order to estimate the model parameters. This is also the approach that we rely on below. However, it should be

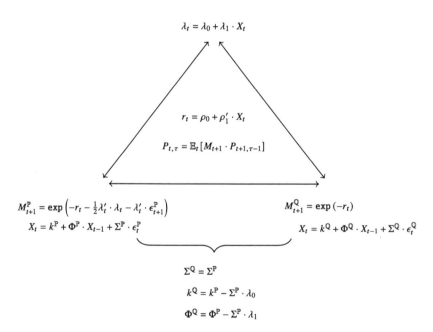

Figure 29 Building blocks for arbitrage-free models.

---

[35] One exception to this rule is the Smith and Wilson (2000) model, which use is prescribed in the context of European Solvency II calculations for insurance companies, see CEIOPS (2010). This model is fitted directly to prices via discount functions.

mentioned that there is another strand of literature using fixed income returns, as the basis for fitting model parameters; see among others, Adrian et al. (2013).

5.3 Implementing the Joslin, Singleton and Zhu (2011) Model

Although the MATLAB code for estimating the Joslin et al. (2011) model is available on the Internet,[36] we still choose to implement the model here. Our implementation will most likely be less efficient, compared to the code made available by the authors. The JSZ code available on the net typically converges within seconds: this is hard to beat, and originates from the clever step-wise estimation approach suggested by Joslin et al. (2011). We will also implement the model in a step-wise fashion, but integrate the code into our TSM-class. While it may seem as poor judgement not simply to use what is already available on the net, in our context, where we may want to include exogenous variables and to do conditional projections, we would anyway have to adapt the JSZ code to our particular needs. So, in the end, it may be easier (and more fun) to implement the model ourselves.

In section 4.2.1 we met the JSZ model, and saw how the SRB model is a constrained member of the of JSZ family. Here we will take a deep-dive and present the model parameters that need to be estimated and how we achieve model convergence.

Following the traditional linear yield curve modelling set-up, the three factors included in the Joslin et al. (2011) model are governed by VAR(1) dynamics. In their paper, JSZ write up the dynamics in difference form, we will however continue using the level-form as we have done throughout this Element:

$$X_t = k^{\mathbb{P}} + \Phi^{\mathbb{P}} \cdot X_{t-1} + \Sigma e_t^{\mathbb{P}} \qquad (5.1)$$
$$X_t = k^{\mathbb{Q}} + \Phi^{\mathbb{Q}} \cdot X_{t-1} + \Sigma e_t^{\mathbb{Q}} \qquad (5.2)$$
$$r_t = \rho_0 + \rho_1 \cdot X_t \qquad (5.3)$$

where r_t is a linear function of the factors, and the residual covariance is given by $\Sigma\Sigma'$. JSZ normalise their model by requiring that $\Phi^{\mathbb{Q}}$ is in Jordan form, that is,

$$\Phi^{\mathbb{Q}} = J(\gamma^{\mathbb{Q}}) = \begin{bmatrix} J_1 & 0 & \cdots & 0 \\ 0 & J_2 & \cdots & 0 \\ \vdots & \vdots & \cdots & \vdots \\ 0 & 0 & \cdots & J_n \end{bmatrix} \qquad (5.4)$$

---

[36] See, www-bcf.usc.edu/ sjoslin/.

and

$$J_i = \begin{bmatrix} \gamma_i^{\mathbb{Q}} & 1 & 0 & \cdots & 0 \\ 0 & \gamma_i^{\mathbb{Q}} & 1 & \cdots & 0 \\ 0 & 0 & \gamma_i^{\mathbb{Q}} & \cdots & 0 \\ \vdots & \vdots & \vdots & \cdots & \vdots \\ 0 & 0 & 0 & \cdots & \gamma_i^{\mathbb{Q}} \end{bmatrix} \qquad (5.5)$$

where the i'th eigenvalue is denoted by $\gamma_i^{\mathbb{Q}}$. With this in place, it turns out that the likelihood function can be partitioned in a convenient way:

$$f(y_t|y_{t-1}; \theta) = \underbrace{f(y_t|X_t, \Sigma_X^{\mathbb{P}}, \rho_0, \rho_1; \gamma^{\mathbb{Q}}, k_\infty^{\mathbb{Q}}, \Sigma_y)}_{\text{translates factors into yields}}$$

$$\times \underbrace{f(X_t|X_{t-1}; k^{\mathbb{P}}, \Phi^{\mathbb{P}}, \Sigma_X^{\mathbb{P}})}_{\text{evolves factors over time}} \qquad (5.6)$$

where the parameters to be estimated, $\theta = \{\gamma^{\mathbb{Q}}, k_\infty^{\mathbb{Q}}, \Sigma_y, \Sigma_X^{\mathbb{Q}}, k^{\mathbb{P}}, \Phi^{\mathbb{P}}, \Sigma_X^{\mathbb{P}},$ $\rho_0, \rho_1\}$, are neatly separated into one group that converts yield curve factors into yield (i.e. the $\mathbb{Q}$-measure parameters), and the parameters that cater for the time-series evolution of the factors under the empirical $\mathbb{P}$ measure. As a consequence, our traditional state-space set-up:

$$y_\tau = a_\tau + b_\tau \cdot X_t + \Sigma_y u_t \qquad (5.7)$$
$$X_t = k^{\mathbb{P}} + \Phi^{\mathbb{P}} \cdot X_t + \Sigma_X^{\mathbb{P}} e_t^{\mathbb{P}} \qquad (5.8)$$

can be broken down into two distinct operations where, first, the state equation is estimated, and second, the observation equation is estimated. From (4.22) and (4.24) we know that the no-arbitrage restriction imposes the following functional form on the parameters that enter the observation equation:

$$A_\tau = A_{\tau-1} + B'_{\tau-1} k^{\mathbb{Q}} + \frac{1}{2} B'_{\tau-1} \Sigma \Sigma' B'_{\tau-1} \qquad (5.9)$$

$$B_\tau = - \left[\sum_{k=0}^{\tau-1} \left(\Phi^{\mathbb{Q}} \right)^k \right]' \cdot \rho_1, \qquad (5.10)$$

and

$$a_\tau = -\frac{A_\tau}{\tau}$$

$$b_\tau = -\frac{B_\tau}{\tau}.$$

In addition, the JSZ normalisation implies the following parameter constraints:

$$r_t = \rho_0 + \rho_1' \cdot X_t,$$

$$\rho_0 = 0,$$

$$\rho_1 = \iota, \tag{5.11}$$

$$k^{\mathbb{Q}} = \begin{bmatrix} k_\infty^{\mathbb{Q}} \\ 0 \\ \vdots \\ 0 \end{bmatrix}. \tag{5.12}$$

With these constraints and (5.4), exact identification of the model is achieved. In practice, this means that we in some sense uncover the structural parameters that govern the yield curve dynamics and cross-sectional behaviour, at its most fundamental level. It is noted that $k_\infty^{\mathbb{Q}}$ is the long-run constant for the short rate under the $\mathbb{Q}$ measure, such that the long-run mean is $r_\infty^{\mathbb{Q}} = \frac{-k_\infty^{\mathbb{Q}}}{\gamma_1^{\mathbb{Q}}}$, when $\gamma_1^{\mathbb{Q}}$ is not a repeated root.

As we saw in section 4.2.1, JSZ use principal components as the staring point for setting up their model. So, together with (5.2), the dynamics of the PCA factors, $\mathcal{P}$, can be written in the following way, where W denotes the PCA weights:

$$\mathcal{P}_t = W \cdot y_t. \tag{5.13}$$

To be clear about the notation used, we denote by $a_{J,\tau}$ and $b_{J,\tau}$ the constant and the factor loadings for the yield curve model where the underlying process for X_t is in its most fundamental form (i.e. where $\Phi^{\mathbb{Q}}$ is in Jordan form):

$$\mathbb{E}[y_t] = a_{J,\tau} + b_{J,\tau} \cdot X_t. \tag{5.14}$$

Using (5.13), the PCA-based model can now be written in terms of the parameters that define the Jordan basis form:

$$\mathcal{P}_t = W \cdot \mathbb{E}[y_t]$$
$$= W \cdot (a_{J,\tau} + b_{J,\tau} \cdot X_t)$$
$$= W \cdot a_{J,\tau} + W \cdot b_{J,\tau} \cdot X_t$$

$$\Updownarrow$$

$$W \cdot b_{J,\tau} \cdot X_t = \mathcal{P}_t - W \cdot a_{J,\tau}$$
$$X_t = (W \cdot b_{J,\tau})^{-1} \cdot \mathcal{P}_t - (W \cdot b_{J,\tau})^{-1} \cdot W \cdot a_{J,\tau}$$
$$= (W \cdot b_{J,\tau})^{-1} \cdot (\mathcal{P}_t - W \cdot a_{J,\tau}) \tag{5.15}$$

To complete the model, such that it can be estimated, expression (5.15) is inserted into (5.14):

$$
\begin{aligned}
\mathbb{E}[y_t] &= a_{J,\tau} + b_{J,\tau} \cdot (W \cdot b_{J,\tau})^{-1} \cdot \mathcal{P}_t - b_{J,\tau} \cdot (W \cdot b_{J,\tau})^{-1} \cdot W \cdot a_{J,\tau} \\
&= a_{J,\tau} - b_{J,\tau} \cdot (W \cdot b_{J,\tau})^{-1} \cdot W \cdot a_{J,\tau} + b_{J,\tau} \cdot (W \cdot b_{J,\tau})^{-1} \cdot \mathcal{P}_t \\
&= \left(I - b_{J,\tau} \cdot (W \cdot b_{J,\tau})^{-1} \cdot W \right) \cdot a_{J,\tau} + b_{J,\tau} \cdot (W \cdot b_{J,\tau})^{-1} \cdot \mathcal{P}_t \\
&= a_{\mathcal{P},\tau} + b_{\mathcal{P},\tau} \cdot \mathcal{P}_t
\end{aligned}
$$

where

$$
a_{\mathcal{P},\tau} = \left(I - b_{J,\tau} \cdot (W \cdot b_{J,\tau})^{-1} \cdot W \right) \cdot a_{J,\tau} \tag{5.16}
$$

$$
b_{\mathcal{P},\tau} = b_{J,\tau} \cdot (W \cdot b_{J,\tau})^{-1} \tag{5.17}
$$

Via equations (5.16) and (5.17), JSZ create a link between the dynamics that characterise the time-series dynamics and cross-sectional behaviour of yields, as represented by the Jordan form, and the parameters that govern the yield curve, when using principal components as underlying factors.

As mentioned earlier, JSZ make their MATLAB code available on the net, and their suite of functions works extremely well and converges exceptionally fast. My implementation below is much less general than the JSZ code, and it does not converge as fast as their code does. However, the educational benefits of making our own implementation hopefully outweigh the programming deficiencies. To estimate a version of the Joslin et al. (2011) model the following steps are followed:

1. ρ_0 and ρ_1 are determined by the normalisation constraints, so no short-rate regression is needed.
2. Use principal component analysis to identify the factors $\mathcal{P}$ and the weights W.
3. Find $k^{\mathbb{P}}$, $\Phi^{\mathbb{P}}$, and $\Sigma_{\mathcal{P}}^{\mathbb{P}}$ using linear regression, or maximum likelihood (if constraints are imposed on the parameters), from the time-series evolution of $\mathcal{P}_t$.
4. Make a first guess on the eigenvalues contained in $\gamma^{\mathbb{Q}}$, and for $k_\infty^{\mathbb{Q}}$.
5. Calculate $a_{J,\tau}$ and $b_{J,\tau}$ using the recursive equations in (5.9) and (5.10).
6. Use (5.16) and (5.17) to find $a_{\mathcal{P},\tau}$ and $b_{\mathcal{P},\tau}$.
7. Then find $\gamma^{\mathbb{Q}}$, and for $k_\infty^{\mathbb{Q}}$ as the solution to the minimisation problem below:

$$
\left\{ \hat{\gamma}^{\mathbb{Q}}, \hat{k}_\infty^{\mathbb{Q}} \right\} = \operatorname*{argmin}_{\gamma^{\mathbb{Q}}, k_\infty^{\mathbb{Q}}} \sum_t \sum_\tau (y - (a_{\mathcal{P}} + b_{\mathcal{P}} \cdot \mathcal{P}))^2 \tag{5.18}
$$

where y is the whole panel of yield curve observations spanning all dates and maturities. After having obtained the parameter estimates of the Jordan form of the model, the remaining parameters of the PCA-founded model can be determined. This is done here, starting with the short-rate equation:

$$
\begin{aligned}
r_t &= \rho_{J,0} + \rho_{J,1} \cdot X_t \\
&= \rho_{J,0} + \rho_{J,1} \cdot (W \cdot b_{J,\tau})^{-1} (\mathcal{P}_t - W \cdot a_{J,\tau}) \\
&= \rho_{J,0} - \rho_{J,1} \cdot (W \cdot b_{J,\tau})^{-1} \cdot W \cdot a_{J,\tau} + \rho_{J,1} \cdot (W \cdot b_{J,\tau})^{-1} \cdot \mathcal{P}_t \\
&= \rho_{P,0} + \rho_{P,1} \cdot \mathcal{P}_t
\end{aligned}
$$

where

$$
\rho_{P,0} = \rho_{J,0} - \rho_{J,1} \cdot (W \cdot b_{J,\tau})^{-1} \cdot W \cdot a_{J,\tau} \tag{5.19}
$$

$$
\rho_{P,1} = \rho_{J,1} \cdot (W \cdot b_{J,\tau})^{-1} . \tag{5.20}
$$

And, then for the $\mathbb{Q}$ dynamics of the factors:

$$
X_t = m^J + \Phi^J \cdot \left(X_{t-1} - m^J \right)
$$

$\Updownarrow$

$$
(W \cdot b_{J,\tau})^{-1} \cdot (\mathcal{P}_t - W \cdot a_{J,\tau}) = m^J + \Phi^J \cdot (W \cdot b_{J,\tau})^{-1} \\
\cdot (\mathcal{P}_{t-1} - W \cdot a_{J,\tau}) - \Phi^J \cdot m^J
$$

$\Updownarrow$

$$
(W \cdot b_{J,\tau})^{-1} \cdot \mathcal{P}_t = (W \cdot b_{J,\tau})^{-1} \cdot W \cdot a_{J,\tau} + m^J + \Phi^J \cdot (W \cdot b_{J,\tau})^{-1} \\
\cdot (\mathcal{P}_{t-1} - W \cdot a_{J,\tau}) - \Phi^J \cdot m^J
$$

$\Updownarrow$

$$
(W \cdot b_{J,\tau})^{-1} \cdot \mathcal{P}_t = \Phi^J \cdot (W \cdot b_{J,\tau})^{-1} \mathcal{P}_{t-1} \\
+ (I - \phi^J) \cdot \left(m^J + (W \cdot b_{J,\tau})^{-1} \cdot W \cdot a_{J,\tau} \right)
$$

$\Updownarrow$

$$
\mathcal{P}_t = (W \cdot b_{J,\tau}) \cdot \Phi^J \cdot (W \cdot b_{J,\tau})^{-1} \mathcal{P}_{t-1} \\
+ (W \cdot b_{J,\tau}) (I - \Phi^J) \cdot \left(m^J + (W \cdot b_{J,\tau})^{-1} \cdot W \cdot a_{J,\tau} \right). \tag{5.21}
$$

This means that the parameters of the dynamic evolution of the principal components can be found in the following way:[37].

$$
\Phi_P^{\mathbb{Q}} = (W \cdot b_{J,\tau}) \cdot \Phi^J \cdot (W \cdot b_{J,\tau})^{-1} . \tag{5.22}
$$

---

[37] Note that (5.21) is written in the constant form, and not in mean-adjusted form. Consequently, the mean is found via the generic expression: $m = (I - \Phi)^{-1} \cdot c$

$$m_{\mathcal{P}}^{\mathbb{Q}} = \left(I - (W \cdot b_{J,\tau}) \cdot \Phi^J \cdot (W \cdot b_{J,\tau})^{-1} \right)^{-1} (W \cdot b_{J,\tau})$$
$$\cdot (I - \Phi^J) \cdot \left(m_{\mathcal{J}}^{\mathbb{Q}} + (W \cdot b_{J,\tau})^{-1} \cdot W \cdot a_{J,\tau} \right).$$

$$(5.23)$$

The notation may have gotten a bit out of hand here. I hope it is still roughly clear, what we have achieved (or rather what Joslin et al. (2011) have achieved): by specifying the term structure model in its most fundamental form, via the Jordan basis, helped clarify which of the variables are central for its empirical implementation and, by afterwards rotating the model to one that relies on principal components as underlying factors, a link was established to data and we are therefore able to estimate the model. In addition, it was shown in equation (5.6), that the $\mathbb{P}$ and $\mathbb{Q}$ measures can be separated – this is of course important from a model-forecasting perspective: basically, this separation principle tell us that superior forecasting performance of a model is unrelated to whether or not it belongs to the family of arbitrage-free models. And, it directs our attention to what may facilitate superior forecasting performance, namely the careful selection of exogenous variables to include, and to the number of factors that the model specification relies on.

As far as notation goes, the intention was that whenever a J appears, as a super- or subscript, it means that the parameter belongs to the Jordan form of the model, and whenever a $\mathcal{P}$ appears, it indicates that the parameter belongs to the model based on principal components. Hopefully, this is not too confusing after all.

5.4 Implementing the Arbitrage-Free SRB Model

Similar to the previous section, a very short implementation guideline is provided here for the arbitrage-free SRB model. This model is also integrated into the TSM class (for completeness). Two-, three-, and four-factor models are supported.

A step-wise estimation algorithm is used (following Nyholm (2018)), which can be seen as a special case of Andreasen and Christensen (2015) and Rios (2015):

1. Conditional on $\gamma^{\mathbb{Q}}$, the arbitrage-free yield loading, b_τ, is known in closed-form from (4.30).
2. Using the yield equation, as in (5.7), the yield factors can be found as: $X = b_\tau^{-1} \cdot y'$, where b_τ^{-1} is the pseudo-inverse of b_τ. This is similar to JSZ's approach in equation (5.13), where PCA weights are used to construct the underlying yield curve factors, although here we use b_τ^{-1} as the weighting

matrix (because we want to impose a certain economic interpretation onto the extracted factors).

3. The optimal value for γ is found via grid-search, as the γ that minimises $\sum_t \sum_\tau (y - b_\tau(\gamma) \cdot X)^2$.

4. Using the extracted factors and (5.8), the parameters governing the $\mathbb{P}$-measure dynamics can be found.

5. Recalling that Φ^Q is a function of γ^Q, the last remaining parameter, m^Q, is found as the solution to $\underset{m^Q}{\operatorname{argmin}} \sum_t \sum_\tau (y - (a_\tau + b_\tau \cdot X))^2$.

5.5 Constructing a Model with the Short Rate and the Ten-Year Term Premium as Underlying Factors

A specific factor structure can help communicate the results of the model more easily to third parties (including decision makers), by better supporting a given narrative and communication style. For example, as we have seen, the underlying economic building blocks of the yield curve are the rate expectation and the term premium components. Often, in economic analysis, yield curve levels and changes around important events, such as, among other things, governing council meetings, major economic news release dates, and when some unexpected news hits the market, are typically broken down into these components to give a reading of how the financial market participants interpret the event. It is naturally important to know the degree to which market participants see an event as affecting the future economic environment (the rate expectations) and how it affects their perception of current and future risks (the term premium component). Such decompositions are typically done on the basis of term structure models that use principal components as underlying factors, and where the factors therefore have interpretations as the level, the slope, and the curvature; and, most often, such models fall in the camp that excludes arbitrage by construction.

So, the aim of the current section is to build an empirical model that includes the short rate, the term premium, and curvature factors, as underlying yield curve factors. This is, perhaps surprisingly, not done very often and the literature on models having this kind of factor structure is very scarce. Actually, to the best of my knowledge, a notable exception from this generalisation is the seminal paper by Creal and Wu (2017).

As always, our approach is modest and it cuts a fair number of corners. The first corner we cut is the one where the arbitrage-free models rest. By relying on a purely empirical model, we are able to finalise its implementation quickly – and we can then look at how to build an arbitrage-free model, with the same factor structure, at a later stage. The following steps are applied:

1. Extraction of observable factors: We rely on the SRB3 model to generate the two factors that are directly attainable – the short rate, the ten-year term premium. Any reasonable term structure model could, in principle, be used to this end. So, now we have the two first elements of X, denoted by $X_{(1:2)}$.

2. Finding the loading structure $b_{\tau,(1:2)}$: The yield loadings $b_{\tau,(1:2)}$ that match $X_{(1:2)}$ are obtained by inversion (or linear regression) $y = X_{(1:2)} \cdot b'_{\tau,(1:2)}$ $\Leftrightarrow b'_{\tau,(1:2)} = X^{-1}_{(1:2)} \cdot y$, where the pseudo-inverse is used to obtain $X^{-1}_{(1:2)}$.

3. Obtaining the remaining factors: The third and fourth factors are obtained via PCA performed on the residuals from the model using the two factors obtained in step 1, and the loading structure found in step 2. The residuals are found as: $e = y - X_{(1:2)} \cdot b'_{\tau,(1:2)}$, and the first two factors (i.e. the ones having the largest eigenvalues) are sampled as $X_{(3:4)}$. That is, the PCA is performed on the covariance matrix, $\Omega_y = 1/T \cdot e'e$.

4. Finding the loading structure $b_{\tau,(1:4)}$: Similar to step 2, b_τ is found as: $b'_\tau = X^{-1} \cdot y$, where X hold the time series of all four factors.

Steps 1–4 complete the yield equation of the model, and since the factors contained in X are observable, the parameters that govern their dynamic evolution can be obtained by VAR analysis, as it is done in all the models that we have looked at so far. For convenience, we include this empirical model in our TSM class, that accompany this Element.

6 Scenario Generation

6.1 Introduction

In this section, we bring together elements from the other sections, and show concrete examples of how yield curve models can be used in a risk management context. What we will look at is unconditional and conditional forecasting, as well as scenario generation. To this end, three case studies will be solved:

(1) A horse race between the models we have looked at so far. Starting in January 1994, the models are evaluated against each other in terms of how well they predict future yield developments.

(2) Macroeconomic variables are included, and a subset of the models are used to generate conditional forecasts.

(3) Scenarios are constructed where the future path of the yield curve is forced to pass through a set of exogenously determined future fixed points.

We are naturally using the same US yield curve data in this section that we have been using throughout this Element.

6.1.1 The Horse Race

Eighteen different model specifications are tested. Their differences fall along three dimensions (i) whether they impose arbitrage constraints, or not; (ii) whether bias correction is performed on the VAR dynamics, or not; and (iii) and whether they rely on two, three, or four factors.

The pseudo out-of-sample forecasting experiment is carried out in the following way:

1. Sample data from June 1961 till January 1994.
2. Estimate the model under consideration.
3. Perform model forecasts for the horizon of one month to twelve months ahead, for each of the maturity points covered by the data sample, that is, for the $\{0.25, 1, 2, \ldots, 10\}$ year segments of the yield curve.
4. Calculate and store the differences between observed and forecasted yields.
5. Add one month to the sample, and repeat the above steps.
6. Repeat the process for the 282 data points covered by the evaluation sample, that is, from February 1994 to June 2017 (we lose 1-year of data due to the twelve-month forecasting horizon).
7. Repeat the above for each of the eighteen models to be evaluated.

Tables 15, 16, and 17, show the resulting forecast RMSE for each model at forecast horizons of one, two, three, six, and twelve months ahead. Only a representative set of yield curve segments (maturities) are shown, and these are the three-month and the five and 10-year segments. For example, the first data row of Table 15 shows the ability of the dynamic Nelson-Siegel (DNS) model to forecast the three-month maturity-segment of the yield curve: one-month ahead the DNS model misses observed yields with an RMSE of 18 basis points, two-months ahead the model misses with an RMSE of 27, and so on for the three, six and twelve-months projection horizons, with RMSEs of, 38, 67, and 122 basis points, respectively. For a model-free comparison, the last data line in each of the tables shows the RMSE of the random walk model.

It is interesting to see that the forecasting performance reported here is very similar to the results of Diebold and Li (2006), both in terms of size and pattern across maturity segments and forecasting horizons – with one significant difference, which is addressed in the following. It is recalled that Diebold and Li (2006) conducted their analysis on US data covering the period from 1985 to 2000, and that the forecasting experiment they conducted was based on pseudo out-of-sample forecasts beginning in 1994. Our analysis extends the data sample to cover historical data going back to 1961 and our forecast also starts in 1994, but extends to 2018. Still, results are quite well aligned. To

Table 15 Forecast RMSEs for the three-month yield curve segment (basis points)

	Forecast horizon				
	1-month	2-month	3-month	6-month	12-month
DNS	18	27	38	67	122
DNS (bc)	17	27	38	66	111
DSS	18	28	39	68	122
DSS (bc)	18	28	39	66	122
SRB-3	18	27	38	67	122
SRB-3 (bc)	17	27	38	66	111
SRB-4	18	28	39	68	122
SRB-4 (bc)	18	28	39	67	122
JSZ	29	51	70	111	166
JSZ (bc)	26	44	60	91	133
AFSRB-2	30	31	39	67	122
AFSRB-2 (bc)	32	35	43	68	122
AFSRB-3	18	27	38	67	122
AFSRB-3 (bc)	17	28	39	67	122
AFSRB-4	30	45	63	122	200
AFSRB-4 (bc)	18	28	39	68	122
SRTPC1C2	44	47	53	74	122
SRTPC1C2 (bc)	38	42	50	74	122
Random walk	38	42	50	74	122

The RMSE of model forecasts calculated for the period covering January 1994 to July 2018 are shown. Each model is re-estimated each at each monthly observation point that is included in the evaluation period (using an expanding data sample), that is, for each of the 282 months that falls in the period between January 1994 and July 2017. Twelve months ahead forecasts are generated at each of the 282 observation points covered by the evaluation sample (this is why the last month estimations are performed is July 2017). The table shows the RMSE of the forecasts for one, two, three, six, and, twelve-months ahead, for the three-month yield curve segment. Model names featuring a '(bc)' have been bias corrected using Pope (1990). The actual models that hides behind the shown abbreviations can be found in the MATLAB TSM class that accompany this Element.

illustrate the similarity of the produced forecasting performance, some representative figures are reported here. Table 5 in Diebold and Li (2006) shows that the RMSE of the three-months, five-year and ten-year maturity points, forecasted six-months ahead are 52, 78, and 72, respectively. In comparison, our study gives the following RMSEs: 67, 74, 61. Differences of similar sizes are seen for the tested maturities and forecasting horizons. So, there is a much smaller

Table 16 Forecast RMSEs for the five-year yield curve segment
(basis points)

	Forecast horizon				
	1-month	**2-month**	**3-month**	**6-month**	**12-month**
DNS	30	44	53	74	100
DNS (bc)	29	42	51	70	92
DSS	27	41	50	71	97
DSS (bc)	27	41	49	69	91
SRB-3	30	44	53	74	100
SRB-3 (bc)	29	42	51	70	92
SRB-4	28	42	51	72	98
SRB-4 (bc)	27	41	50	69	91
JSZ	29	41	49	69	93
JSZ (bc)	29	42	50	67	85
AFSRB-2	34	47	55	77	100
AFSRB-2 (bc)	33	45	53	72	95
AFSRB-3	30	44	53	75	100
AFSRB-3 (bc)	30	43	51	71	93
AFSRB-4	67	77	84	100	133
AFSRB-4 (bc)	29	41	50	70	92
SRTPC1C2	44	53	60	78	100
SRTPC1C2 (bc)	44	53	61	79	100
Random walk	44	53	61	79	100

The RMSE of model forecasts calculated for the period covering January 1994 to July 2018 are shown. Each model is re-estimated each at each monthly observation point that is included in the evaluation period (using an expanding data sample), is for each of the 282 months that falls in the period between January 1994 and July 2017. Twelve months ahead forecasts are generated at each of the 282 observation points covered by the evaluation sample (this is why the last month estimations are performed is July 2017). The table shows the RMSE of the forecasts for one, two, three, six, and, twelve-months ahead, for the five-year yield curve segment. Model names featuring a '(bc)' have been bias corrected using Pope (1990). The actual models that hides behind the shown abbreviations can be found in the MATLAB TSM class that accompany this Element.

difference between the numbers produced by Diebold and Li (2006) and our results, despite of the differences in the historical and forecast-evaluation periods.

There might be some who are of the opinion that the documented differences are large – roughly 10 basis points difference in term of standard deviation is not small, they may say. To assess whether the size of the difference is large

Table 17 Forecast RMSEs for the ten-year yield curve segment (basis points)

| | \multicolumn{5}{c}{Forecast horizon} | | | | |
	1-month	2-month	3-month	6-month	12-month
DNS	28	40	45	61	75
DNS (bc)	29	40	46	61	73
DSS	27	39	45	61	76
DSS (bc)	28	40	46	62	74
SRB-3	28	40	45	61	75
SRB-3 (bc)	29	40	46	61	73
SRB-4	27	39	45	61	76
SRB-4 (bc)	27	40	45	62	74
JSZ	31	44	52	75	111
JSZ (bc)	30	42	48	67	86
AFSRB-2	38	47	52	65	74
AFSRB-2 (bc)	39	49	54	67	77
AFSRB-3	29	40	45	60	74
AFSRB-3 (bc)	29	41	46	61	73
AFSRB-4	49	49	51	61	79
AFSRB-4 (bc)	28	40	46	62	73
SRTPC1C2	45	52	57	70	86
SRTPC1C2 (bc)	46	53	59	74	87
Random walk	46	53	59	74	87

The RMSE of model forecasts calculated for the period covering January 1994 to July 2018 are shown. Each model is re-estimated each at each monthly observation point that is included in the evaluation period (using an expanding data sample), is, for each of the 282 months that falls in the period between January 1994 and July 2017. Twelve months ahead forecasts are generated at each of the 282 observation points covered by the evaluation sample (this is why the last month estimations are performed is July 2017). The table shows the RMSE of the forecasts for one, two, three, six, and, twelve-months ahead, for the ten-year yield curve segment. Model names featuring a '(bc)' have been bias corrected using Pope (1990). The actual models that hides behind the shown abbreviations can be found in the MATLAB TSM class that accompany this Element.

or not, it may be illustrative to consider the standard error on the forecasts themselves. Inspecting the estimated models suggest that a comparable (i.e for the same maturity point and forecast horizon) forecast error is in the range of 20–30 basis points, so, to my reading, the differences between the Diebold and Li (2006) results and our results are immaterial.

Now, as mentioned previously there is one important difference between our results and those of Diebold and Li (2006). And, this relates to the behaviour of the short end of the curve. Starting with the Fed's response to the 2007/2008 financial crises by lowering the policy rate (see the top panel of Figure 2), the dynamics of the short end has been under the control of the monetary authority and has remained at very low levels until around year 2017. In addition, the Fed's asset purchase programmes, implemented during this period, have impacted the term structure of term premia. However, our forecasting results imply that the dynamics of longer maturities of the curve can be well approximated by the same DGP as before 2007 – only the short end is materially impacted – as is clear from the performance of the three-month segment of the curve shown in Table 15.

If we had been asked to make an unconditional guess, we would probably have said that the precision of the model forecasts would deteriorate as the forecast-horizon is increased. And, this is also what Tables 15, 16, and 17 confirm. Furthermore, being aware of the implemented policy measures since 2007/2008, we would also have said that the dynamics of the short end would be forecasted poorly, and that a shadow-short-rate model may alleviate this problem (the reason why the SSR model is not included in the horse race is because it is very time consuming to re-estimate this model 282 times). Finally, based on the separation of the likelihood function as derived by Joslin et al. (2011), see equation (5.6), we may also have reached the conclusion – since all tested models are based on a VAR(p) model for the factor dynamics – that their forecasting performance must be reasonably close; although differences may materialise due to a marginally better performance of, for example, a VAR(3) model, compared to VAR(2) and VAR(4) alternatives.

One of the practical conclusions that can be drawn from this horse race is that the choice of yield curve model has little impact on the precision of the unconditional forecasting performance. It does not seem feasible to choose the 'best' model on the basis of its forecasting skills, when forecasts are made unconditionally. We have confirmed this empirically via the results of the performed horse race, as shown in Tables 15, 16, and 17. And, theoretical considerations also support this conclusion, as argued previously.

What then, should guide our choice of model set-up? One element could be models' conditional forecasting performance; but we are not now going to conduct another horse race to explore different conditioning datasets – this would take too much time, as there are so many different constellations of macroeconomic variables that may be relevant. Another element is more subjective, yet important, and it relates to the factor structure that better fits the narratives we aim to support with our model. And, this of course depends on the business context in which the model is used. So, unfortunately, all the hard work that went in to producing the results shown in Tables 15, 16, and 17, while perhaps helpful from a general perspective, will not solve the model-selection problem for us.

6.1.2 Conditional Projections

In many practical applications, we are interested in generating conditional yield curve scenarios. For example, in the context of strategic fixed income asset allocation, our objective is to assess risk and return characteristics of bond indices and portfolios in a setting where the investment horizon is long. For this purpose, unconditional forecasts are not overly useful, because the underlying VAR model that governs the dynamic evolution of the yield curve factors (and therefore also the yields) will typically converge to its sample mean before the end of the investment horizon. There are, therefore limits to what kind of relevant questions such model projections can answer. Instead, when deciding on long-term asset allocations, it is relevant to know what the yield curve will look like, if one or the other macroeconomic environment materialises, and how the yield curve converges to such scenario-based economic outcomes. In effect, the yield curve model becomes a tool that can help illustrate the consequence of various, more or less realistic, economic scenario developments on expected returns and risks along the maturity dimension of the investable asset universe. So, rather then hoping for a yield curve model that will generate accurate point forecasts, we seek a model that links macroeconomic variables to yield curve developments, such that accurate conditional yield distributions can be generated (as opposed to accurate point estimates).

The reason why macroeconomic variables are pulled to the forefront here is that we may have a better grasp of what value such variables would take in different possible future scenarios, and it would be harder for us to directly predict how the yield curve would evolve. This is why we build a bridge between the dynamic evolution of yield curves and macroeconomic (or other) variables, such that we can generate scenarios for these bridge variables and subsequently extract the yield curve evolution, because this is what we are genuinely interested in.

As mentioned in the previous section, there are many macro variables to choose from. Out of convenience, we chose to use the same type of macroeconomic variables as used in Diebold, Rudebusch and Aruoba (2006), namely manufacturing capacity utilisation (CU) and annual price inflation (INFL)[38].

---

[38] The variable INFL is the twelve-month percent change in the Personal Consumption Expenditures Excluding Food and Energy (Chain-Type Price Index), (FRED code PCEPILFE). The used CU variable has FRED code MCUMFN. Diebold et al. (2006) also include the federal funds

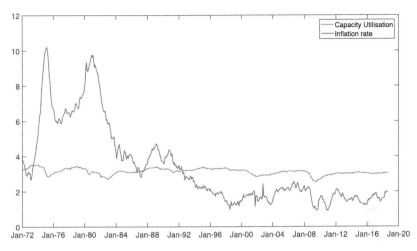

Figure 30 Capacity utilisation and inflation

US macroeconomic variables observed monthly since 1972. Manufacturing capacity utilisation (CU) and annual price inflation (INFL) are shown. Capacity utilisation (FRED code MCUMFN) is divided by 25 to align its scale. The inflation rate is calculated as the twelve-month percent change in the Personal Consumption Expenditures Excluding Food and Energy (Chain-Type Price Index), (FRED code PCEPILFE).

These data are obtained from the FRED database, and are shown in Figure 30. These two variables gauge the level of real economic activity relative to potential, and the inflation rate. The macroeconomic variables are observable at a monthly frequency since January 1972, and our conditional forecasting experiment is therefore limited to using data from this date onwards.

We then form a set of possible macroeconomic scenarios. Although the conditional yield distributions were mentioned previously as a main reason for this exercise, to keep things manageable in terms of visual representations, we show only the mean paths of the yield curve. The presented framework can easily be used to also generate distributions.

Since the objective is to extract the model-implied trajectories for the yield curve factors β^y, conditional on the macroeconomic variables β^{macro}, we first need to estimate the parameters that govern the joint evolution of $\beta = [\beta^y, \beta^{macro}]$. For demonstration purposes alone we do this in the context of the SRB3 model (any of the term structure models included in these lecture note can naturally be used). After the model parameters have been identified, we then use the Kalman filter to extract the model-implied conditional projections of interest. The game plan is the following:

---

rate in their study, but since we will rely on a multi-factor short-rate based model (SRB3), we already have the short rate included among the yield curve factors that we model.

1. Estimate the SRB3 model by including the two macro variables as exogenous variables (using the TSM class).

2. Set up the VAR(1)-part of the model (i.e. the part involving the dynamic evolution of the yield curve factors) in a MATLAB SSM model. This allows us to easily calculate the conditional projections for the yield curve factors using MATLAB's pre-programmed Kalman filter.

3. Make scenario projections for the macroeconomic variables over a five-year period. To exemplify, four scenario developments are examined: (1) random walk (INLF and CU stay constant at their levels as observed at the end of the sample period); (2) exponential growth in inflation until a level of 4 per cent is reached, after which the inflation rate normalises over a period of twelve months, and it then stays constant at 2.5 per cent until the end of the projection horizon; (3) a linear drop in inflation to a level of 1.75 per cent followed by a linear recovery; (4) a steady increase in economic growth over a period of four years, while the inflation rate is under control.

4. The conditional-scenario projections for the yield curve factors are converted into yields using the estimated-SRB3 model's loading structure.

It is important to emphasise that the parametrisation of the model that is used here has not been validated, nor has it undergone any testing/calibration to ensure that its economic narrative is sound: in other words, the model is used exactly as it comes, directly from the machine-room. The purpose here is, of course, not to construct a model that can enter directly into the SAA/policy process. The objective is simply to illustrate how the provided tool box can be used to make conditional yield curve projections.

It is left to the reader to investigate and inspect the outcome of each of the sketched scenarios using Figures 31, 32, 33, and 34.

It is recalled that the mapping between the projected yield curve factors and the scenario yields is given by the observation equation of our well-known yield curve state-space model:

$$Y = a + b \cdot X_t + \Sigma_Y \cdot u_t \tag{6.1}$$

So far, we have plotted only the mean scenarios (i.e. $E[Y]$). But, it is (of course) possible to use this framework to generate distributions around the shown mean paths. This can be done by drawing innovations for the state and observation equations and by feeding these though Σ_X and Σ_Y, respectively. Another often-used method is to block-bootstrap the historical residuals, possibly only sampled from historical periods that are judged to be similar to the one characterising the projection horizon.

(a)

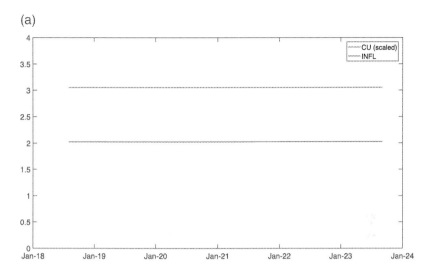

(b)

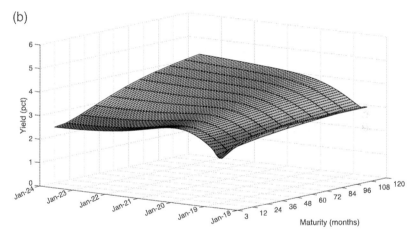

Figure 31 Scenario 1: Random walk for inflation and economic growth

The (a) panel shows the macroeconomic scenario as illustrated by the assumed evolution of the macroeconomic variables. The macroeconomic developments are only dictated for the period of time that defines the scenario. After this period, the Kalman filter is used to find the relevant projections. The yield curve factors of the model are also obtained via the Kalman filter as projections that are calculated conditional on the macroeconomic developments. The (b) panel shows the corresponding development in the yield curve. The scenario spans a horizon of five years.

(a)

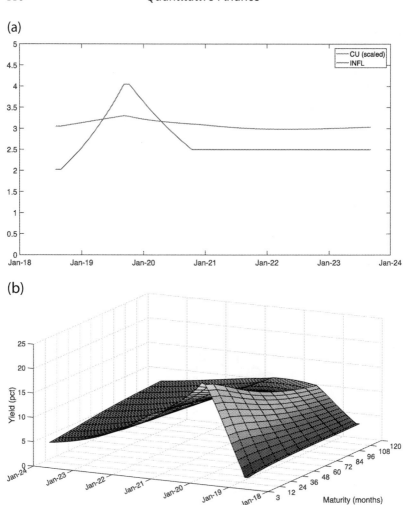

(b)

Figure 32 Scenario 2: Exponential growth in inflation

The (a) panel shows the macroeconomic scenario as illustrated by the assumed evolution of the macroeconomic variables. The macroeconomic developments are only dictated for the period of time that defines the scenario. After this period, the Kalman filter is used to find the relevant projections. The yield curve factors of the model are also obtained via the Kalman filter as projections that are calculated conditional on the macroeconomic developments. The (b) panel shows the corresponding development in the yield curve. The scenario spans a horizon of five years.

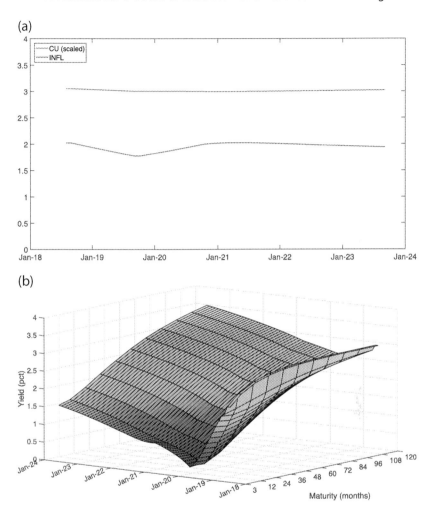

Figure 33 Scenario 3: A sudden drop in inflation

The (a) panel shows the macroeconomic scenario as illustrated by the assumed evolution of the macroeconomic variables. The macroeconomic developments are only dictated for the period of time that defines the scenario. After this period, the Kalman filter is used to find the relevant projections. The yield curve factors of the model are also obtained via the Kalman filter as projections that are calculated conditional on the macroeconomic developments. The (b) panel shows the corresponding development in the yield curve. The scenario spans a horizon of five-years.

(a)

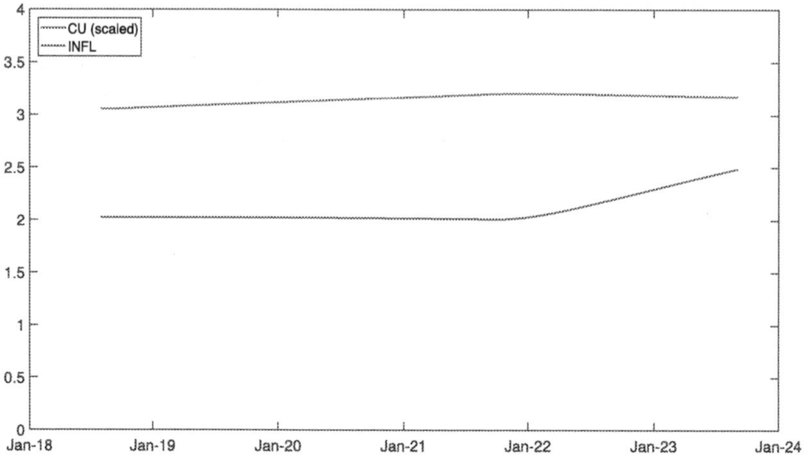

(b)

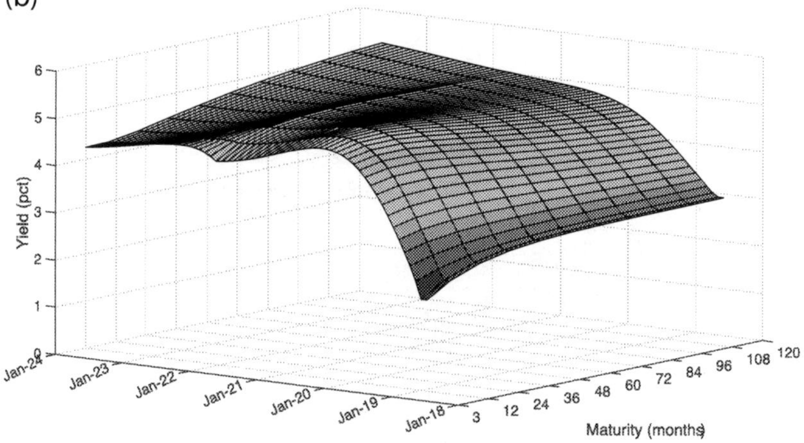

Figure 34 Scenario 4: Steady economic growth

The (a) panel shows the macroeconomic scenario as illustrated by the assumed evolution of the macroeconomic variables. The macroeconomic developments are only dictated for the period of time that defines the scenario. After this period, the Kalman filter is used to find the relevant projections. The yield curve factors of the model are also obtained via the Kalman filter as projections that are calculated conditional on the macroeconomic developments. The (b) panel shows the corresponding development in the yield curve. The scenario spans a horizon of five-years.

(a)

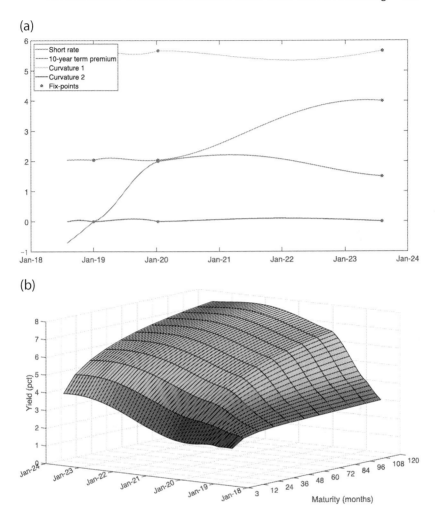

(b)

Figure 35 A yield curve scenario using fixed-point projections

The (a) panel shows the development of the yield curve factors of the SRTPC1C2-model, i.e. the short rate, the ten-year term premium, and the two curvature factors. The projected scenario is defined by three fixed-point vectors that the factors are required to pass through, (1) after six months where the ten-year term premium equals 0.00% (at the start of the projection-horizon sample (July 2018) the ten-year term premium is estimated to be around −0.70%); (2) after an additional eighteen months, the 10-year term premium equals 4.00%; and (3) at the end of the sixty-month projection horizon the ten-year term premium equals 1.5% and the short rate equals 4.00%. The resulting factor trajectories and yield curve evolutions are displayed in. The (b) panel shown the corresponding yield curve projection.

6.1.3 Fix-Point Scenarios

Sometimes we may be able to construct scenarios directly using the yield curve factors; this is particularly the case when our chosen model is built on yield curve factors that have interpretations that we can relate to and that have straight-forward economic interpretations. For example, we may be interested in a scenario where the curve steepens by $x\%$ or to a certain level, or perhaps a scenario where the yield curve steepens to some predefined level. Such scenarios can be used, for example, to analyse the size of portfolio losses and gains given the materialisation of some future shape and location of the yield curve. The point is, contrary to the previous section where the yield curve and its dynamic evolution was tied to macroeconomic variables, that sometimes we are able to directly specify scenarios exclusively in terms of the future values that the yield curve factors are assumed to take on.

To cater for the generation of such scenarios, a neat little reformulation of the VAR model is helpful. Let X_{t+h}^{target} be the sequence of future fixed points that the factors are assumed to take on. $h = \{h_1, h_2, \ldots, h_n\}$ is a vector of future horizons, that define the scenario factor values (and thus naturally the scenario yield curves). In order to illustrate this process, we will focus on a single future horizon, but the process naturally generalises to multiple horizons, as we shall see in the empirical illustration to follow.

Starting with the VAR(1) model that governs the dynamic evolution of the yield curve factors (and suppressing the expectations operator for ease of notation), and making a projection for the horizon h_1, gives the following:

$$X_{t+h_1} = \mu + \Phi^{h_1}(X_t - \mu). \tag{6.2}$$

We now want to ensure that this projection exactly meets a given future set of yield curve factor values, such that $X_{t+h_1} = X_{t+h_1}^{target}$. We also want to retain the factor interpretation that is embedded in our chosen term structure model. In other words, we need to leave the eigenvectors of Φ unchanged during this exercise, because it is the eigenvectors that define the direction of the factors and thus their economic interpretation. This leaves us with the persistency parameters (the eigenvalues of Φ), and the mean m to be eligible for changing. Lets implement the changes via the presistency parameters, and write Φ using the eigenvalue decomposition:

$$X_t = \mu + V \cdot D \cdot V^{-1} \cdot (X_t - \mu), \tag{6.3}$$

where V contains the eigenvectors, and D holds eigenvalues on the diagonal. We can then write:

$$X_{t+h_1}^{target} - \mu = V \cdot D^{h_1} \cdot V^{-1} \cdot (X_t - \mu)$$

$$\Updownarrow$$

$$D^{h_1} \cdot V^{-1} \cdot (X_t - \mu) = V^{-1} \cdot \left(X_{t+h_1}^{\text{Target}} - \mu\right)$$

$$\Updownarrow$$

$$D^{h_1} = V^{-1} \cdot \left(X_{t+h_1}^{\text{Target}} - \mu\right) \odot \left(V^{-1} \cdot (X_t - \mu)\right)^{-1}, \qquad (6.4)$$

where $\odot$ represents the element-by-element multiplication. The last line works because D is diagonal.

Intuitively, it makes sense to change the persistency part of the system to force the yield curve factors to pass through a certain future fix point. The persistency of the model (the eigenvalues) is what makes the model converge to its sample mean: the higher the persistency (the higher the eigenvalues) the slower the convergence to historical means. So, by keeping the eigenvectors fixed, the economic interpretation of the factors remains unchanged, while the persistency is changed such that the desired fix-point values can be met at the desired projection horizon.

To illustrate this process, we again generate a scenario over the coming five years, now using the SRTPC1C2-model, hat is, the one where we have included the short rate and the 10-year term premium as yield curve factors (together with two curvature factors). Having the short rate and the term premium as underlying factors allows to us make scenarios where future fixed-point values are specified exogenously for the value that these factors may take on at future dates covered by the projection horizon.

Following a period of central bank intervention in the fixed income markets via bond purchases, as seen in the USA from 2008 to 2018, where the purpose of such interventions is to compress the term premium – and thereby the yield curve – it is likely that we have in mind particular future trajectories for the term premium and the short end of the yield curve, and it is therefore handy to be able to model these factors explicitly in the context of a formal modelling-and-projection framework. But, the relevance of having a direct handle on these factors naturally extends beyond the quantitative easing example provided here, and is of a general interest in monetary policy modelling as well as strategic investment analysis.

In the current example, it is assumed that we have three fix-points: (1) after six months where the ten-year term premium equals 0.00% (at the start of the projection-horizon sample (July 2018) the ten-year term premium is es-timated to be around -0.70%); (2) after an additional eighteen months, the ten-year term premium equals 4.00%; and (3) at the end of the sixty-month projection horizon, the ten-year term premium equals 1.5% and the short rate equals 4.00%. The resulting factor trajectories and yield curve evolutions are displayed in Figure 35.

The familiar relationship between factors and yields recalled in equation (6.1) is also used here to translate projected yield curve factors into yield evolutions.

In the LHS panel of Figure 35 it is observed that the projections for the short rate and the ten-year term premium pass through the scenario fixed-points at the pre-specified future dates, and that the RHS panel of Figure 35, traces out the scenario yields that follow as a logical consequence of the yield curve factor trajectories.

MATLAB code

> filename: Scenario_and_forecasting.m

```
1    %% Scenario generation and forecasting
2    %
3    % preparing the data
4    %
5    warning('off','all')
6    path_=[pwd,'\MATLAB_classes'];
7    addpath(path_);
8    load('Data_GSW.mat');
9    GSW_          = GSW;                   % creates an instance of the GSW class
10   GSW_.tau      = [3 12:12:120]';       % vector of maturities
11   GSW_.beta     = GSW_factors(:,2:5);   % yield curve factors
12   GSW_.lambda   = GSW_factors(:,6:7);   % lambdas
13   GSW_          = GSW_.getYields;       % getting yields
14
15   dates = GSW_factors(:,1);
16   Y     = GSW_.yields;
17   tau   = GSW_.tau;
18   nTau  = size(tau,1);
19
20   figure
21       plot(dates,Y(:,11))
22       date_ticks = datenum(1960:4:2020,1,1);
23       set(gca, 'xtick', date_ticks);
24       datetick('x','mmm-yy','keepticks')
25
26   figure('units','normalized','outerposition',[0 0 1 1])
27       plot(US_MacroVariables(:,1),[US_MacroVariables(:,2)./25 ...
28                       US_MacroVariables(:,3) ],'LineWidth',2)
29       date_ticks = datenum(1972:4:2020,1,1);
30       set(gca, 'xtick', date_ticks);
31       datetick('x','mmm-yy','keepticks')
32       set(gca, 'FontSize', 18),
33       legend('Capacity Utilisation','Inflation rate')
34    %  print -depsc MacroVariables
35
36
37   %% The horse-race
38   % The following models are included in the horce-race
39   % -------------------------------------------------
40   % DNS          -> Dynamic Nelson-Siegel model
41   % DNS_bc       -> Dynamic Nelson-Siegel model, bias corrected
42   % DSS          -> Dynamic Svensson-Soderlind model
43   % DSS_bc       -> Dynamic Svensson-Soderlind model, bias corrected
44   % SRB3         -> Short-Rate based 3-factor model
```

```
45   %  SRB3_bc      -> Short-Rate based 3-factor model, bias corrected
46   %  SRB4         -> Short-Rate based 4-factor model
47   %  SRB4_bc      -> Short-Rate based 4-factor model, bias corrected
48   %  JSZ          -> Joslin, Singleton, Zhu (2011)
49   %  JSZ_bc       -> Joslin, Singleton, Zhu (2011), bias corrected
50   %  AFSRB        -> Arbitrage-free SRB model with 2,3, or 4 factors
51   %  AFSRB_bc     -> Arbitrage-free SRB model with 2,3, or 4 factors, bias c.
52   %  SRTPC1C2     -> Model with Short rate, 10-year term premium,
53   %                       and 2 additional empirical factors
54   %  SRTPC1C2_bc  -> Model with Short rate, 10-year term premium,
55   %                       and 2 additional empirical factors, bias corrected
56   %
57   % Note that program execution could possibly be improved by combining
58   %      the pseudo out-of-sample forecasts, performed for each model,
59   %      inside one loop. However, with an eye to clarity of the code,
60   %      a slower model-by-model implementation is used.
61   %
62   fDate      = datenum('31-Jan-1994'); % start date for the horse-race
63   horizon    = 12;                     % forecast horizon
64   startIndx  = find(fDate==dates,1,'first');
65   nIter      = GSW_.nObs - startIndx - horizon;
66
67   %
68   % ... DNS
69   %
70   DNS_fErr = NaN(horizon+1,GSW_.nTau,nIter);
71   for ( j=1:nIter )
72       estYields      = Y(1:startIndx+j,:);
73       oYields        = Y(startIndx+j-1:startIndx+j-1+horizon,:);
74       A_TSM          = [];
75       A_TSM          = TSM;
76       A_TSM.yields   = estYields;
77       A_TSM.tau      = tau;
78       A_TSM.DataFreq = 12;
79       A_TSM.nF       = 3;
80       A_TSM.biasCorrect = 0;
81       A_TSM          = A_TSM.getDNS;
82       castY          = [];
83       A_SSM          = TSM2SSM;
84       A_SSM.TSM      = A_TSM;
85       A_SSM          = A_SSM.getMdl;
86       castY          = [ A_SSM.Data(startIndx+j-1,:); forecast(A_SSM.Mdl, ...
87                                   horizon, A_SSM.Data(startIndx+j-1,:) )];
88       DNS_fErr(:,:,j)   = oYields-castY(:,1:11);
89   end
90   DNS_fRMSE = 100.*sqrt(mean((DNS_fErr.^2),3));
91
92   %
93   % ... DNSbc
94   %
95   DNSbc_fErr = NaN(horizon+1,GSW_.nTau,nIter);
96   for ( j=1:nIter )
97       estYields      = Y(1:startIndx+j,:);
98       oYields        = Y(startIndx+j-1:startIndx+j-1+horizon,:);
99       A_TSM          = [];
100      A_TSM          = TSM;
101      A_TSM.yields   = estYields;
102      A_TSM.tau      = tau;
103      A_TSM.DataFreq = 12;
104      A_TSM.nF       = 3;
105      A_TSM.biasCorrect = 1;
106      A_TSM          = A_TSM.getDNS;
107      castY          = [];
108      A_SSM          = TSM2SSM;
109      A_SSM.TSM      = A_TSM;
110      A_SSM          = A_SSM.getMdl;
111      castY          = [ A_SSM.Data(startIndx+j-1,:); forecast(A_SSM.Mdl, ...
112                                  horizon, A_SSM.Data(startIndx+j-1,:) )];
113      DNSbc_fErr(:,:,j)   = oYields-castY(:,1:11);
```

```
114   end
115   DNSbc_fRMSE = 100.*sqrt(mean((DNSbc_fErr.^2),3));
116
117   %
118   % ... DSS
119   %
120   DSS_fErr = NaN(horizon+1,GSW_.nTau,nIter);
121   for ( j=1:nIter )
122       estYields       = Y(1:startIndx+j,:);
123       oYields         = Y(startIndx+j-1:startIndx+j-1+horizon,:);
124       A_TSM           = [];
125       A_TSM           = TSM;
126       A_TSM.yields    = estYields;
127       A_TSM.tau       = tau;
128       A_TSM.DataFreq  = 12;
129       A_TSM.nF        = 3;
130       A_TSM.biasCorrect = 0;
131       A_TSM           = A_TSM.getDSS;
132       castY           = [];
133       A_SSM           = TSM2SSM;
134       A_SSM.TSM       = A_TSM;
135       A_SSM           = A_SSM.getMdl;
136       castY           = [ A_SSM.Data(startIndx+j-1,:); forecast(A_SSM.Mdl, ...
137                           horizon, A_SSM.Data(startIndx+j-1,:) )];
138       DSS_fErr(:,:,j) = oYields-castY(:,1:11);
139   end
140   DSS_fRMSE = 100.*sqrt(mean((DSS_fErr.^2),3));
141
142   %
143   % ... DSSbc
144   %
145   DSSbc_fErr = NaN(horizon+1,GSW_.nTau,nIter);
146   for ( j=1:nIter )
147       estYields       = Y(1:startIndx+j,:);
148       oYields         = Y(startIndx+j-1:startIndx+j-1+horizon,:);
149       A_TSM           = [];
150       A_TSM           = TSM;
151       A_TSM.yields    = estYields;
152       A_TSM.tau       = tau;
153       A_TSM.DataFreq  = 12;
154       A_TSM.nF        = 3;
155       A_TSM.biasCorrect = 1;
156       A_TSM           = A_TSM.getDSS;
157       castY           = [];
158       A_SSM           = TSM2SSM;
159       A_SSM.TSM       = A_TSM;
160       A_SSM           = A_SSM.getMdl;
161       castY           = [ A_SSM.Data(startIndx+j-1,:); forecast(A_SSM.Mdl, ...
162                           horizon, A_SSM.Data(startIndx+j-1,:) )];
163       DSSbc_fErr(:,:,j) = oYields-castY(:,1:11);
164   end
165   DSSbc_fRMSE = 100.*sqrt(mean((DSSbc_fErr.^2),3));
166
167
168   %
169   % ... SRB3
170   %
171   SRB3_fErr = NaN(horizon+1,GSW_.nTau,nIter);
172   for ( j=1:nIter )
173       estYields       = Y(1:startIndx+j,:);
174       oYields         = Y(startIndx+j-1:startIndx+j-1+horizon,:);
175       A_TSM           = [];
176       A_TSM           = TSM;
177       A_TSM.yields    = estYields;
178       A_TSM.tau       = tau;
179       A_TSM.DataFreq  = 12;
180       A_TSM.nF        = 3;
181       A_TSM.biasCorrect = 0;
182       A_TSM           = A_TSM.getSRB3;
```

```
183    castY           = [];
184    A_SSM           = TSM2SSM;
185    A_SSM.TSM       = A_TSM;
186    A_SSM           = A_SSM.getMdl;
187    castY           = [ A_SSM.Data(startIndx+j-1,:); forecast(A_SSM.Mdl, ...
188                                  horizon, A_SSM.Data(startIndx+j-1,:) )];
189    SRB3_fErr(:,:,j) = oYields-castY(:,1:11);
190  end
191  SRB3_fRMSE = 100.*sqrt(mean((SRB3_fErr.^2),3));
192
193
194  %
195  % ... SRB3bc
196  %
197  SRB3bc_fErr = NaN(horizon+1,GSW_.nTau,nIter);
198  for ( j=1:nIter )
199    estYields       = Y(1:startIndx+j,:);
200    oYields         = Y(startIndx+j-1:startIndx+j-1+horizon,:);
201    A_TSM           = [];
202    A_TSM           = TSM;
203    A_TSM.yields    = estYields;
204    A_TSM.tau       = tau;
205    A_TSM.DataFreq  = 12;
206    A_TSM.nF        = 3;
207    A_TSM.biasCorrect = 1;
208    A_TSM           = A_TSM.getSRB3;
209    castY           = [];
210    A_SSM           = TSM2SSM;
211    A_SSM.TSM       = A_TSM;
212    A_SSM           = A_SSM.getMdl;
213    castY           = [ A_SSM.Data(startIndx+j-1,:); forecast(A_SSM.Mdl, ...
214                                  horizon, A_SSM.Data(startIndx+j-1,:) )];
215    SRB3bc_fErr(:,:,j) = oYields-castY(:,1:11);
216  end
217  SRB3bc_fRMSE = 100.*sqrt(mean((SRB3bc_fErr.^2),3));
218
219
220  %
221  % ... SRB4
222  %
223  SRB4_fErr = NaN(horizon+1,GSW_.nTau,nIter);
224  for ( j=1:nIter )
225    estYields       = Y(1:startIndx+j,:);
226    oYields         = Y(startIndx+j-1:startIndx+j-1+horizon,:);
227    A_TSM           = [];
228    A_TSM           = TSM;
229    A_TSM.yields    = estYields;
230    A_TSM.tau       = tau;
231    A_TSM.DataFreq  = 12;
232    A_TSM.nF        = 4;
233    A_TSM.biasCorrect = 0;
234    A_TSM           = A_TSM.getSRB4;
235    castY           = [];
236    A_SSM           = TSM2SSM;
237    A_SSM.TSM       = A_TSM;
238    A_SSM           = A_SSM.getMdl;
239    castY           = [ A_SSM.Data(startIndx+j-1,:); forecast(A_SSM.Mdl, ...
240                                  horizon, A_SSM.Data(startIndx+j-1,:) )];
241    SRB4_fErr(:,:,j) = oYields-castY(:,1:11);
242  end
243  SRB4_fRMSE = 100.*sqrt(mean((SRB4_fErr.^2),3));
244
245
246  %
247  % ... SRB4bc
248  %
249  SRB4bc_fErr = NaN(horizon+1,GSW_.nTau,nIter);
250  for ( j=1:nIter )
251    estYields       = Y(1:startIndx+j,:);
```

```
252        oYields        = Y(startIndx+j-1:startIndx+j-1+horizon,:);
253        A_TSM          = [];
254        A_TSM          = TSM;
255        A_TSM.yields   = estYields;
256        A_TSM.tau      = tau;
257        A_TSM.DataFreq = 12;
258        A_TSM.nF       = 4;
259        A_TSM.biasCorrect = 1;
260        A_TSM          = A_TSM.getSRB4;
261        castY          = [];
262        A_SSM          = TSM2SSM;
263        A_SSM.TSM      = A_TSM;
264        A_SSM          = A_SSM.getMdl;
265        castY          = [ A_SSM.Data(startIndx+j-1,:); forecast(A_SSM.Mdl, ...
266                                   horizon, A_SSM.Data(startIndx+j-1,:) )];
267        SRB4bc_fErr(:,:,j) = oYields-castY(:,1:11);
268    end
269    SRB4bc_fRMSE = 100.*sqrt(mean((SRB4bc_fErr.^2),3));
270
271
272    %
273    % ... JSZ
274    %
275    JSZ_fErr = NaN(horizon+1,GSW_.nTau,nIter);
276    for ( j=1:nIter )
277        estYields      = Y(1:startIndx+j,:);
278        oYields        = Y(startIndx+j-1:startIndx+j-1+horizon,:);
279        A_TSM          = [];
280        A_TSM          = TSM;
281        A_TSM.yields   = estYields;
282        A_TSM.tau      = tau;
283        A_TSM.DataFreq = 12;
284        A_TSM.nF       = 3;
285        A_TSM.biasCorrect = 0;
286        A_TSM          = A_TSM.getJSZ;
287        castY          = [];
288        A_SSM          = TSM2SSM;
289        A_SSM.TSM      = A_TSM;
290        A_SSM          = A_SSM.getMdl;
291        castY          = [ A_SSM.Data(startIndx+j-1,:); forecast(A_SSM.Mdl, ...
292                                   horizon, A_SSM.Data(startIndx+j-1,:) )];
293        JSZ_fErr(:,:,j) = oYields-castY(:,1:11);
294    end
295    JSZ_fRMSE = 100.*sqrt(mean((JSZ_fErr.^2),3));
296
297
298    %
299    % ... JSZ_bc
300    %
301    JSZbc_fErr = NaN(horizon+1,GSW_.nTau,nIter);
302    for ( j=1:nIter )
303        estYields      = Y(1:startIndx+j,:);
304        oYields        = Y(startIndx+j-1:startIndx+j-1+horizon,:);
305        A_TSM          = [];
306        A_TSM          = TSM;
307        A_TSM.yields   = estYields;
308        A_TSM.tau      = tau;
309        A_TSM.DataFreq = 12;
310        A_TSM.nF       = 3;
311        A_TSM.biasCorrect = 1;
312        A_TSM          = A_TSM.getJSZ;
313        castY          = [];
314        A_SSM          = TSM2SSM;
315        A_SSM.TSM      = A_TSM;
316        A_SSM          = A_SSM.getMdl;
317        castY          = [ A_SSM.Data(startIndx+j-1,:); forecast(A_SSM.Mdl, ...
318                                   horizon, A_SSM.Data(startIndx+j-1,:) )];
319        JSZbc_fErr(:,:,j) = oYields-castY(:,1:11);
320    end
```

```
321    JSZbc_fRMSE = 100.*sqrt(mean((JSZbc_fErr.^2),3));
322
323
324    %
325    % ... AFSRB2
326    %
327    AF2_fErr = NaN(horizon+1,GSW_.nTau,nIter);
328    for ( j=1:nIter )
329        estYields    = Y(1:startIndx+j,:);
330        oYields      = Y(startIndx+j-1:startIndx+j-1+horizon,:);
331        A_TSM        = [];
332        A_TSM        = TSM;
333        A_TSM.yields = estYields;
334        A_TSM.tau    = tau;
335        A_TSM.DataFreq = 12;
336        A_TSM.nF     = 2;
337        A_TSM.biasCorrect = 0;
338        A_TSM        = A_TSM.getAFSRB;
339        castY        = [];
340        A_SSM        = TSM2SSM;
341        A_SSM.TSM    = A_TSM;
342        A_SSM        = A_SSM.getMdl;
343        castY        = [ A_SSM.Data(startIndx+j-1,:); forecast(A_SSM.Mdl, ...
344                                 horizon, A_SSM.Data(startIndx+j-1,:) )];
345        AF2_fErr(:,:,j) = oYields-castY(:,1:11);
346    end
347    AF2_fRMSE = 100.*sqrt(mean((AF2_fErr.^2),3));
348
349
350    %
351    % ... AFSRB2
352    %
353    AF2bc_fErr = NaN(horizon+1,GSW_.nTau,nIter);
354    for ( j=1:nIter )
355        estYields    = Y(1:startIndx+j,:);
356        oYields      = Y(startIndx+j-1:startIndx+j-1+horizon,:);
357        A_TSM        = [];
358        A_TSM        = TSM;
359        A_TSM.yields = estYields;
360        A_TSM.tau    = tau;
361        A_TSM.DataFreq = 12;
362        A_TSM.nF     = 2;
363        A_TSM.biasCorrect = 1;
364        A_TSM        = A_TSM.getAFSRB;
365        castY        = [];
366        A_SSM        = TSM2SSM;
367        A_SSM.TSM    = A_TSM;
368        A_SSM        = A_SSM.getMdl;
369        castY        = [ A_SSM.Data(startIndx+j-1,:); forecast(A_SSM.Mdl, ...
370                                 horizon, A_SSM.Data(startIndx+j-1,:) )];
371        AF2bc_fErr(:,:,j) = oYields-castY(:,1:11);
372    end
373    AF2bc_fRMSE = 100.*sqrt(mean((AF2bc_fErr.^2),3));
374
375    %
376    % ... AFSRB3
377    %
378    AF3_fErr = NaN(horizon+1,GSW_.nTau,nIter);
379    for ( j=1:nIter )
380        estYields    = Y(1:startIndx+j,:);
381        oYields      = Y(startIndx+j-1:startIndx+j-1+horizon,:);
382        A_TSM        = [];
383        A_TSM        = TSM;
384        A_TSM.yields = estYields;
385        A_TSM.tau    = tau;
386        A_TSM.DataFreq = 12;
387        A_TSM.nF     = 3;
388        A_TSM.biasCorrect = 0;
389        A_TSM        = A_TSM.getAFSRB;
```

```
390      castY         = [];
391      A_SSM         = TSM2SSM;
392      A_SSM.TSM     = A_TSM;
393      A_SSM         = A_SSM.getMdl;
394      castY         = [ A_SSM.Data(startIndx+j-1,:); forecast(A_SSM.Mdl, ...
395                                horizon, A_SSM.Data(startIndx+j-1,:) )];
396      AF3_fErr(:,:,j) = oYields-castY(:,1:11);
397  end
398  AF3_fRMSE = 100.*sqrt(mean((AF3_fErr.^2),3));
399
400
401  %
402  % ... AFSRB3_bc
403  %
404  AF3bc_fErr = NaN(horizon+1,GSW_.nTau,nIter);
405  for ( j=1:nIter )
406      estYields     = Y(1:startIndx+j,:);
407      oYields       = Y(startIndx+j-1:startIndx+j-1+horizon,:);
408      A_TSM         = [];
409      A_TSM         = TSM;
410      A_TSM.yields  = estYields;
411      A_TSM.tau     = tau;
412      A_TSM.DataFreq = 12;
413      A_TSM.nF      = 3;
414      A_TSM.biasCorrect = 1;
415      A_TSM         = A_TSM.getAFSRB;
416      castY         = [];
417      A_SSM         = TSM2SSM;
418      A_SSM.TSM     = A_TSM;
419      A_SSM         = A_SSM.getMdl;
420      castY         = [ A_SSM.Data(startIndx+j-1,:); forecast(A_SSM.Mdl, ...
421                                horizon, A_SSM.Data(startIndx+j-1,:) )];
422      AF3bc_fErr(:,:,j) = oYields-castY(:,1:11);
423  end
424  AF3bc_fRMSE = 100.*sqrt(mean((AF3bc_fErr.^2),3));
425
426
427  %
428  % ... AFSRB4
429  %
430  AF4_fErr = NaN(horizon+1,GSW_.nTau,nIter);
431  for ( j=1:nIter )
432      estYields     = Y(1:startIndx+j,:);
433      oYields       = Y(startIndx+j-1:startIndx+j-1+horizon,:);
434      A_TSM         = [];
435      A_TSM         = TSM;
436      A_TSM.yields  = estYields;
437      A_TSM.tau     = tau;
438      A_TSM.DataFreq = 12;
439      A_TSM.nF      = 4;
440      A_TSM.biasCorrect = 0;
441      A_TSM         = A_TSM.getAFSRB;
442      castY         = [];
443      A_SSM         = TSM2SSM;
444      A_SSM.TSM     = A_TSM;
445      A_SSM         = A_SSM.getMdl;
446      castY         = [ A_SSM.Data(startIndx+j-1,:); forecast(A_SSM.Mdl, ...
447                                horizon, A_SSM.Data(startIndx+j-1,:) )];
448      AF4_fErr(:,:,j) = oYields-castY(:,1:11);
449  end
450  AF4_fRMSE = 100.*sqrt(mean((AF4_fErr.^2),3));
451
452
453  %
454  % ... AFSRB4_bc
455  %
456  AF4bc_fErr = NaN(horizon+1,GSW_.nTau,nIter);
457  for ( j=1:nIter )
458      estYields     = Y(1:startIndx+j,:);
```

```
459        oYields          = Y(startIndx+j-1:startIndx+j-1+horizon,:);
460        A_TSM            = [];
461        A_TSM            = TSM;
462        A_TSM.yields     = estYields;
463        A_TSM.tau        = tau;
464        A_TSM.DataFreq = 12;
465        A_TSM.nF         = 4;
466        A_TSM.biasCorrect = 1;
467        A_TSM            = A_TSM.getAFSRB;
468        castY            = [];
469        A_SSM            = TSM2SSM;
470        A_SSM.TSM        = A_TSM;
471        A_SSM            = A_SSM.getMdl;
472        castY            = [ A_SSM.Data(startIndx+j-1,:); forecast(A_SSM.Mdl, ...
473                                    horizon, A_SSM.Data(startIndx+j-1,:) )];
474        AF4bc_fErr(:,:,j) = oYields-castY(:,1:11);
475    end
476    AF4bc_fRMSE = 100.*sqrt(mean((AF4bc_fErr.^2),3));
477
478
479    %
480    % ... SRTPC1C2
481    %
482    SRTPC1C2_fErr = NaN(horizon+1,GSW_.nTau,nIter);
483    for ( j=1:nIter )
484        estYields        = Y(1:startIndx+j,:);
485        oYields          = Y(startIndx+j-1:startIndx+j-1+horizon,:);
486        A_TSM            = [];
487        A_TSM            = TSM;
488        A_TSM.yields     = estYields;
489        A_TSM.tau        = tau;
490        A_TSM.DataFreq = 12;
491        A_TSM.nF         = 4;
492        A_TSM.biasCorrect = 0;
493        A_TSM            = A_TSM.getSRTPC1C2;
494        castY            = [];
495        A_SSM            = TSM2SSM;
496        A_SSM.TSM        = A_TSM;
497        A_SSM            = A_SSM.getMdl;
498        castY            = [ A_SSM.Data(startIndx+j-1,:); forecast(A_SSM.Mdl, ...
499                                    horizon, A_SSM.Data(startIndx+j-1,:) )];
500        SRTPC1C2_fErr(:,:,j) = oYields-castY(:,1:11);
501    end
502    SRTPC1C2_fRMSE = 100.*sqrt(mean((SRTPC1C2_fErr.^2),3));
503
504
505    %
506    % ... SRTPC1C2bc
507    %
508    SRTPC1C2bc_fErr = NaN(horizon+1,GSW_.nTau,nIter);
509    for ( j=1:nIter )
510        estYields        = Y(1:startIndx+j,:);
511        oYields          = Y(startIndx+j-1:startIndx+j-1+horizon,:);
512        A_TSM            = [];
513        A_TSM            = TSM;
514        A_TSM.yields     = estYields;
515        A_TSM.tau        = tau;
516        A_TSM.DataFreq = 12;
517        A_TSM.nF         = 4;
518        A_TSM.biasCorrect = 1;
519        biasCorrect      = 1;
520        A_TSM            = A_TSM.getSRTPC1C2;
521        castY            = [];
522        A_SSM            = TSM2SSM;
523        A_SSM.TSM        = A_TSM;
524        A_SSM            = A_SSM.getMdl;
525        castY            = [ A_SSM.Data(startIndx+j-1,:); forecast(A_SSM.Mdl, ...
526                                    horizon, A_SSM.Data(startIndx+j-1,:) )];
527        SRTPC1C2bc_fErr(:,:,j) = oYields-castY(:,1:11);
```

```
528    end
529    SRTPC1C2bc_fRMSE = 100.*sqrt(mean((SRTPC1C2bc_fErr.^2),3));
530
531    %% preparing output tables
532    %
533    % RMSE of all models
534    %        For maturities      : 3m 1Y 5Y 10Y
535    %        and forecasts adead : 1m 2m 3m 6m 12m
536    %
537
538    ahead = [2;3;4;7;13];
539    %
540    % ... for the 3m maturity segment
541    %
542    ZZmat_3m = [  DNS_fRMSE(ahead,1)';
543                  DNSbc_fRMSE(ahead,1)';
544                  DSS_fRMSE(ahead,1)';
545                  DSSbc_fRMSE(ahead,1)';
546                  SRB3_fRMSE(ahead,1)';
547                  SRB3bc_fRMSE(ahead,1)';
548                  SRB4_fRMSE(ahead,1)';
549                  SRB4bc_fRMSE(ahead,1)';
550                  JSZ_fRMSE(ahead,1)';
551                  JSZbc_fRMSE(ahead,1)';
552                  AF2_fRMSE(ahead,1)';
553                  AF2bc_fRMSE(ahead,1)';
554                  AF3_fRMSE(ahead,1)';
555                  AF3bc_fRMSE(ahead,1)';
556                  AF4_fRMSE(ahead,1)';
557                  AF4bc_fRMSE(ahead,1)';
558                  SRTPC1C2_fRMSE(ahead,1)';
559                  SRTPC1C2bc_fRMSE(ahead,1)'];
560
561    %
562    % ... for the 1Y maturity segment
563    %
564    ZZmat_1Y = [  DNS_fRMSE(ahead,2)';
565                  DNSbc_fRMSE(ahead,2)';
566                  DSS_fRMSE(ahead,2)';
567                  DSSbc_fRMSE(ahead,2)';
568                  SRB3_fRMSE(ahead,2)';
569                  SRB3bc_fRMSE(ahead,2)';
570                  SRB4_fRMSE(ahead,2)';
571                  SRB4bc_fRMSE(ahead,2)';
572                  JSZ_fRMSE(ahead,2)';
573                  JSZbc_fRMSE(ahead,2)';
574                  AF2_fRMSE(ahead,2)';
575                  AF2bc_fRMSE(ahead,2)';
576                  AF3_fRMSE(ahead,2)';
577                  AF3bc_fRMSE(ahead,2)';
578                  AF4_fRMSE(ahead,2)';
579                  AF4bc_fRMSE(ahead,2)';
580                  SRTPC1C2_fRMSE(ahead,2)';
581                  SRTPC1C2bc_fRMSE(ahead,2)'];
582
583
584    %
585    % ... for the 5Y maturity segment
586    %
587    ZZmat_5Y = [  DNS_fRMSE(ahead,6)';
588                  DNSbc_fRMSE(ahead,6)';
589                  DSS_fRMSE(ahead,6)';
590                  DSSbc_fRMSE(ahead,6)';
591                  SRB3_fRMSE(ahead,6)';
592                  SRB3bc_fRMSE(ahead,6)';
593                  SRB4_fRMSE(ahead,6)';
594                  SRB4bc_fRMSE(ahead,6)';
595                  JSZ_fRMSE(ahead,6)';
596                  JSZbc_fRMSE(ahead,6)';
```

```
597                    AF2_fRMSE(ahead,6)';
598                    AF2bc_fRMSE(ahead,6)';
599                    AF3_fRMSE(ahead,6)';
600                    AF3bc_fRMSE(ahead,6)';
601                    AF4_fRMSE(ahead,6)';
602                    AF4bc_fRMSE(ahead,6)';
603                    SRTPC1C2_fRMSE(ahead,6)';
604                    SRTPC1C2bc_fRMSE(ahead,6)'];
605
606    %
607    % ... for the 10Y maturity segment
608    %
609    ZZmat_10Y = [ DNS_fRMSE(ahead,11)';
610                    DNSbc_fRMSE(ahead,11)';
611                    DSS_fRMSE(ahead,11)';
612                    DSSbc_fRMSE(ahead,11)';
613                    SRB3_fRMSE(ahead,11)';
614                    SRB3bc_fRMSE(ahead,11)';
615                    SRB4_fRMSE(ahead,11)';
616                    SRB4bc_fRMSE(ahead,11)';
617                    JSZ_fRMSE(ahead,11)';
618                    JSZbc_fRMSE(ahead,11)';
619                    AF2_fRMSE(ahead,11)';
620                    AF2bc_fRMSE(ahead,11)';
621                    AF3_fRMSE(ahead,11)';
622                    AF3bc_fRMSE(ahead,11)';
623                    AF4_fRMSE(ahead,11)';
624                    AF4bc_fRMSE(ahead,11)';
625                    SRTPC1C2_fRMSE(ahead,11)';
626                    SRTPC1C2bc_fRMSE(ahead,11)'];
627
628    ZZZ_tex_3msegment = latex(vpa(sym(ZZmat_3m),2));
629    ZZZ_tex_1Ysegment = latex(vpa(sym(ZZmat_1Y),2));
630    ZZZ_tex_5Ysegment = latex(vpa(sym(ZZmat_5Y),2));
631    ZZZ_tex_10Ysegment = latex(vpa(sym(ZZmat_10Y),2));
632
633    %% RW forecasts
634    %
635    RW_fErr = NaN(horizon+1,GSW_.nTau,nIter);
636    for ( j=1:nIter )
637        RW_cast        = Y(startIndx+j-1,:);
638        oYields        = Y(startIndx+j-1:startIndx+j-1+horizon,:);
639        RW_fErr(:,:,j) = oYields-RW_cast;
640    end
641    RW_fRMSE = 100.*sqrt(mean((SRTPC1C2bc_fErr.^2),3));
642
643    ZZ_RW = RW_fRMSE(ahead,[1 2 6 11])';
644
645    ZZZ_tex_RW = latex(vpa(sym(ZZ_RW),2));
646
647    %%  Plots
648    %
649
650    %
651    % ... 1Y maturity, 12 months ahead
652    %
653    hori = 13;
654    matu = 11;
655    figure
656        subplot(2,1,1), plot(dates(startIndx+1:end-12,1),Y(startIndx+1:end-12,matu))
657        datetick('x','mmm-yy')
658        subplot(2,1,2), plot(dates(startIndx+1:end-12,1),squeeze(DNS_fErr(hori,matu,:).^2))
659        hold on
660        subplot(2,1,2), plot(dates(startIndx+1:end-12,1),squeeze(JSZbc_fErr(hori,matu,:).^2))
661        hold on
662        subplot(2,1,2), plot(dates(startIndx+1:end-12,1),squeeze(AF2_fErr(hori,matu,:).^2))
663        datetick('x','mmm-yy'), legend('DNS','JSZ','AFSRB2')
664
665    %% Conditional forecasting exercise
```

```
666    %
667    nCast          = 60;
668    indxStart      = find(dates==US_MacroVariables(1,1),1,'first');
669                                     % index to match yield and macro data
670    datesX         = dates(indxStart:end,1);
671    datesCast      = (dates(end,1):31:dates(end,1)+(nCast)*31)';
672    SRB3           = TSM;
673    SRB3.yields    = Y(indxStart:end,:);
674    SRB3.tau       = tau;
675    SRB3.DataFreq  = 12;
676    SRB3.nF        = 3;
677    SRB3.eXo       = [US_MacroVariables(:,2)./25 US_MacroVariables(:,3)];
678    SRB3           = SRB3.getSRB3;
679    %
680    % ... convert the VAR part of the model into SSM format
681    %
682    SRB3_SSM       = TSM2SSM;
683    SRB3_SSM.TSM = SRB3;
684    SRB3_SSM       = SRB3_SSM.getMdl;
685    nX             = SRB3_SSM.TSM.nF+SRB3_SSM.TSM.nVarExo;  % number of factors and exogenous
686                     variables
687    AA             = [ SRB3_SSM.Mdl.A(1:nX,1:nX*2);
688                       zeros(nX,nX) eye(nX) ];
689    BB             = [ SRB3_SSM.Mdl.B(1:nX,1:nX); zeros(nX,nX)];
690    CC             = eye(nX*2);
691    stateType      = [ zeros(1,nX), ones(1,nX) ];
692    castMdl        = ssm(AA,BB,CC,'statetype',stateType);  % VAR model as SSM model
693
694    beta_Cast      = [ NaN( size(SRB3_SSM.Mdl.B,2), nCast); ones(nX,nCast)];
695    beta_Cast(1:nX,1) = SRB3_SSM.TSM.beta(:,end);
696                                     % start projections at last obs of factors
697
698    % ......................................
699    % ... Conditional forecasting examples
700    % ......................................
701
702    %
703    % 0: unconditional forecast
704    %
705    beta_0   = beta_Cast;
706
707    filter_0 = [ [SRB3_SSM.TSM.beta(:,end)' ones(1,size(BB,2))] ;
708                 filter(castMdl,beta_0') ];
709    Y_0      = [SRB3_SSM.Mdl.C(1:nTau,1:nX*2)*filter_0']';
710
711    figure('units','normalized','outerposition',[0 0 1 1])
712        surf(tau./12,datesCast,Y_0)
713        date_ticks = datenum(2018:1:2024,1,1);
714        set(gca, 'ytick', date_ticks);
715        datetick('y','mmm-yy','keepticks')
716        xticks(0:1:11), xticklabels({tau}),
717        xlabel('Maturity (months)'), zlabel('Yield (pct)'),
718        zlim([0 5])
719        view([-53 16]),
720        ytickangle(25),
721        set(gca, 'FontSize', 18)
722        %print -depsc Forecast_Y0
723
724    figure('units','normalized','outerposition',[0 0 1 1])
725        plot(datesCast,filter_0(:,4:5),'LineWidth',2)
726        date_ticks = datenum(2018:1:2024,1,1);
727        set(gca, 'xtick', date_ticks);
728        datetick('x','mmm-yy','keepticks')
729        ylabel(' (pct)'), legend('CU (scaled)', 'INFL')
730        ylim([0 4])
731        set(gca, 'FontSize', 18)
732        %print -depsc Forecast_X0
733
734    %
```

```
735   % 1: random walk assumption on macro variables
736   %
737   beta_1          = beta_Cast;
738   beta_1(4:5,2:nCast) = repmat(beta_1(4:5,1),1,nCast-1);
739
740   filter_1 = [ [SRB3_SSM.TSM.beta(:,end)' ones(1,size(BB,2))]  ;
741               filter(castMdl,beta_1') ];
742   Y_1      = [SRB3_SSM.Mdl.C(1:nTau,1:nX*2)*filter_1']';
743
744   figure('units','normalized','outerposition',[0 0 1 1])
745       surf(tau./12,datesCast,Y_1)
746       date_ticks = datenum(2018:1:2024,1,1);
747       set(gca, 'ytick', date_ticks);
748       datetick('y','mmm-yy','keepticks')
749       xticks(0:1:11), xticklabels({tau}),
750       xlabel('Maturity (months)'), zlabel('Yield (pct)'),
751       zlim([0 6])
752       view([-53 16]),
753       ytickangle(25),
754       set(gca, 'FontSize', 18)
755       %print -depsc Forecast_Y1
756
757   figure('units','normalized','outerposition',[0 0 1 1])
758       plot(datesCast,filter_1(:,4:5),'LineWidth',2)
759       date_ticks = datenum(2018:1:2024,1,1);
760       set(gca, 'xtick', date_ticks);
761       datetick('x','mmm-yy','keepticks')
762       legend('CU (scaled)', 'INFL')
763       ylim([0 4])
764       set(gca, 'FontSize', 18)
765       %print -depsc Forecast_X1
766
767   %
768   % 2: Inflation overshooting, and increased CU
769   %
770   nn     = 12;
771   beta_2 = beta_Cast;
772   a      = beta_Cast(5,1);
773   b      = 2*a;
774   a1     = 2.5;
775   g1     = (b/a)^(1/nn);
776   g2     = (a1/b)^(1/nn);
777   infl_  = [a*g1.^(0:nn) b*g2.^(0:nn) ];
778   cu_    = linspace(beta_Cast(4,1),beta_Cast(4,1)+0.25,nn+1);
779
780   beta_2(4,1:length(cu_))   = cu_;
781   beta_2(5,1:length(infl_)) = infl_;
782   beta_2(5,length(infl_):end) = 2.5;
783
784   filter_2 = [[SRB3_SSM.TSM.beta(:,end)' ones(1,size(BB,2))]; filter(castMdl,beta_2')];
785   Y_2      = [SRB3_SSM.Mdl.C(1:nTau,1:nX*2)*filter_2']';
786
787   figure('units','normalized','outerposition',[0 0 1 1])
788       surf(tau./12,datesCast,Y_2)
789       date_ticks = datenum(2018:1:2024,1,1);
790       set(gca, 'ytick', date_ticks);
791       datetick('y','mmm-yy','keepticks')
792       xticks(0:1:11), xticklabels({tau}),
793       xlabel('Maturity (months)'), zlabel('Yield (pct)'),
794       zlim([0 25])
795       view([-64 25]),
796       ytickangle(25),
797       set(gca, 'FontSize', 18)
798       %print -depsc Forecast_Y2
799
800   figure('units','normalized','outerposition',[0 0 1 1])
801       plot(datesCast,filter_2(:,4:5),'LineWidth',2)
802       date_ticks = datenum(2018:1:2024,1,1);
803       set(gca, 'xtick', date_ticks);
```

```
804        datetick('x','mmm-yy','keepticks')
805        legend('CU (scaled)', 'INFL')
806        ylim([0 5])
807        set(gca, 'FontSize', 18)
808        %print -depsc Forecast_X2
809
810
811    %
812    % 3: New drop in inflation
813    %
814    nn       = 12;
815    beta_3 = beta_Cast;
816    a        = beta_Cast(5,1);
817    b        = a-0.25;
818    a1       = 2;
819    g1       = (b/a)^(1/nn);
820    g2       = (a1/b)^(1/nn);
821    infl_    = [a*g1.^(0:nn) b*g2.^(0:nn) ];
822    cu_      = linspace(beta_Cast(4,1),beta_Cast(4,1)-0.05,nn+1);
823
824    beta_3(4,1:length(cu_))    = cu_;
825    beta_3(5,1:length(infl_)) = infl_;
826    %beta_3(5,length(infl_):end) = 2.5;
827
828    filter_3 = [ [SRB3_SSM.TSM.beta(:,end)' ones(1,size(BB,2))] ;
829    filter(castMdl,beta_3') ];
830    Y_3      = [SRB3_SSM.Mdl.C(1:nTau,1:nX*2)*filter_3']';
831
832    figure('units','normalized','outerposition',[0 0 1 1])
833        surf(tau./12,datesCast,Y_3)
834        date_ticks = datenum(2018:1:2024,1,1);
835        set(gca, 'ytick', date_ticks);
836        datetick('y','mmm-yy','keepticks')
837        xticks(0:1:11), xticklabels({tau}),
838        xlabel('Maturity (months)'), zlabel('Yield (pct)'),
839        zlim([0 4])
840        view([-53 16]),
841        ytickangle(25),
842        set(gca, 'FontSize', 18)
843        %print -depsc Forecast_Y3
844
845    figure('units','normalized','outerposition',[0 0 1 1])
846        plot(datesCast,filter_3(:,4:5),'LineWidth',2)
847        date_ticks = datenum(2018:1:2024,1,1);
848        set(gca, 'xtick', date_ticks);
849        datetick('x','mmm-yy','keepticks')
850        legend('CU (scaled)', 'INFL','location','NW')
851        ylim([0 4])
852        set(gca, 'FontSize', 18)
853        %print -depsc Forecast_X3
854
855
856    %
857    % 4: high growth, inflation under control
858    %
859    nn       = 36;
860    beta_4 = beta_Cast;
861    a        = beta_Cast(5,1);
862    b        = a;
863    a1       = 2;
864    g1       = (b/a)^(1/nn);
865    g2       = (a1/b)^(1/nn);
866    infl_    = [a*g1.^(0:nn/2) b*g2.^(0:nn/2) ];
867    cu_      = linspace(beta_Cast(4,1),beta_Cast(4,1)+0.15,nn+1);
868
869    beta_4(4,1:length(cu_))    = cu_;
870    beta_4(5,1:length(infl_)) = infl_;
871    %beta_4(5,length(infl_):end) = 2.5;
872
```

```
873    filter_4 = [ [SRB3_SSM.TSM.beta(:,end)' ones(1,size(BB,2))]  ;
874    filter(castMdl,beta_4') ];
875    Y_4      = [SRB3_SSM.Mdl.C(1:nTau,1:nX*2)*filter_4']';
876
877    figure('units','normalized','outerposition',[0 0 1 1])
878        surf(tau./12,datesCast,Y_4)
879        date_ticks = datenum(2018:1:2024,1,1);
880        set(gca, 'ytick', date_ticks);
881        datetick('y','mmm-yy','keepticks')
882        xticks(0:1:11), xticklabels({tau}),
883        xlabel('Maturity (months)'), zlabel('Yield (pct)'),
884        zlim([0 6])
885        view([-53 16]),
886        ytickangle(25),
887        set(gca, 'FontSize', 18)
888        %print -depsc Forecast_Y4
889
890    figure('units','normalized','outerposition',[0 0 1 1])
891        plot(datesCast,filter_4(:,4:5),'LineWidth',2)
892        date_ticks = datenum(2018:1:2024,1,1);
893        set(gca, 'xtick', date_ticks);
894        datetick('x','mmm-yy','keepticks')
895        legend('CU (scaled)', 'INFL','location','NW')
896        ylim([0 4])
897        set(gca, 'FontSize', 18)
898        %print -depsc Forecast_X4
899
900    %% Fix-point projections
901    %
902    % h_target:  is the number of periods ahead at which the target is met
903    % X_target:  is the fix-point forecast for the yield curve factor
904    % V       :  id the eigenvector of Phi
905
906    % % Function that calculate the adjusted mean
907    % m_target      = @(X_t, Phi, X_target,h_target) ...
908    %                      1/h_target*((eye(length(X_t))-Phi)^(-1)*(X_target-Phi*X_t));
909
910    % Function that calculates
911    D_target = @(X_t, V, m, X_target, h_target) ...
912                        diag(((V^(-1)*(X_target-m))./(V\(X_t-m))).^(1/h_target));
913
914    % ... Using the model with factors equal to the: short rate, term premium,
915    %             and C1 and C2
916    %
917    nCast       = 60;
918    datesCast = (dates(end,1):31:dates(end,1)+(nCast-1)*31)';
919
920    SR_TP = TSM;
921    SR_TP.yields   = GSW_.yields;
922    SR_TP.tau      = GSW_.tau;
923    SR_TP.nF       = 3;
924    SR_TP.DataFreq = 12;
925    SR_TP          = SR_TP.getSRTPC1C2;  % est model with SR,TP,C1,C2
926
927    % ... Generating scenarios
928    %
929    % ... Scenario 1:  (a) TP goes to 0% in 6 months,
930    %                  (b) Thereafter TP goes to 2% after additional 12 months
931    %                      while short rate stays low
932    %                  (c) At the end of the 60 months projection horizon,
933    %                      the short rate converges to 4% and the TP to 3%
934
935    X_t1        = SR_TP.beta(:,end);
936    X_t1(2,1)   = 0;
937    X_t2        = SR_TP.beta(:,end);
938    X_t2(2,1)   = 2;
939    X_t3        = SR_TP.beta(:,end);
940    X_t3(1,1)   = 4.00;
941    X_t3(2,1)   = 1.50;
```

```
942  h1              = 6;
943  h2              = 12;
944  h3              = 42;
945  beta_proj       = NaN(SR_TP.nF+1,h1+h2+h3);
946  beta_proj(:,1)  = SR_TP.beta(:,end);
947
948  [V,D] = eig(SR_TP.PhiP);
949  D_1   = D_target( beta_proj(:,1), V, SR_TP.mP, X_t1, h1-1 );
950  for ( j=2:h1+1 )
951      beta_proj(:,j) = SR_TP.mP + (V*(D_1)*V^(-1)) * ...
952                                  (beta_proj(:,j-1) - SR_TP.mP);
953  end
954  D_2   = D_target( beta_proj(:,h1), V, SR_TP.mP, X_t2, h2 );
955  for ( j=h1+1:h1+h2+1 )
956      beta_proj(:,j) = SR_TP.mP + (V*(D_2)*V^(-1)) * ...
957                                  (beta_proj(:,j-1) - SR_TP.mP);
958  end
959  D_3   = D_target( beta_proj(:,h1+h2), V, SR_TP.mP, X_t3, h3 );
960  for ( j=h1+h2+1:h1+h2+h3 )
961      beta_proj(:,j) = SR_TP.mP + (V*(D_3)*V^(-1)) * ...
962                                  (beta_proj(:,j-1) - SR_TP.mP);
963  end
964  beta_proj = real(beta_proj);
965  Y_proj    = (SR_TP.B*real(beta_proj))';
966  fDates    = cumsum([h1;h2;h3]);
967
968  figure('units','normalized','outerposition',[0 0 1 1])
969      surf(tau./12,datesCast,Y_proj)
970      date_ticks = datenum(2018:1:2024,1,1);
971      set(gca, 'ytick', date_ticks);
972      datetick('y','mmm-yy','keepticks')
973      xticks(0:1:11), xticklabels({tau}),
974      xlabel('Maturity (months)'), zlabel('Yield (pct)'),
975      zlim([0 8])
976      view([-53 16]),
977      ytickangle(25),
978      set(gca, 'FontSize', 18)
979      %print -depsc Y_fixed_point_1
980
981  figure('units','normalized','outerposition',[0 0 1 1])
982      plot(datesCast,beta_proj,'LineWidth',2),
983      hold on
984      plot(datesCast(fDates,1),beta_proj(:,fDates)','*b','LineWidth',5), ...
985          legend('Short rate','10-year term premium','Curvature 1','Curvature 2',
986          'Fix-points','Location','NW')
987      hold off
988      date_ticks = datenum(2018:1:2024,1,1);
989      set(gca, 'xtick', date_ticks);
990      datetick('x','mmm-yy','keepticks')
991      set(gca, 'FontSize', 18)
992      %print -depsc beta_fixed_point_1
```

Appendix
On the Included MATLAB Codes and Scripts

This Element is intended for students and practitioners as a gentle and intuitive introduction to the field of discrete-time yield curve modelling. I strive to be as comprehensive as possible, while still adhering to the overall premise of putting a strong focus on practical applications. Some experience difficulties when embarking on the vast field of yield curve modelling approaches. It is my hope that the materials covered here can ease the entry into this interesting and useful field.

To emphasise the applied nature of the text, I have included MATLAB transcripts where relevant, as well as a set of MATLAB object oriented classes that, among other things, facilitate the estimation of all the included yield curve models. Virtually all the empirical examples and results shown in the text can be replicated using the supplied MATLAB materials. Of course, no warranty is provided for the MATLAB codes, and bugs are very likely still lurking around; if you find any, then please do not hesitate to report them to me.

An overview of the MATLAB classes that I have programmed to help digest the presented content is given in the following. In addition to these functionalities, I provide MATLAB scripts at the end of each of the empirically tilted chapters. To provide an overview, a list of these script files is also provided. Note that all the provided codes can be inspected in MATLAB by typing edit and then the name of the code you want to see. It is recommended that the accompanying MATLAB files are stored in a separate directory, and that the path (with sub-folders) is added to the MATLAB path.

The data that are used throughout the text are contained in the MATLAB files: Data_YCM.mat, Data_TSM.mat and Data_GSW.mat.

To illustrate how shadow-short rate models work, I have created a small graphical MATLAB add-in. This add-in can be installed by double clicking on the file name: *ShadowRateExample.mlappinstall*. More information on this is provided in Chapter 3.5.

GSW.m is a class-file that can be used to convert Gurkaynak, et al. (2006) yield curve factors, and in general Svensson and Söderlind (1997) factors, into yields at a set of pre-specified maturity points. The help file for this class is shown.

GSW

```
Usage:  .getYields  -> converts factors and lambdas into zero yields
        .getForwards -> converts factors and lambdas into forwards

GSW: converts Gurkaynak, Sack and Wright yield curve factors into
     yield and forward curves for a user-selected set of maturities.

     The conversion is based on the Svensson-Soderlind model as
     applied by GSW in their Fed working paper:
         "The U.S. Treasury Yield Curve: 1961 to the Present"
         Refet S. Gurkaynak, Brian Sack, and Jonathan H. Wright
         2006-28

     Gurkaynak, Sack and Wright data can be downloaded from the
     Fed homepage (http://www.federalreserve.gov/pubs/feds/2006/200628/200628abs.html).

Input:
    beta    :  GSW yield curve factors          (nObs-by-4)
    lambda  :  holds the time-decay parameters (nObs-by-2) [called tau by GSW]
    tau     :  vector of maturities (in months)(nTau-by-1)
               e.g. 24 is provided for a 2year maturity
Output.
    yields   :  zero-coupon yield curves
    forwards :  forward curves

    Activate calculations:
                        getYields   -> obtains zero coupon curves
                        getForwards -> obtains instantaneous forward curves
```

TSM

```
Usage:  .getDNS       -> Dynamic Nelson-Siegel model and related metrics
        .getDSS       -> Dynamic Svensson-Soderlind model and related metrics
        .getSRB3      -> Short-Rate based 3-factor model and related metrics (following Nyholm 2018)
        .getSRB4      -> Short-Rate based 4-factor model and related metrics (following Nyholm 2018)
        .getJSZ       -> Joslin, Singleton, Zhu (2011)
        .getAFSRB     -> Arbitrage-free SRB model with 2,3, or 4 factors
        .getSRTPC1C2  -> Model with Short rate, 10-year termpremium, and 2 additional empirical factors
        .getSSR3      -> Shadow-short rate model with 3 factors (following Coche, Nyholm, Sahakyan 2018)

TSM : Dynamic term structure models of the Nelson-Siegel family.
      Arbitrage constraints are not imposed in this modelling
      framework. See Nelson-Siegel(1987), Diebold-Li(2011), Nyholm(2018)
      for references.

      Small sample bias correction using Pope's closed form solution
      can be invoked via the flagg "biasCorrect=1".

      The basic model setup is the following:

          Y_t(tau) = B(lambda) * beta_t + e_t
          beta_t   = mP + PhiP * (beta_{t-1}-mP) + v_t

      The model is estimated using two-step OLS.

      B(lambda) specifies the applied model. The following
      alternatives are valid:
```

Input:

```
    yields  :  panel of yields         ( nObs-by-nTau )
    nF      :  number of factors       ( used only for the arbitrage-free models )
    tau     :  vector of maturities ( nTau-by-1 )
    mP_pre  :  pre-specified mean for the betas
    DataFreq :  Data frequency of the yield curve data. This is
               relevant for the calculation of Term Premia.
               The frequency is provided as the
               "number of observations per year" to allow for
               flexibility, so, e.g.:
```

	DataFreq		Interpretation
	360	=	daily
	52	=	weekly
	12	=	Monthly

```
    Z        :  panel of exogenous variables that can affect the
               yield curve factors via the VAR model. They are
               treated as unspanned factors as they do not impact
               the pricing of bonds
```

Output:

```
    beta   :  panel of extracted factors
    lambda :  optimal lambda values
    Yfit   :  fitted yields
    RMSE   :  Root mean squared error of yield residuals (in Basis points)
    e_t    :  residuals from the yield equation
    v_t    :  residuals from the beta equation
    PhiP   :  matrix of autoregressive parameters
```

```
mP    : estimated mean of the betas
rho1  : vector that defines the short rate as a function of
          the yield curve factors
TP    : term premia calculated at the maturities tau
Er    : expectations component (risk free term structure)
```

TSM.m is a class-file that allows for the estimation of various term structure models. The help file for this class is reproduced in the following.

TSM2SSM.m is a class that translates an estimated TSM model into MAT-LAB's state-space format. This is, for example, relevant if we want to use MATLAB's built-in Kalman filter routines to generate conditional projections for the estimated yield curve factors. Once a TSM model has been estimated, the TSM2SSM class can be used to translate the model into SSM format. The help file for this class file is shown here.

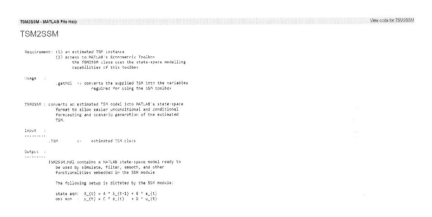

EX_Script_Classes.m is a script file that provides information on how class files are run. Many more examples are given in the codes listed here and found at the end of each section of the Element:

1. Empirical_Investigation_of_Observed_Yields.m
2. P_and_Q_Measure_Vasicek_State_Space.m
3. P_and_Q_Measure_Vasicek_2_step_approach.m
4. Basic_yield_curve_setup.m
5. Modelling_yields_under_Q.m
6. P_and_Q_Measure_1.m[39]
7. Scenario_and_forecasting.m

---

[39] Used just for illustration, not shown as end-chapter code.

References

Adrian, T., Crump, R. K. & Mönch, E. (2013). Pricing the term structure with linear regressions. *Journal of Financial Economics, 110,* 110–38.

Andreasen, M. & Christensen, B. J. (2015). The sr approach: A new estimation procedure for non-linear and non-gaussian dynamic term structure models. *Journal of Econometrics, 184,* 420–51.

Ang, A. & Piazzesi, M. (2003). A no-arbitrage vector autoregression of term structure dynamics with macroeconomic and latent variables. *Journal of Monetary Economics, 50*(4), 745–87.

Bauer, M. D. & Rudebusch, G. D. (2014). *Monetary policy expectations at the zero lower bound.* (Working Paper, Federal Reserve Bank of San Francisco)

Bauer, M. D., Rudebusch, G. D. & Wu, J. C. (2012). Correcting estimation bias in dynamic term structure models. *Journal of Business & Economic Statistics, 30,* 454–67.

Black, F. (1995). Interest rates as options. *Journal of Finance, 50*(5), 1371–6.

Campbell, J. Y. (2018). *Financial decisions and markets: A course in asset pricing.* Princeton University Press, Princeton, NJ.

CEIOPS. (2010). *Risk-free interest rates, extrapolation method. qis 5 background document.* (Technical report, https://eiopa.europa.eu/)

Christensen, J. H. E., Diebold, F. X. & Rudebusch, G. D. (2011). The affine arbitrage-free class of Nelson-Siegel term structure models. *Journal of Econometrics, 164,* 4–20.

Christensen, J. H. E. & Rudebusch, G. D. (2013). *Estimating shadow-rate term structure models with near-zero yields.* (Working Paper, Federal Reserve Bank of San Francisco)

Coche, j., Nyholm, K. & Sahakyan, V. (2017). *Forecasting the term structure of interest rates close to the effective lower bound.* (Work in progress)

Cochrane, J. H. (2005). *Asset pricing: Revised edition.* Princeton University Press.

Creal, D. D. & Wu, J. C. (2017). Monetary policy uncertainty and economic fluctuations. *International Economic Review, 58*(4), 1317–54.

Dai, Q. & Singleton, K. (2000). Specification analysis of affine term structure models. *Journal of Finance, 55,* 1943–78.

Diebold, F. X. & Li, C. (2006). Forecasting the term structure of government bond yields. *Journal of Econometrics, 130,* 337–64.

Diebold, F. X. & Rudebusch, G. D. (2013). *Yield curve modeling and forecasting: The Dynamic Nelson-Siegel approach.* Princeton University Press, Princeton, New Jersey, USA.

Diebold, F. X., Rudebusch, G. D. & Aruoba, S. B. (2006). The macroeconomy and the yield curve: A dynamic latent factor approach. *Journal of Econometrics, 131*, 309–38.

Duffie, D. & Kan, R. (1996). A yield-factor model of interest rates. *Mathematical Finance, 6*, 379–406.

Engsted, T. & Pedersen, T. Q. (2014). Bias-correction in vector autoregressive models: A simulation study. *Econometrics, 2*, 45–71.

Eser, F., Lemke, W., Nyholm, K., Radde, S. & Vladu, A. L. (2019). *Tracing the impact of the ecb's asset purchase programme on the yield curve.* (ECB working paper, no 2293)

Greenwood, R. & Vayanos, D. (2014). Bond supply and excess bond returns. *Review of Financial Studies, 27*, 663–713.

Gurkaynak, R. S., Sack, B. & Wright, J. H. (2006). *The US treasury yield curve: 1961 to present.* (Federal Reserve Board Working Paper)

Gürkaynak, R. S. & Wright, J. H. (2012). Macroeconomics and the term structure. *Journal of Economic Literature, 50*(2), 331–67.

Hamilton, J. D. (1994). *Time series analysis.* Princeton University Press, Princeton, NJ.

Hull, J. C. (2006). *Options, futures, and other derivatives.* Prentice Hall, USA.

Johnson, R. A. & Wichern, D. W. (1992). *Applied multivariate statistical analysis.* Prentice-Hall, Englewood Cliffs, NJ.

Joslin, S., Singleton, K. J. & Zhu, H. (2011). A new perspective on gaussian dynamic term structure models. *Review of Financial Studies, 24*, 926–70.

Julier, S. J. & Uhlmann, J. K. (1997). A new extension of the Kalman filter to nonlinear systems. In *Proceedings of aerosense: The 11th international symposium on aerospace/defence sensing, simulation and controls.*

Julier, S. J. & Uhlmann, J. K. (2004). Unscented filtering and nonlinear estimation. In *Proceedings of the IEEE* (Vol. 92, p. 401–22).

Karatzas, I. & Shreve, S. E. (1996). *Brownian motion and stochastic calculus.* Springer, New York.

Kim, D. H. & Priebsch, M. A. (2013). *Estimation of multi-factor shadow-rate term structure models.* (Unpublished manuscript, Federal Reserve Board)

Kim, D. H. & Wright, J. H. (2005). *An arbitrage-free three-factor term structure model and the recent behavior of long-term yields and distant-horizon forward rates.* (Finance and Economics Discussion Series 2005-33. Board of Governors of the Federal Reserve System, Washington, D.C)

Krippner, L. (2013). Measuring the stance of monetary policy in zero lower bound environments. *Economics Letters, 118*(1), 135–38.

Krippner, L. (2015a). *A comment on wu and xia (2015), and the case for two-factor shadow short rates.* (CAMA Working Paper 48/2015)

Krippner, L. (2015b). *Zero lower bound term structure modeling.* Palgrave Macmillan, US.

Lemke, W. & Vladu, A. L. (2017). *Below the zero lower bound: a shadow-rate term structure model for the euro area.* (European Central Bank Working Paper)

Li, C., Niu, L. & Zeng, G. (2012). *A generalized arbitrage-free Nelson-Siegel term structure model with macroeconomic fundamentals.* (Xiamen University, Working Paper)

Li, C. & Wei, M. (2013). Term structure modeling with supply factors and the federal reserves large-scale asset purchase programs. *International Journal of Central Banking, 9,* 3–39.

Litterman, R. & Scheinkman, J. (1991). Common factors affecting bond returns. *Journal of Fixed Income, 47,* 54–61.

Luenberger, D. G. (1998). *Investment science.* Oxford University Press, USA.

Lütkepohl, H. (1991). *Introduction to multiple time series analysis.* Springer-Verlag, Berlin.

Mikosch, T. (1998). *Elementary stochastic calculus, with finance in view.* World Scientific, advanced series on statistical science and probability, vol. 6.

Nelson, C. & Siegel, A. (1987). Parsimonious modeling of yield curves. *Journal of Business, 60,* 473–89.

Niu, L. & Zeng, G. (2012). *The discrete-time framework of the arbitrage-free Nelson-Siegel class of term structure models.* (Xiamen University, Working Paper)

Nyholm, K. (2008). *Strategic asset allocation in fixed-income markets: A MATLAB-based users guide.* John Wiley and Sons, UK.

Nyholm, K. (2018). *A flexible short-rate based four factor arbitrage-free term structure model with an explicit monetary policy rule.* (www.kennyholm.com)

Pope, A. L. (1990). Biases of estimators in multivariate non-gaussian autoregressions. *J. Time Ser. Anal, 11,* 249–258.

Rebonato, R. (2018). *Bond pricing and yield curve modelling.* Cambridge University Press, UK.

Rebonato, R., Mahal, S., Joshi, M., Bucholz, L. & Nyholm, K. (2005). Evolving yield curves in the real-world measures: A semi-parametric approach. *Journal of Risk, 7,* 29–62.

Rios, A. D. D. L. (2015). A new linear estimator for gaussian dynamic term structure models. *Journal of Business & Economic Statistics, 33,* 282–295.

Smith, A. & Wilson, T. (2000). *Fitting yield curves with long term constraints.* (Technical report, Bacon and Woodrow, August 2000)

Svensson, L. & Söderlind, P. (1997). New techniques to extract market expectations from financial instruments. *Journal of Monetary Economics, 40,* 383-429.

Taylor, J. B. (1993). Discretion versus policy rules in practice. *Carnegie-Rochester Conference Series on Public Policy, 39,* 195–214.

Vasicek, O. (1977). An equilibrium characterization of the term structure. *Journal of Financial Economics, 5,* 177–88.

Vayanos, V. & Vila, J. (2009). *A preferred-habitat model of the term structure of interest rates.* (NBER Working Paper)

Wan, E. A. & Merwe, R. V. D. (2001). Chapter 7: The unscented kalman filter. In *Kalman filtering and neural networks* (pp. 221–80). Wiley.

Wu, J. C. & Xia, F. D. (2015). *Measuring the macroeconomic impact of monetary policy at the zero lower bound.* (NBER Working Paper No. w20117)

Acknowledgements

This Element started as a manuscript supporting an internal course that I gave at the Risk Management Directorate of the European Central Bank. I am grateful to Fernando Monar, my head of division at the time (now Director of Risk Management), for supporting and encouraging me to write up the materials in a structured way, and for giving input on the content.

As with my book, Nyholm (2008), I also own immense debt and gratitude to Carlos Bernadell.

Many colleagues and friends have helped, pushed, and challenged me to obtain a better understanding of the topics covered in this Element.

My colleagues in the Capital Markets Division have been a constant source of inspiration and insight into the many ways that term structure models can be used to illuminate the transmission of monetary policy to the economy: I want to thank (in alphabetical order) Søren Autrup, Magdalena Grothe, Mike Joyce, Daniel Kapp, Gregory Kidd, Wolfgang Lemke, Nikolaj Orloff, Andreea Vladu, and Flemming Würtz.

In the Risk Analysis Division, I want the thank the following colleagues for many insightful discussion on how to design and apply term-structure models to help answer questions in the field of strategic asset allocation for fixed income portfolios (in alphabetical order): Luca Bortolussi, Diego Caballero, Siobhán Devin, Lisette Ho-Spoida, Johannes Krämer, Marco Marrazzo, Alexandru Penciu, Vlad Pretrescu, and Thomas Werner.

I also want to thank Vahe Sahakyan and Joachim Coche at the Bank for International Settlements for excellent collaboration over the years.

I owe Riccardo Rebonato a great debt of thanks for his encouragements and detailed reading (and correction) of previous versions of the manuscript. This Element would be far less interesting to read without his insightful suggestions. Thank you.

I also want to thank an anonymous referee for his/her thorough review of the manuscript.

Finally, and needless to say, any remaining errors in the manuscript and the accompanying MATLAB codes are solely my responsibility.

Disclaimer: The materials and views presented in this Element do not necessarily reflect the views of my employer, the European Central Bank. All MATLAB code and other materials are provided without warranty.

Cambridge Elements $\equiv$

Quantitative Finance

Riccardo Rebonato
EDHEC Business School

Editor Riccardo Rebonato is Professor of Finance at EDHEC Business School and holds the PIMCO Research Chair for the EDHEC Risk Institute. He has previously held academic positions at Imperial College, London, and Oxford University and has been Global Head of Fixed Income and FX Analytics at PIMCO, and Head of Research, Risk Management and Derivatives Trading at several major international banks. He has previously been on the Board of Directors for ISDA and GARP, and he is currently on the Board of the Nine Dot Prize. He is the author of several books and articles in finance and risk management, including *Bond Pricing and Yield Curve Modelling* (2017, Cambridge University Press).

About the Series

Cambridge *Elements in Quantitative Finance* aims for broad coverage of all major topics within the field. Written at a level appropriate for advanced undergraduate or graduate students and practitioners, *Elements* combines reports on original research covering an author's personal area of expertise, tutorials and masterclasses on emerging methodologies, and reviews of the most important literature.

Cambridge Elements ☰

Quantitative Finance

Printed in the United States
By Bookmasters